IRANIAN RAPPERS

AND

PERSIAN PORN

IRANIAN RAPPERS

AND

PERSIAN PORN

[A HITCHHIKER'S ADVENTURES IN THE NEW IRAN]

JAMIE MASLIN

Skyhorse Publishing

Skyhorse Publishing books may be purchased in bulk at special discounts for sales promotion, corporate gifts, fund-raising, or educational purposes. Special editions can also be created to specifications. For details, contact the Special Sales Department, Skyhorse Publishing, 555 Eighth Avenue, Suite 903, New York, NY 10018 or info@skyhorsepublishing.com.

www.skyhorsepublishing.com

10 9 8 7 6 5 4 3 2 1

Library of Congress Cataloging-in-Publication Data
Maslin, Jamie.
Iranian rappers and Persian porn : a hitchhiker's adventures in the new Iran / Jamie Maslin.
    p. cm.
ISBN 978-1-60239-791-0
1. Iran—Description and travel. 2. Iran—Social life and customs—21st century.
3. Maslin, Jamie—Travel—Iran. I. Title.
DS259.2.M38 2009
955.06'1092—dc22
2009023710

Printed in the United States of America

CONTENTS

Introduction

From Iran's scorching deserts to its lush forested mountains, from sprawling chaotic cities to ancient historical sites, I witnessed a subtle yet perceptible breeze of discontent stirring through the country, a breeze that foretold an approaching storm.

That storm erupted for the world to see in 2009 when thousands of predominantly young Iranians took to the streets of Tehran, Tabriz, Esfahan, and elsewhere, to protest the reelection of incumbent president Mahmoud Ahmadinejad, amid allegations of vote fraud from rival candidate Mir-Hossein Mousavi.

Despite the Western press giving the impression that the election was unquestionably rigged and that Mir-Hossein Mousavi and his supporters were robbed of victory by Ahmadinejad, the evidence available thus far does not back this up. The only reliable independent polls conducted before the vote by a Western polling organization—carried out by the nonprofit Center for Public Opinion and the New America Foundation whose work with ABC News and the BBC earned them an Emmy Award—predicted a substantial victory of two to one for Ahmadinejad.

During his first election in 2005, Ahmadinejad received just over 60 percent of the vote, and the above polling organizations predicted roughly the same figure in the 2009 elections, which appears to be what he received.

Indications of vote tampering exist, but it seems their scale would have been insufficient to swing the final outcome. Ahmadinejad would have won regardless, and by a substantial degree–perhaps not surprising given that he is a sitting president perceived by many Iranians as someone standing up to the country's archenemy, the United States, whose armed forces sandwich Iran between Iraq in the west and Afghanistan in the east.

The irony of such slanted media coverage is that it has portrayed the defeated Mir-Hossein Mousavi as something of an American hero. He is anything but, for when serving as Iran's prime minister in the eighties, he is believed to have been responsible for orchestrating the attacks on the U.S. embassy and the U.S. Marine Corps barracks in Beirut. These attacks killed 241 U.S. personnel.

Whether or not vote fraud occurred, and whether or not Mousavi is the great upholder of freedom and democracy that much of the Western media portray him to be, what I came to witness in Iran was a generation longing for greater freedoms. Not just freedom to say what they choose and to write what they wish, but in more elementary ways too–to socialize at parties, to openly have a boyfriend or girlfriend, to hold hands.

Two thirds of Iran's 71 million people are below the age of thirty, and half are younger than twenty-five. In the country's metropolitan areas in particular, there is a huge willingness to break the county's Islamic laws, often at great personal risk, in order to have a more interesting and exciting life. Alcohol, pornography, illegal books, and forbidden music abound.

The longing for greater freedom is not the sole preserve of Iran's youth, but is clear to see in older generations too. I witnessed cab drivers purposefully wind their car windows down in order to yell expletive-peppered abuse at passing mullahs; shopkeepers draw their finger symbolically across their throat whilst gesturing toward obligatory pictures of the country's late supreme leader, Ayatollah Khomeini; and others who simply expressed a discontent toward the government.

But just as I witnessed an appetite for domestic change, so too did I see a deep distrust of the American and British brand of freedom, and outright cynicism, often amongst those most vocal in demanding greater freedoms within Iran, regarding our platitudes on "democracy" and "liberation." There will scarcely be an Iranian on either side of the recent election protests–and there were huge numbers out in support of Ahmadinejad too–not well aware of the U.S. and Britain's role in destroying secular Iranian democracy in 1953, something which Iranians are taught from a young age, and in which U.S. president Barack Obama recently acknowledged American involvement.

It was then that the CIA launched its first ever coup, over-throwing the democratically elected government of Mohammad Mossadegh, and installing a brutal dictator, the Shah, in his place, whose secret police, the SAVAK, tortured citizens in the most horrendous ways imaginable. The CIA's methods included a campaign of shootings and bombings that were blamed on Mossadegh in order to stir up protests and opposition against him.

With such a past, the irony of the United States decrying the electoral process in Iran, but remaining mute regarding ally nations such as Saudi Arabia that have no elections whatsoever, will not be lost on many within the country.

The Iranians I met wanted change, but on their terms, not the West's. For this, there is appetite aplenty in the new Iran.

Prologue

"Iran? Are you insane?" I'd received similar melodramatic responses from other friends, one of whom said he didn't want to switch on his television set and see me paraded around in an orange jumpsuit as the latest al Qaeda hostage about to receive "the chop." He wasn't talking about a vasectomy.

Hardly anyone I talked to had any notion that Iran was anything other than an Axis of Evil terrorist hotbed. In fact, no one seemed to have any idea what the place was like at all. "They're all desert nomads, right?" asked a colleague of mine. Hardly. But I confess that I was almost as ignorant when I first applied for my Iranian visa, and as a result intended to spend as little time as possible in the country.

My plan was to travel overland all the way from England to China, following, as best I could, the famed "Silk Route" of renowned thirteenth-century Venetian explorer Marco Polo. To do this, I would have to venture through the Islamic Republic of Iran. Initially assuming it to be far too dangerous for a Westerner to dawdle through, I planned to skip quickly across the top of the country en route to its northeastern border, where I would then travel at a more leisurely pace through such mysterious lands as Turkmenistan, Uzbekistan, Kyrgyzstan, Tajikistan, and finally China itself.

I chose China as my destination because my brother had lived in Shanghai for the last five years but I had yet to make the trip out there to visit. For transport, I had made up my mind to hitchhike. I'd done plenty of hitching before, most notably from Normandy, France, to the tiny British colony of Gibraltar. I'd also hitched all the way across Australia, but this trip would far exceed that in length.

A myriad of reasons motivated me to make this trip; not least was the fact that to my mind it was an epic journey, and up until that point my journeys had been far from epic, and I had yet to travel anywhere truly exotic, different, or challenging. I had spent a good few years backpacking abroad, but on the whole I had only really visited English-speaking former British colonies where the only discernible differences from my native Britain were the warmer weather and the colder beer. It had been great fun and a worthy experience, but hardly a different and fascinating new world. I hoped this trip would redress the balance.

The travels of my former girlfriend, Ashley, were the antithesis of mine. She had spent eight years as a humanitarian aid worker for Doctors Without Borders, during which time she visited some of the most war-torn countries on the planet. This included two years in Sierra Leone, two in Lebanon, and two in southern Sudan. I had immense respect for her work and had always loved to hear of her many adventures. Some of her tales were exciting, some poignant and moving, others downright funny—all were an inspiration and made me want to visit a more enigmatic part of the world.

All I needed to see my plan come to fruition was enough money to fund it—quickly, so I didn't have to travel through Central Asia in the depths of winter. Winters in that part of the world could be brutal, and, since my accommodation would predominately be my flimsy little tent, it made travel at that time of year unappealing if not unfeasible.

For the last few months, I had been religiously saving every penny earned from my boring and underpaid temporary office job, but this was only a secondary source of funding. The main slice of traveling cash would come from something I'd done on three previous occasions when in dire need of money–taking part in medical research in a voluntary clinical trial.

For clinical or medical trials, healthy people volunteer to take an experimental medicine that is in the final stages of development with a pharmaceutical company, such as a new headache pill or asthma inhaler. They're then monitored on a hospital ward for a designated period of time before receiving a handsome, tax-free check for their troubles, normally in the order of one or two thousand British pounds for just a couple weeks of their time. Two grand (roughly four thousand U.S. dollars) was just what I needed to add to the eight hundred pounds I'd saved. That would enable me to stick around in China for a while, and, more importantly, get me back again.

Clinical trials aren't such a bad way of spending a week or two. You get free food and accommodation, a common room with satellite TV, free Internet access, loads of DVDs, game consoles, books, board games, and best of all there are lots of pretty nurses to chat to–when they're not siphoning your blood or demanding a periodic urine sample, that is.

The downside to the trials is that the medicines, thus far, have been untested on humans. I'd felt no side effects during the three previous trials I'd taken part in, but whether I'd been lucky and got one of the placebos, which make up 25 percent of the doses given, I don't know.

I phoned the hospital and secured my place on a trial for a new flu drug. The pretrial screening seemed but a formality, since I had passed all the previous screenings and was of average height, average weight, and a nonsmoker. After several tests, however, the doctor gave me the bad news that I had been rejected from the study because my heartbeat was two-beats-a-minute too fast for this particular trial. I was gutted. The next available trial, *if* I passed the screening, was months away, meaning I'd have to travel in the depths of winter. My failing the trial had put an end to my epic overland journey to China before it had even begun.

So what was I to do? I had about fourteen hundred dollars to my name and two brand-new, unused visas in my passport, one for Uzbekistan, the other for the Islamic Republic of Iran. The first had been a piece of cake to acquire but the second had been very difficult. It had taken over two months to secure, despite the fact that I'd used a Tehran-based visa agency which had promised speedy service and liaised on my behalf with the Iranian Ministry of Foreign Affairs. It had been so difficult to come by that it now seemed a terrible waste not to use it, especially as I had read that if I didn't use it, it would effectively guarantee the embassy's turning down any subsequent applications.

With this in mind I decided, somewhat apprehensively, to hitchhike to Tehran instead of Shanghai, and to travel the country from north to south and east to west. It was apparently dirt cheap, so I figured my funds would just about stretch this far. Plus, it was over halfway to China–over three thousand miles away–a more than respectable hitchhiking destination, although perhaps not quite the monumental overland marathon I'd hoped for with China.

My only concern was Iran's ominous reputation as an "Axis of Evil" breeding ground for angry Islamic fundamentalists. And since two of its bordering neighbors, Iraq and Afghanistan, were in total chaos, I wondered if Iran might not be the smartest of holiday destinations. Most of my friends thought likewise and encouraged me to go elsewhere for my vacation–somewhere "safer."

I could well understand their concerns, for I had similar fears myself, most of which had been formed after watching a TV documentary showing graphic footage of human rights abuses in Iran. It had made a powerful and lasting impression on me. In the program, a man was shown having his hand cut off, another was shown screaming in utter agony as his eyeball was sliced out with a scalpel–punishment for looking at something immoral–and worst of all was footage of women being stoned to death. The women were wrapped up like mummies in thick white sheeting and buried in the ground up to their chests to prevent any movement as the blows rained in. Gradually, the sheets turned from white to red. It was horrific and scared the hell out of me.

But any fear of hitching to and traveling around the Islamic Republic was superseded by my fear of staying in England in a dead-end job I hated. I thus made up my mind to hitchhike to Iran come–what–may.

The more I thought about it, the more I became curious as to whether the country's ominous reputation was well-founded, or if much of it was just media propaganda. I couldn't remember having ever seen a positive or heartwarming news story from Iran, and it seemed to me that whenever it featured on the nightly news, either crazed, head-banging mobs or grim, black-cloaked women were shown. Even the famous Iranian embassy siege in London seemed to indicate a country that was trouble. Did normal people live there at all, I wondered? Whatever the truth, I wanted to see and experience the real Iran for myself and to spend as much time as I could with the people of the country whilst immersing myself in their culture.

My planning, or lack of planning, for this new adventure of mine consisted simply of photocopying the relevant pages from both a European and Turkish road atlas, on which I plotted my intended hitchhiking route with a thick red marker, then buying a trusty *Lonely Planet Iran*, and getting myself packed.

I was desperate to get moving.

Arriving at the train station, I headed toward the seaside town of Dover, where I would catch the ferry to France and begin my long hard hitch to the Middle East.

CHAPTER ONE

Close Encounters of the Mustachioed Kind

To hitchhike is to experience the very best and worst of humanity. Often when hitching, I've been lucky enough to meet people who have shown to me a kindness and generosity so great as to be humbling–a kindness which, had our situations been reversed, I fear I would not have shown to them.

Unfortunately though, whilst hitching you also get to encounter your fair share of moronic idiots, who, upon seeing you standing by the side of the road with a thumb held optimistically in the air, flick you, by way of response, a middle finger. Or even, as I experienced once in Australia, throw a bag of half-eaten McDonald's at you. From my experience though, the good normally far outweighs the bad, and to travel this way generally leaves me with a greater faith in humanity.

I'd had an interesting two and a half weeks. I'd hitchhiked all the way from France to eastern Turkey, stopping off at places of interest en route to Iran, which was now only one or two day's hitching to the east. I'd met some wonderful people in the process and had traveled through France, Belgium, Germany, Austria, Hungary, Croatia, Serbia, Bulgaria, and Turkey.

I now stuck out my thumb for an approaching truck. It stopped, but in hindsight I wish it hadn't. Writing this now, months later, still sends a shiver up my spine.

I jumped in and was happy to take the weight off my feet and dump my horrible backpack. I said "Malatya," to the driver who responded with an "Ooh" as if to say, "That's a big journey!"

He was a Saddam Hussein look-alike, although he was in better shape than the original and had a bushier trademark 'stache.

I asked Saddam on numerous occasions to make sure we were definitely going to Malatya. Although he spoke no English, Saddam established a sort of standing joke to my question and would shake his head and say, "Istanbul." When I gave him a concerned look, he'd laugh and say, "Malatya, Malatya." It wasn't a rib tickler by any stretch of the imagination, but at least he grasped where I wanted to go.

On our way through dramatic mountain gorges and fields of tobacco plantations, we pulled over next to some children who were selling apples opposite their families' nomadic tents. They were young guys of about twelve or thirteen, and they filled up a carrier bag full of green apples for Saddam, which they weighed on a small scale. Saddam smiled at them and reached inside the truck, where he produced a handheld scale of his own. He weighed the bag, indicated it was lighter than they claimed, and demanded more apples for his money. The kids knew they'd been rumbled but took it with a smile and even handed me a free apple for the road. Things got weird not long after this.

We traveled along a dusty section of road and onto the highway heading directly to Malatya, which was by now due east. We'd been traveling for a few minutes, when Saddam veered abruptly off the highway and onto a gravelly track heading north toward what looked like a deserted industrial site. I protested immediately and pointed in the direction of Malatya whilst saying the city's name forcefully several times. Saddam put his foot down on the accelerator and tried his previous joke of "Istanbul, Istanbul!" It hadn't been funny before, and it certainly wasn't now.

He sped along the bumpy track, going too fast for me to get out, as I continued protesting, "Malatya! Malatya!" He ignored me completely now and drove at full throttle until he slowed down in the middle of an eerie-as-hell area straight out of a cheap B horror movie. The truck swung round to face the way we came and then came to a halt in the center of a deserted field. The highway was in front of us now along with a vast, disused industrial factory, quite a distance away. To the right of the factory were, I think, three unfinished or abandoned apartment blocks, which wouldn't have looked out of place in neighboring Iraq's bombed-out front line. On our immediate right was a small orchard enclosed by barbed wire. Behind us were more fields stretching off into the distance. There was, effectively, no place for me to go unless I got out and hiked back toward the highway. Just to add to the foreboding setting, it was now beginning to get dark.

Saddam got out of the truck and gestured for me to follow. "Like hell," I thought, and stayed put, saying, "No!" He tried again to persuade me to join him but I was having none of it.

As if thinking this over for a second, he stood in front of the truck and looked around at our location. Slowly moving off, he headed toward the orchard. Unhooking a section of the barbed wire fence, he gained entry and stepped inside. I tried to see what he was up to through the small trees, but in the disappearing light it was difficult to be sure. From what I could make out, though, it looked like Saddam had gone into a small shed and was rummaging around for something. I immediately thought he had foul play in mind. It just didn't seem likely he was tending to his prize tomato plants or new geraniums, and I began to wonder seriously if he was after some sort of weapon.

Under normal circumstances, I was sure I could take him in a fight, but if my gut feeling was right and he was getting "tooled up," then that was another matter altogether.

My adrenaline started to elevate, and I decided to equal the odds a bit, grabbing my six-inch camping knife from the side pocket of my backpack. I attached it to my belt and flicked open its sheath, just in case I needed it in a hurry. I'd only ever used it for carving wood, but if need be and things got serious, then it would do the job. Before leaving England, I'd sharpened it to such a degree that it would shave the hairs off my arm, so I figured that as long as Saddam didn't have a gun then I'd be okay. If he did, I'd be fucked.

Part of me tried to discount the feeling of danger as complete paranoia and to tell myself, "Hey, this can't be happening," and "It's probably all very innocent," but a much more powerful part of me knew something was wrong. A good ten minutes passed agonizingly slowly, but still there was no sign of Saddam. With the passing of time, my thoughts, like the sky, got darker and darker. It seemed to me, rightly or wrongly, that he was waiting for me to venture inquisitively into the orchard to see where he'd got to–fat chance.

I got more freaked out as time ticked by. What the hell was he doing? Was he waiting for it to get dark? My heart pounded and my breathing quickened as I thought through my options. The way I saw it, I could either give him the benefit of the doubt and stick where I was until he returned, or assume the worst and get the hell out of here on foot. I chose the latter. Grabbing my backpack, I slipped from the driver's side of the truck unnoticed and headed out across the field in the direction of the highway and disused factory.

It was a long walk, and luckily the field was ploughed and too bumpy for him to follow in his truck if he noticed I was gone. About a third of the way across the field, I looked back and saw Saddam run to his truck and drive off at speed. He'd obviously noticed I was gone and as insane and surreal as it sounds, now appeared to be coming after me.

My adrenaline accelerated rapidly as I ran all manner of nightmare scenarios through my head. He drove along the outskirts of the field slightly parallel to my direction of travel, and although there was a good distance between us, he would easily be able to close the gap if the track he was driving along veered back toward my route further up ahead. For the life of me, though, I couldn't make out if this was the case, as the little light that was left just wasn't enough to see for certain.

Turning around wasn't an option; I needed to get to the highway, not head off deeper into the unknown. I was also convinced that I could batter Saddam to a pulp unless he had his own little weapon of mass destruction, and I felt genuinely pissed off that he was messing with and underestimating me. I shook my head at the insanity of the situation. I just wanted to be in a nice hotel with a hot shower not dealing with this demented shit in a deserted field.

I watched his truck like a hawk as it approached the far side of the factory just hoping upon hope that there wasn't an unseen track that would enable him to head in my direction.

"Please say he's not turning there."

He turned.

The lonely realization that I was going to have to confront him hit me hard. I didn't even try to increase my pace as there was no point now—he would intercept me before I reached the highway, and that was that. Saddam skidded to an abrupt halt about five hundred feet away and got out of the truck. I continued forward taking several deep breaths, desperately trying to control the buildup of adrenaline running wild through my veins. Every footstep felt heavy as I went on high alert ready for fight or flight. I still hoped it would be the latter.

Fear gnarled away at me shouting, "What if he's armed!? What if he's fucking armed!?" I tethered the thought as I walked closer and repeated to myself that if he was armed, then I wouldn't hesitate to reach for my knife. But in reality it was the last thing I wanted to do–I just wanted to be rid of him and hit the highway unhindered.

When I got within twenty feet of him, Saddam walked toward me aggressively and ordered me, with a pointed finger and some yelled Turkish expletives, back into the truck. My adrenaline went through the roof now and I was ready to go for him big-time but was still very much in favor of the flight option. Under normal circumstances, in, say, a pub in England, I would have stood my ground, but out here in the middle of a deserted Turkish field, it was a different matter. If I could get away from him then I would and my ego be dammed.

As such, I tried to simply walk around him. This strategy proved to be worthless, as he quickly moved toward me and tried to grab my arm, which I held out blocking his advance. I pulled violently away but with the weight of my backpack, I spun almost completely around. He grabbed my pack instantly and with both hands tried to wrestle it and me to the ground.

I fought wildly to remain upright as he yanked the pack and me from side to side. Its weight and size were a great lever for him, and I struggled to get the upper hand. Through sheer aggression, as opposed to technique, I managed to get him in front of me again, where I now grabbed his wrists like a vice. His face was real close, and the perfect distance for me to head butt, but my backpack, still strapped to me, made this maneuvering impossible.

Instead, I shoved him back with both hands as hard as I could yelling, "Fucking get back! Stay where you fucking are!" There was no need for translation. I stepped backward to create some space between us, in the hope he'd now back off without things getting any worse than they already were. No chance. He reached down for a jagged rock and began to come at me with it. That was it: if he had a weapon then so would I. I drew my knife and really thought I was going to have to butcher the bastard into several Sunday roasts.

I flashed the gleaming blade at him and bellowed, "Drop the stone! Fucking get back!"

He stopped dead in his tracks, his eyes going from me, to the knife, then back to me again. I got the impression he was figuring out if I had the balls to use it. And the truth of the matter was, I was very reluctant to do so, but if push came to shove and he tried to batter me with the rock, then I'm sure I would have plunged the weirdo.

I yelled once more, "Drop it! Fucking get back!"

He looked again at the knife then thankfully saw sense and slowly backed off, dropping the rock in the process, before getting into his truck. I didn't waste time sticking around in case he changed his mind or had a weapon in the cab. Instead, I quickly moved off the track where he could only follow me on foot. I watched as he started the truck up and raced off toward the highway, leaving me alone in the darkness.

A number of stray dogs started barking eerily in the distance. This was not what I wanted. Going as fast as I could, I headed toward the highway. This whole area gave me the creeps; I wanted out of it and quick. I came to an abrupt halt when my path was blocked by a high barbed wire fence on the opposite side of the factory. It looked like I might have to make a long and unappealing detour around it, but mercifully I found a hole in the fence large enough for me and my pack to squeeze through. It was now completely dark, and as I walked toward the highway I wondered if Saddam was still around.

I felt drained, and on reaching the road I hailed the first shared minibus that came along—hitching could wait for another day. I jumped in the back of the partially filled van, and as it pulled away, the gravity of what had just happened hit me. I felt desperately lonely and wanted to talk to someone very badly. But of course not being a Turkish speaker, I remained in silence and just thought things over again and again and again.

As we approached the city, I said to the guy sitting next to me, "Hotel? Malatya?" He hadn't a clue what I wanted, but a mid-twenties girl a couple of seats in front of me turned around and asked clearly if I spoke English. This was more like it. I explained that I was looking for a cheap hotel in the center of town. If there weren't any cheap ones then to hell with my tight budget, I was going to spend whatever it cost tonight to get a good bed in a place I could get my head together.

She explained that she and her friend would walk me to a hotel. I thanked her many times and began to relax. As we pulled into a thriving bus station, her friend reached over to the driver and paid the fare for all three of us. I didn't argue. We got out of the van and now in the light I saw them properly for the first time.

I was taken aback by the English speaker's friend, whose eyes were almost identical to my ex-girlfriend's. The similarity was uncanny and I'm sure it was the crazy incident in the field minutes earlier, but I desperately wanted to hold her. Of course I did nothing of the sort. I followed the girls like a lost puppy through the streets and began to think of them as my guardian angels.

The English-speaking girl explained that they were taking me to a hotel that was both cheap and beautiful–it was also full. On we walked through crowded city streets to a second establishment called the Hotel Aygun. She explained that she was leaving now but her friend would do the negotiations for me inside. Farewells and thank-yous were exchanged, and I headed inside with her friend. How well her negotiation skills worked I don't know, but she got me a room and it seemed a reasonable enough price at the time, although I can't remember the cost. In the few words of English she spoke, she said, "Goodbye" and "Nice to meet you." I really didn't want her to go as I desperately wanted company but, since she didn't speak any English, it wasn't like I could ask her to come for a drink or anything, and what's more, all I really wanted was a hug. I said, "Goodbye."

CHAPTER TWO

Hitchhiking to the Axis of Evil

I made good initial progress after leaving Malatya, and had hoped to reach Iran by nightfall but had made the mistake of accepting a less-than-slow lift when hitching out of the Turkish town of Elazig. Here, I was picked up by a kindly old truck driver called Ilhan, whose vehicle was in a terrible state of repair and looked as old as he did. I stuck with him though, as Ilhan was traveling some 220 odd miles along my route to the small town of Horasan, which was only 130 miles from the Iranian border. We spent most of the day on the road but covered a fraction of the distance we should have, since the vehicle was overheating terribly with smoke billowing from the engine as we drove. The farther we traveled, the more fatigued the truck became. It was slow enough on flat straight roads, but when it got to hills, it really began to struggle and ascended these at next to walking pace. This took forever as there were numerous long twisting mountainous roads along our route and every time we approached one of these, we had to jump out and dowse the engine with water from a number of old plastic bottles in the cab.

Whenever we passed a stream or roadside water fountain, it was my job to sink the bottles in the cool water, filling them up for use later on. This procedure, as well as our speed, ate away at our time, and it soon became apparent that I wasn't going to get to Iran anytime tonight. Realistically, I would probably get there by midday tomorrow. I resigned myself to this and wasn't really bothered; it didn't matter to me whether it was today, tomorrow, or even next week that I arrived there, so long as I did arrive.

The farther east we went, the better the landscape became, and we drove through some of the finest scenery I'd seen so far on my journey. Parts of it reminded me of the rugged Scottish Highlands, although there was a slightly different tinge to the color of the hills. Numerous nomadic people lived out here in this vast rolling landscape, as indicated by their tents visible from the road. Although I was hugely excited about being so close to my final destination of Iran, I was so impressed with the scenery in eastern Turkey that I flirted with the idea of stopping off for a few days and trying to befriend some nomads.

We drove late into the night before pulling up next to a deserted gas station in the Turkish town of Erzurum. Ilhan took the bed at the back of the cab, whilst I tried to nestle down in front. This was none too easy since there was a huge gap between the seats with the gear stick protruding in the middle. To make matters worse, as soon as Ilhan's head hit the pillow, he began to snore. Not your normal snoring, mind you, but strong enough to give the local seismologists a scare.

My industrial–strength wax earplugs wouldn't touch it, and being a very light sleeper, I knew I was in for a ghastly tormented night. I rolled about uncomfortably trying to sleep, but it was no good, and I decided to cut my losses and head outside with my sleeping bag. Even with the doors shut and several feet away from the truck, the snores resonated at a ridiculous level.

Outside was a complete mess, strewn with piles of broken glass and trash, and illuminated by a big red light near the deserted garage, and a bright white light out on the road. Next to the garage was a small slope leading down to a patch of waste ground, which backed onto several houses. From these the vicious barking of dogs emanated.

Looking down the slope, I surveyed the waste ground, which appeared slightly flatter and less carpeted with glass than the area immediately outside the truck. I decided it was home. Lying on my side to minimize the effect of the streetlight, I got as good a rest as could be expected under the circumstances–bugger all. After a while, though, I went into that state where you're neither fully awake nor fully asleep, although you are getting some limited benefit. This semi–peaceful state shattered like a falling mirror in an instant. I awoke to the sound of dogs barking wildly and opened my eyes to a waking nightmare. To my horror, I saw through sleep–blurred eyes four bloodthirsty–looking dogs running out of the darkness at me, less than forty feet away. In a nanosecond, my adrenaline hit fever pitch and I scrambled madly to my feet, only to fall straight back down again since my legs were still in my sleeping bag. The dogs closed the gap, their barking now chillingly close.

I got up again and ripped off the sleeping bag in a panicked flurry, throwing it behind me as I ran like a man possessed toward the slope and the safety of the truck. I powered up the hill, stumbling on the rocky surface and smashing my shin against a boulder in the process. Finally, I reached the top. I spun around, panting like my pursuers, and looked down at them whilst my heart thundered away in my chest. They were going crazy at the bottom of the slope, growling and barking away, but although they could have scaled it, they seemed to have reached an invisible boundary that they wouldn't venture past. The waste ground was clearly their domain and not to be invaded. I backed off farther, not wanting to test this theory out, and not long afterward they did the same, disappearing into the darkness from which they had come.

My sleeping bag was still down there, but the thought of going to retrieve it didn't exactly appeal right now. It took a while before I plucked up the courage, and when I did so, I was on hyper alert and at running speed in and out. The prospect of the truck's cab and Ilhan's snoring seemed strangely appealing now. I climbed back inside the warmth of the cab and resigned myself to a disrupted night. The snoring was still deafening but it was far preferable to a mad dog attack. It was one of the worst night's "sleep" I've ever had.

In the morning, Ilhan arose with a contented smile looking well-rested and ready to face the day ahead. We arrived at Horasan, which was a small rural place, by midmorning and bade each other farewell, since Ilhan was heading north. I stood out like a sore thumb here and received many strange looks from the locals who clearly weren't used to seeing European hitchhikers this far east. Some young lads, one of whom spoke a few words of English, came over to where I was standing and tried to persuade me to catch a bus to Iran instead. I hadn't hitched this far through mad dog and psychopath attack to cheat on the last section and pay for a ride, so I shook my head with a smile.

Opposite where I waited was a load of livestock being transferred from one truck to another. It wasn't a nice sight: in the process one poor cow stumbled and fell to the ground, where it was beaten repeatedly with a stick. It just made it harder for the animal to get back up again and was sickening to watch; the blows came in thick and fast, and echoed off its body.

Half an hour later, I got a lift in a very modern and fast truck. It drove along at speeds Ilhan's poor vehicle could only have dreamt about, which felt worrying given the huge size of the truck and the small width of the roads. The driver spoke no English, but instead of silence I was treated to some religious chanting coming from the stereo. At one point, the driver put his hand on his heart and mumbled some chanted words reverently to himself. He looked across at me to make sure I was taking it all very seriously. I tried my best to look pensive but was more concerned with his one-handed high-speed prayer driving.

We parted company in a small rural Turkish village, the name of which I never learnt, next to a bridge over a river that was blocked by several goats and cows ambling along to get to the embankment nearby. They took a good while to clear, and on seeing me and my backpack, their young herder shouted a warm English "hello." He looked rather pleased with himself when I responded with the same.

A few minutes later, another modern truck responded to my request for a lift and pulled up some distance from where I stood, creating a huge cloud of dust. I ran over, opened the door, climbed the steps leading up to the cab, and was just about to haul myself inside when the driver stopped me by indicating that I should take off my shoes first. He pointed to his immaculate carpet, then to his feet, and shook his head with a smile. I climbed down the steps again, pulled my shoes off, and got in.

This proved to be my final lift all the way to Iran and the end of my hitchhiking proper for this trip. I was extremely pleased. It turned out to be a conversation-free ride since the driver spoke as much English as I did Turkish or Farsi, the Iranian language, but we managed to establish early on what each other's names were. His was Kerim, and he was driving all the way to Tehran, the capital of Iran.

The landscape we drove through was beautiful, but the music he played at a deafening volume was anything but, with eighties Irish crooner Chris de Burgh blaring from the stereo. This was my first encounter with the peculiar popularity of de Burgh all over Iran, and although not my first choice of auditory stimulation, it did, at the time, make a welcome change from the likes of repetitive religious chanting.

The last settlement before the Iranian border is the small Turkish town of Dogubayazit, known affectionately to travelers as "doggie biscuit." Just twenty-two miles from Iran and at an elevation of some 6,000 feet, Dogubayazit commands spectacular views of Turkey's highest peak, Mount Ararat, which rises majestically from a plain to reach nearly 17,000 feet.

At one time, Dogubayazit had been a significant trading town thanks to its location near an ancient trading route that ran from northwestern Iran to the shores of the Black Sea. But when the trading route's importance declined, so did that of the town, and today this predominantly Kurdish settlement provides services for people stopping off between Turkey and Iran, and for those visiting Mount Ararat.

The snow-capped Mount Ararat dominates the town's surrounding landscape. It is considered a holy site by the Armenians and is, according to some, the resting place of Noah's ark. Genesis 8:4 states that the ark came to rest on the "mountains of Ararat." The counterargument to this handy pinpointing of the ark's location is that *Ararat* was the Assyrian way of saying "the empire of Urartu," which was a whole geographical region, not simply a mountain. Still, many people are adamant that it's somewhere up the mountain, and numerous expeditions have set off in vain to try to find it.

We stopped in Dogubayazit at a café for lunch, which included meat of uncertain origin, tomatoes, bread, and olives. We were less than thirty minutes from the border, and it was now that I looked properly at my *Lonely Planet* guidebook for the very first time. For sure, I'd browsed the pictures before, but I felt planning anything before I arrived in Iran and got a feel for the place was premature. As I began to skim the pages, however, I wished I'd read more before I'd got so close to the border.

Of particular concern was a section about changing money, and its advice not to do so at Bazargan just inside the Iranian border, which was exactly where I had planned to do it, as it would be my first stop in Iran. Apparently, foreigners received extreme hassle from the crafty money changers there and were often ripped off in the process. I didn't like the sound of this.

In the money changer's favor I now learnt, was the confusion between the rials written on Iranian bank notes and the tomans commonly referred to by the locals. Since one toman equates to ten rials, this quirky local practice is the equivalent of American shopkeepers asking for ten cents when they really require a dollar. To confuse matters further, the shopkeepers at the bazaars will, on occasion, ask for one toman when they actually mean one hundred rials, or even a thousand.

According to my guidebook, the money changers were perfectly aware of this confusion and did their best to exploit it with foreigners, whilst stirring in random references to the dollar just to muddy the waters further. I didn't plan to change a penny in Bazargan now. I mimed to Kerim and the other guys at the café, all of whom he seemed to know, that I needed to exchange some money before I arrived in Iran.

These kindly chaps explained, via a man from the shop next door who spoke a little English, that they would be more than happy to help me out and personally exchange my U.S. dollars, for what they assured me was a better than average rate. I politely declined. After further discussions and negotiations, one of them agreed, for a small fee, to take me to a proper money changer not far away in the center of town. I jumped into his car, leaving Kerim and my backpack behind in the truck, and went through the crowded twisting streets to a small currency exchange shop. I only wanted to exchange enough for the next few days until I managed to locate a proper bank inside Iran. I swapped the Turkish lira equivalent of about sixty dollars, and in return received a huge wad of green Iranian currency graced with the image of the Ayatollah Khomeini. As soon as I returned to the café, we set off for Iran.

The queue of trucks stretched for a hell of a long distance from the border, which is considered to be one of the most congested bottlenecks in West Asia. The thought of waiting in the truck for hours didn't appeal, so I thanked Kerim for the ride and headed off on foot toward Iran.

* * *

I approached the border with some trepidation. Thoughts of the gruesome documentary I'd seen before leaving and of the chaos in nearby Iraq filled my mind, and I wondered what sort of reception I, as a Westerner, would get in the Islamic Republic of Iran. Britain had meddled often with the country's internal affairs, so would the Iranian people be cold or even hostile? I thought back on my encounter with Saddam, which, along with last night's canine–interrupted sleeping arrangements, I could well have done without. I hoped there wouldn't be any similar close shaves awaiting me in Iran.

The initial reception, it turned out, couldn't have been nicer. I was directed by friendly, smiling officials to one of two border queues situated inside an airport–style customs building. In here, I saw for the first time a picture I would see again and again during my Iranian tour: a portrait of Iran's late supreme religious leader, Ayatollah Khomeini. Alongside this was a picture of the current religious leader, Ayatollah Ali Khamenei. There was also a sign for a prayer room and one for a human quarantine area. On seeing these pictures and signs, I felt a quiet sense of achievement at having made it this far and having finally reached my elusive destination. The nervousness I'd experienced moments ago evaporated and was replaced with an intense excitement.

I joined the back of a large line leading to a couple of kiosks where it appeared that passports and visas were being checked and stamped. Just beyond this was a larger area where a group of people were busy arranging their luggage in readiness for joining another queue, at the end of which luggage was being presented for inspection at a customs desk. After less than a minute lined up behind the locals, I was spotted by an official who immediately approached me. My previous apprehension returned when I was then asked for my passport and told simply, "Follow me." I was paranoid at having been singled out and was half–expecting a thorough interrogation, followed by an invasive full cavity search, topped off with a spell in "human quarantine."

Instead the official brought me to the front of the line, handed his colleague my passport, and said happily, even excitedly, "Tourist!" His colleague smiled back, stamping my passport in the process, and said in a similar manner, "Welcome to Iran!"

I was now led through the crowd of locals rearranging their luggage. This proved difficult as my tent protruded significantly sideways from my backpack, making it impossible to get past without bumping into people. I apologized profusely and tried to maneuver as carefully through the crowds as possible, but the friendly official couldn't be bothered with any of this cautious nonsense and pushed me from behind shouting "Tourist! Tourist!" in an attempt to clear the crowds.

A generously proportioned Iranian woman in traditional full black chador stood blocking my way. I hunched my shoulders and turned to squeeze respectfully past her, but just as I was about to negotiate this move, the official gave another helpful shove and I hurtled toward her. It was like the second before being in a car crash where paradoxically everything slows down and yet speeds up all at once. I panicked and instinctively tried to stop the collision by throwing out my hands–which collided with her ample hindquarters. My palms sunk in, giving me a big fat fistful of Iranian ghetto booty, and sending her forward with a surprised and startled jolt.

She spun around in disgust and reprimanded me, saying goodness knows what in Farsi. She didn't look too happy and neither was I. It was hardly in keeping with the delicate etiquette surrounding the treatment of women in an Islamic state of which I was well aware.

"I'm awfully sorry," I tried to explain as best I could using hand gestures but the official continued pushing and before I knew it we'd cleared the crowd. Now in the main hall, I made a move to join the back of the "customs" line, but the official shook his head and with a smile whisked me to the front of this also. Luckily, this time I went *around* it rather than through it. The customs guy checking bags was already dealing with someone when we approached, but his colleague pushed me in front of him announcing proudly, "Tourist!"

Now ignoring the local himself, the customs guy gave me a warm smile and said, "Ah, tourist!" I lifted my bag up for inspection but he just smiled again and waved me through.

That was it—I'd cleared the border.

Weren't customs officials meant to be officious bureaucrats, never happier than when exercising their little bit of power? I'd expected nothing less in Iran; I'd imagined they'd be worse than the ones at home and would make British or American officials seem almost cheery and lenient by comparison, but in fact, the opposite was true. I was completely stunned, and didn't quite know what to do next.

In need of a strong caffeine injection, and an opportunity to formulate a plan and get my head together, I headed to a café inside the border control building. Even walking the short distance there, I was approached by several money changers touting for business. Again, I felt pleased to have read up on this before getting here and shook my head at them with a smile as I passed.

The café was packed, and despite pointing to a cup of coffee, I was given tea. I wasn't bothered, so long as it had caffeine in it, and was just about to sit down at one of the tables with a few spare seats when I realized I couldn't, as sitting on one of the seats was a woman. It is considered a big no-no to sit down next to a member of the opposite sex who is not your spouse, a close relative, or a person you're familiar with, unless specifically asked to do so. This etiquette stuff was going to take some getting used to.

I found another table completely free of women and plonked myself down. Whilst sipping away at my tea, I dipped into my guidebook to read about the surrounding area of northwestern Iran. One attraction in particular caught my attention. A church by the name of Kelisa-ye Tadi (the Church of St. Thaddeus), described as one of the most famous and remarkable Christian monuments in Iran, was relatively close by, at fourteen miles from the next town of Maku. Its origins dated back as far as AD 371, and although it had only one service a year, held on the feast of St. Thaddeus when pilgrims traveled from all over Iran to attend, it was open daily for tourists. The guidebook recommended chartering a taxi to get there, which, including the return journey, would apparently cost a very reasonable IR25,000—about three dollars. Not bad for nearly thirty miles. Cabs are cheap in Iran as gasoline only costs an amazing thirty-seven cents a gallon (at the time of writing).

I decided the church would be the first place I'd visit tomorrow, but for now I wanted to get a bus into Maku, the nearest town from the border and once there book into a hotel. I headed outside and got my first glimpse of Iran. It was rugged, blue skied, fresh aired, and very sunny. As the majority of pictures I'd seen of Iran in newspapers and magazines at home were, almost without exception, in black and white and of a depressing nature, I almost felt surprised that the sun was still shining on this side of the border. Naïve, I know. The place was awash with color, and everyone seemed chilled out and had big happy smiles. I started to realize that things in Iran might be very different from the image I had of the place in my mind, and from the one portrayed in the Western media.

I proceeded to turn down several animated money changers, and, after soaking up the mountain scenery for a minute, I started my Iran journey proper.

CHAPTER THREE

Tourist at the Border

A statesmanlike picture of the late Ayatollah Khomeini greeted me in the slightly musty but welcoming lobby of the Hotel Alvand in Maku. Manning the reception desk was an attentive, grandfather–like figure who, in between sipping away at a little glass of tea and chomping on pistachio nuts, negotiated a price for a room. We settled on IR30,000, which, at about three dollars and fifty cents, seemed reasonable enough to me. In addition to handing over the money, I was also required to do likewise with my passport. This I did, assuming that it would be handed back after the appropriate reference number had been jotted down, but off it was taken and locked in a safe.

"Hello, hello, what's all this about?" I thought, and requested it back.

The friendly manager shook his head, and with the help of an English speaker in the lobby explained that whenever you book into a hotel in Iran, by law, you've got to hand over your passport. I wasn't overly keen on this little procedure, but what could I do?

The room was very basic, but after last night's less than salubrious accommodation, it was complete luxury for me. The view from my window was a breathtaking one of the huge rocky mountain gorge in which Maku was situated. A section of it contained a massive overhang of rock, which, if it ever fell down would wipe out a good bit of the town. This bit of the gorge looked well worth a visit.

Lurking suspiciously in the corner of my room were the most unhygienic pair of plastic sandals the world has ever seen. The sandals were a dingy white, imprinted with a nasty black sludge, presumably the result of countless applications of filthy feet and deposits of sweat and dead skin. God knows how many verrucas and fungus infections currently called them home, but one thing was for sure: my feet weren't going anywhere near them. Even looking at them made me feel queasy, so holding them at arm's length, I placed them in the cupboard and set off for the communal shower down the hall with my ten toes out for all to see.

The amount of soap and shampoo I smothered my body with was obscene. I used an industrial quantity of toothpaste, had a shave, and after putting on some clean clothes, which could no longer consist of shorts since exposing your legs in public in Iran is a big no–no even for a man, I felt like a different person and was ready to go exploring.

The air outside seemed to crackle with an electric charge such was my overwhelming excitement and anticipation to finally be here, in Iran! Maku was thriving with traffic and people, and consisted of one long main road lined with all manner of different shops, which were squeezed between the precipitous sides of the aforementioned mountain gorge. The gorge was spectacular and completely dominated the whole area for miles around.

The overhanging rock visible from my hotel window seemed to beckon me, so I decided to hike on up. It looked accessible through a slightly rough area off the main road, lined with lots of abandoned or partially collapsed houses. I was a bit apprehensive at first about going through here, but then thought, "What the hell?" I needn't have worried. The people were all very friendly, and some of them greeted me with a warm, *"Bonjour monsieur"* as I walked through their neighborhood. This greeting I assumed was simply the locals using a Western language they were familiar with rather than me looking French–or at least I hoped so.

After the houses, it was steep, rough terrain where several fallen boulders had blocked my route. I puffed and panted my way over a couple of these before realizing an established path ran nearby. The higher I climbed, the more impressive the mountain overhang became.

From the town below, the overhang had looked quite interesting and maybe worth a visit, but close by it was incredible and far larger than I'd thought. It was a huge tidal wave of rock, looking as if it were just about to break, swallowing everything in its path below. Interestingly, there were a couple of small trees growing almost horizontally from the side of the rock, hundreds of feet above me, clinging tenaciously to life.

I felt dizzy just staring up at it and had to sit down. Whilst gazing up in awe, I was approached by a local guy of about eighteen with a big friendly smile. He spoke no English but gestured for me to follow him. I got up and walked over to what looked like the remains of an old tower or chimney, then climbed up and looked inside, revealing . . . nothing at all.

My friendly guide gestured that I should maybe take a photo of it. I politely declined and pointed to the tsunami of rock above. It was the equivalent of standing next to a mighty elephant and taking a photo of its steaming pile of poop. There was just no comparison between the chimney and the rock face. It was simply too big to get in the viewfinder, and despite trying many different angles, I only managed to capture a mere fraction of its size and, as such, a fraction of its splendor. The local guy left soon after, leaving me to admire the site all by myself.

Whilst sitting, I began to watch a vast flock of birds slowly ebbing and flowing in perfect harmony hundreds of feet above. It was as if they no longer were comprised of individual birds but were instead a single entity. Periodically, their poetic synergy would shatter as the birds scattered wildly in a panicked flurry, but despite my best efforts, I spotted no predators.

By now it was dusk and as the sun began to set, it bathed the gorge below in a soothing orange hue that instilled in me a deep sense of tranquility. I felt so very alive and happy to be me, to be here and to be far away from England.

Just two and a half weeks earlier, I'd been stuck in a job I despised, confined within that office prison. There I'd sat under the artificial glow of strip lighting entering data onto a computer screen. The monotony was mind–numbing. Working there, I'd felt my happiness slipping slowly away from me. There hadn't even been a plant to look at for solace, no windows to offer temporary respite. I was a trapped animal longing desperately for adventure, for rapture, for nature, and to truly feel alive again.

As I gazed out across the wild, rugged expanse of mountains that stretched to the horizon, it all seemed so very far away now. I was happy beyond belief to be exactly where I was, and my spirit soared.

A soft wind hissed gently across the sand–colored rocks as I headed down, this time along a different path, which was far more gradual and went around the neighborhood I'd previously walked through. Near the bottom, I came across a small outdoor volleyball court where a group of guys ranging from about eighteen to thirty were dividing themselves into two teams. This procedure wasn't going too smoothly and an animated debate broke out which seemed to be about which team would get the most athletic–looking player and which would be burdened with the one who looked like he'd eaten all the pies.

I perched myself on a wall overlooking the court in order to watch the debate and reminisced on a similar situation in high school, when I'd been lucky enough to be chosen as one of two team captains. This tried and tested method of captains picking players from a line up was always employed to balance the teams out, and to throw in a bit of ritual humiliation for the fat kids.

It wasn't that I was particularly bad at sports back then, but more that I just couldn't give a damn about them, especially since, at the time, puberty-fuelled growth had not quite kicked in for me, making games like rugby more than just a little on the uneven side. One day, though, when our much-despised pock-faced rugby teacher, Mr. Brown, was being evaluated by a school inspector, I decided it would be fun to mix things up a bit.

Realizing there was little chance that a pupil of my reputation would be picked as a captain, I piped up with a completely out of character, "Excuse me, sir, can I be a captain please? It's just I haven't been one yet and I'd really like the opportunity." Mr. Brown eyed me suspiciously and looked like he was about to refuse, but with the inspector standing next to him, pencil poised above his clipboard and staring his way through the tops of his glasses, he reluctantly agreed.

My fellow captain, Rory, was first to choose from the line up and picked a brawny athletic type who replied with a confident nod.

No such logic with my selection. I picked, to everybody's amazement, most of all his own, Darren Hopton. To say that Hopton was underweight was a gross understatement. The kid was positively skeletal, and about as good at the sport of rugby as I am at synchronized swimming, which is to say no good at all. Hopton couldn't have tackled his grandmother–and she'd been dead for over a decade. But today was his day. It was the first time he'd not been picked last and he seized his moment of glory. Glancing back at the far more athletic players, he puffed out his chest in mock bravado and gave an audible condescending "hah!" their way. Everybody laughed except Mr. Brown.

My most unlikely, and unfortunate, rugby team of misfits ended up getting the drubbing of our lives from the burly cream of the class. But it was well worth it. When we passed the one hundred to zero mark, Mr. Brown, in a fit of frustration, scrapped the game and changed the teams, receiving, I hope, a disapproving scribble on the inspector's clipboard.

The dispute over teams on the volleyball court was finally resolved and the players, most of them wearing work shirts, shoes, and dress pants, not sporting gear, began a game. Three other guys, who were in fact wearing "casuals," sat watching from a bench nearby. Also spectating were lots of younger boys, of around seven to ten years old, who all hung out together in a big group.

It was a pretty even match, but when one particularly good point was scored, everyone applauded. I did likewise and received a couple of gracious nods from the players below. Lots of the little kids now tentatively looked my way. They all whispered together and looked as if they were discussing approaching the strange tourist but didn't quite have the courage in case he wasn't friendly. After a couple more applauded shots, one of the biggest of the kids threw caution to the wind and began his advance. The others stayed a safe distance back and looked on.

He got within a few feet of me and said cautiously, "Hello."

"Hello, salaam," I replied.

That was it—he turned and smiled triumphantly down at his friends, giving them the all clear. They stampeded en masse up to join their friend, and now with an assembled audience he did it again.

"Hello," he said, as if performing a demonstration.

"Hello, salaam," I replied again.

They all wanted to give this a try. To everyone's delight, it worked as well for them as it had done for their friend and the tourist replied "Hello, salaam" in return. Although this was the limit of the conversation, it did nothing to curb their enthusiasm and they tried it repeatedly just to make sure it still worked. Luckily, I was rescued by one of the guys on the bench, who waved me down to join them. I walked over and was immediately offered a glass of tea, or *chay* as it is called in Iran, from a decorative silver tray. There were only three glasses so I hesitated–I didn't want to steal their drink.

I took one though, figuring that as they'd offered, it must be okay and what's more, I fancied a drink. One of them spoke a tiny bit of English, and asked me in a matter-of-fact way for my name, age, occupation, and salary, along with where I was from and whether I was married. On hearing that I wasn't married yet, he expressed his sadness, as if this was a terrible trauma for a male of nearly thirty to bear. I learned later that these questions, including the seemingly tactless ones of how much I earned and whether I was married, are in fact standard Iranian icebreakers, and I was to hear them again and again wherever I went. I kind of liked this forthright approach that rejected the idea of delicately pussyfooting around a new social encounter and instead cut through the BS and went directly for the required information. Perhaps, I wondered, Iranian guys had a similarly frank approach when chatting up women, and asked directly for waist, chest, and leg measurements, along with a full STD history, and whether or not they were up for it.

During my introductions with the guys on the bench, the bigger of the little lads who'd approached me before came over for a piece of the action with the tourist. He attempted his tried and tested "Hello" line again, but before I could answer he got the Farsi equivalent of "Get lost, shorty" from the proper big boys. He looked a little annoyed; after all, he'd been the one who'd found the tourist first and now the big boys had stolen him. He did as he was told though, and walked off sullenly.

Gesturing to the game, I asked the guy who spoke a little English if he played volleyball. Shaking his head, he replied, "Football and box," followed by a brief shadowboxing demonstration.

Having done a bit of this myself, I did likewise with a quick flurry of the noble art. They all liked this so he did his again. I again followed suit. We were buddies now, and to show it he produced a flick knife and began meticulously slicing up an apple and banana for us to share. They were delicious. I stayed around trying to communicate with them long after it got dark, and when it was finally time to leave, they insisted on driving me back to my hotel.

Before going inside to bed, I headed up the street for a stroll; I was struck by the clarity of the stars, which blazed in the clear night sky with an intensity I'd not yet seen on this trip, and I stood for several minutes just looking up. They were spectacular and although I was delighted to be here, I couldn't help but wish I had someone to share this magical sight with.

When I got back to the hotel, the fatigue of the last couple of nights caught up with me and I crashed out exhausted but happy.

* * *

Iranian taxi drivers can be a pain in the ass. I'd spent the last twenty minutes in animated negotiation with a group of hard-nosed cabbies in an attempt to get a ride to my intended destination of today, the church of St. Thaddeus, but things hadn't gone according to plan.

I had made my way out to a little junction just outside of Maku where a group of taxis was parked haphazardly along the road I needed to take to get to the church. Despite my best efforts, none of the crafty cabbies, of which there were about fifteen, was willing to take me unless I paid *way* over the standard price and stumped up an outrageously big tourist fee instead. They didn't say this, of course, but since the prices they were quoting were seven times higher than those in my guidebook, it didn't take a genius to work it out.

Taxis in Iran work in a slightly different way from those in the West, in that they can be hired in two ways, either in the conventional manner, or as a so-called shared taxi. This is where the taxi picks up multiple passengers along a standard route in much the same way as a bus does in the West. Both are interchangeable, though, with the driver going for the best option as it presents itself.

My plan had been to catch a shared cab to the church, as the costs for this were much lower, but the cabbies vetoed this option despite there being other people heading along the same route. They insisted that they would only take me privately, and only to the town nearest the church, Kandi Kelisa, but not to the church itself. And for this they wanted a ridiculous amount of money, IR200,000, which at about twenty dollars was having a laugh to say the least.

The fact that they were all together made them impossible to negotiate with, as a sort of group mentality developed that made none of them want to haggle, or more accurately back down in front of their buddies, and especially not to a tourist. A gangly traffic cop from across the street who had been watching all the commotion and lively negotiations loped over to lend his authority to the drivers' argument. He insisted, in broken English, that their price was an absolute bargain just for me, and that I was a very lucky tourist indeed to have encountered such generous drivers. Yeah right. I shook my head with a laugh. He demanded my passport.

Whoops. I explained as best I could that it was at my hotel in the safe. He didn't seem to mind and thankfully went back to his traffic duties, which seemed to entail standing in the road staring at my frustrated efforts to secure a ride and not much else.

Things took an ominous twist now as I was waved over by three military guys and a man in a dark suit and shades, who were standing across the main road next to a little office.

"Oh shit," I thought.

They asked for my passport and once again, I had to explain where it was. The guy in the suit and shades seemed to be the main man and had the distinct air of a secret policeman of some sort. I soon got them all on my side when I produced my Iranian guidebook, which totally fascinated them. Their officious attitudes melted as they flicked through the glossy color photos, smiling and pointing out places to each other. The guy in the suit now explained, in good English, what I already knew: that the cabbies were trying to rip me off because I was a tourist, and that my best bet was to go back to Maku proper where they didn't have a monopoly, and to get a taxi there.

As I left to go back to Maku, the cabbies waved goodbye sarcastically and had a good-natured giggle at me. That was it; the gauntlet had been thrown.

Once back in Maku, I found it easy to get a driver to agree to take me on a return trip to the church. His price was slightly more than I wanted to pay at IR40,000, but it would be more than worth it to drive past the cabbies at the junction and see their faces drop. I planned not only to wave out of the window but to hold up three fingers, like I had done when trying to negotiate with them, as if to say I had only paid 30,000. It was a bit of a white lie, but I didn't care and couldn't wait to see them all again.

My hopes for revenge were dashed when my driver headed along a different route to get to the church, which went nowhere near their junction. It was a much longer drive than I thought it would be, through a near-deserted, barren, rocky landscape whose stark emptiness was broken only by the occasional wandering goat herder or hovering hawk in the sky, of which I spotted a surprising number. The sky was an intense blue and virtually cloudless, save for a few fluffy cotton wool-like forms drifting low toward the horizon. I didn't see any other cars the whole way there and was amazed at how sparse the area was. It would have been a great place to have had my own car and explore at length.

St. Thaddeus came into view long before we arrived. Although prominent, the church blended in beautifully with the sand-colored rolling hills, as much of the church was composed of a similar shade of rock. Surrounded by a large, fortresslike stone wall, the church was an impressive sight, graced with two large twelve-sided domed towers, one of which also had twelve arched windows. The other tower had four windows and was constructed with alternating black and sand-colored stone. At its western end, the church was constructed with sand-colored rock, and at its far eastern end with black stone. This reflected the other name for the church, "Qareh Kelisa," which translates from Azeri as "black church," although the vast majority of it was anything but black. Its isolated location and the fact it was in Iran, where I had not expected to be looking at early Christian churches, made it all the more interesting.

Contrary to popular belief, Iran has a significant Christian community totaling somewhere in the region of 300,000 worshipers. The religion has a long history in Iran with some of the earliest saints spreading the gospels there. Most Iranian Christians are Armenian, but many other Christian communities exist in the country, including Catholics, Protestants, Adventists, and Nestorians. As a result, you can find churches in nearly all large Iranian towns. For the most part, Iran's Christian community enjoys religious freedom, even to the extent that the country's outright ban on alcohol consumption is annulled for churches, which are allowed to import communion wine. These freedoms do not extend, however, to Muslims who convert to Christianity. In these circumstances, you run the risk of being executed; under Iranian law, this can be punished with the death penalty.

The cab driver and I approached a little booth stationed by the main entrance. There was no one about so we walked straight into the courtyard in search of someone. The janitor was located in a small building off the main church and welcomed us in warmly. For a very small fee, I was given a little leaflet and entrance to the church itself, which the janitor unlocked for me. The taxi driver was allowed in for free, although for now he remained outside.

I stepped out of the roasting sun into the church's mercifully cool interior and, like a good Catholic, made the sign of the cross. It was quite dark inside, with only a few hazy shafts of sunlight from the dome above for lighting, and was unlike any church I'd seen before. The first thing I noticed was a load of internal scaffolding supporting the cracked sections of the structure, of which there were many. Some of the larger cracks ran down from the domes themselves. Growing from these cracks were several wild plants. Strangely, the main flooring area was completely empty; for some reason, all the benches had been piled haphazardly on top of one another in a corner. They looked, quite frankly, like they'd been thrown there to create a barricade of some sort and were in a right old mess. To add to the unloved look were several crosses scratched into the walls, which looked very recent and of a graffiti nature. I walked slowly toward the altar, which was made predominantly from stained and dirty black rock and knelt down. Here I said a brief prayer and whilst doing so was joined by the cabby. On seeing me make the sign of the cross, he put his hand on his heart and bowed respectfully at the altar. I found this interesting as clearly he wasn't a Christian but treated the church with not just respect but a certain reverence. Both of us now had a quiet look around the place.

The first chapel here had been erected in AD 371, which had then been developed into a proper church in the seventh century. Most of what now remained dated to the fourteenth century, although some sections, particularly around the altar, were much older. It was undoubtedly a fascinating piece of architecture and steeped in history, but it was in a very poor state of repair. Up in one of the domes flew two pigeons, their wing beats echoing through the church's empty interior. The place really needed renovation but since it was a Christian rather than an Islamic site, it would have received no state funding.

I wandered outside to have a look at the exterior, which in many ways was far more impressive and cheerful than the inside. Surrounding the walls were wonderful stone carvings going all the way around, some of which appeared Christian and others Islamic. All were extremely beautiful. One even looked like it depicted good old English patron saint St. George slaying a dragon, although I may well be wrong. I attempted walking all the way around the exterior of the fortresslike wall but decided against it when I came across a section with a steep drop.

I spent about an hour at the church and would have spent longer but I could tell the taxi driver was itching to get back. Whilst walking back to his car, we went past a rather strange flock of sheep, a number of which had been spray painted in the most incredible colors and patterns. Some were spotted pink and blue, others orange and green and a couple were painted up like the British union flag. I had to get a photo of this and tried to snap one sheep at close range, but every time I got near, it would scurry off. Seeing my frustration, the helpful cabby lunged at said sheep and held it still from behind, long enough for me to get the picture. The sheep's legs were splayed apart and it looked mighty startled to be held around the hips. But it made for a great photo. Months later when I got the film developed, it looked, for all the world, like the taxi driver was getting down and dirty with a technicolored piece of mutton, and the poor ewe didn't look in the slightest bit happy about it.

We took a different way back, which I hoped would take us past the taxi drivers who'd had a laugh at my expense and that I could now have one at theirs. There was much more life on this route, and we passed through some incredible rural mud–brick villages. These contained the biggest, most out of proportion haystacks I've ever seen. They were huge, oversized things piled up in little square roofless buildings, and extended many times the building's height into the air. Although I had chartered a private cab, when we passed a couple of guys standing by the side of the road in one of the villages, I gestured to the driver to pick them up. He didn't have to think twice and pulled over in an instant. We took them to the next village. Although I'd already experienced some wonderful landscapes in Europe and Turkey, I was still bowled over by this drive, with its huge dramatic gorges and twisting mountain roads.

It was with sheer delight that I spotted the junction up ahead where the sarcastic cabbies were waiting. I couldn't wait to get the last laugh and see their faces drop as we zoomed past and I waved triumphantly at them. I got my three fingers ready to indicate the price and hauled myself partially out of the car's window. Goodness knows what the driver, who gave me a most concerned and confused look, thought I was doing. As we got closer, I noticed to my utter dismay that most of the cabbies were sitting around in the shade of a tree facing the other way. As we drove past, I waved frantically and shouted at the only one facing me and held up my three fingers at him.

He looked extremely confused. I hoped he'd tell the others about the strange tourist he'd seen waving madly from a taxi cab and that they'd work it out, but I wasn't optimistic. I laughed at this and then wished I hadn't; my lips were horrendously cracked from the sun of the last couple of weeks and were excruciatingly painful. Having been on the road for so long, I hadn't had a chance to get any medication, but now it was getting beyond a joke and they needed sorting out, and soon. If not, I sure as hell wouldn't be getting any kisses for the foreseeable future—and I couldn't be having that.

Tomorrow, I would be heading off to the thriving city of Tabriz, so I got myself down to the bus station to book a ticket. This was situated on Maku's one and only main road, Imam Khomeini Ave. Maku, as I was soon to learn, was far from the only place where something was named in honor of Khomeini.

Seyyed Ruhollah Musavi Khomeini was born in a small central Iranian village called Khomein and later moved to the holy city of Qom to study philosophy, law, and theology, which was the family tradition. He earned Shiite Islam's highest clerical title of Ayatollah in the 1920s and pretty much kept to himself teaching and writing for the next few decades.

In 1962, he came to prominence by criticizing the country's American and British installed dictator, the Shah, and his proposals to diminish the clergy's property holdings and give greater freedoms to women. Two years later, the Shah banished him from the country for attacking a bill he had approved that gave American servicemen based in Iran total immunity from arrest. Khomeini attacked the bill by saying that the Shah had "reduced the Iranian people to a level lower than that of an American dog," since if a dog was run over in America then the person responsible could be liable to prosecution, whereas if an American now mowed down an Iranian, he could do so without concern of consequence, as he would be untouchable by the court system. Khomeini fled to Turkey and then Iraq, where he stayed until the late seventies.

The so-called oil price revolution of 1974 was the catalyst for the Shah's eventual downfall. Within the space of a year, the Shah's oil revenue skyrocketed from $4- to $20 billion, but instead of spending this windfall wisely, he was convinced by American arms dealers to waste much of it on quantities of weaponry, which then stood idle, decaying in the desert. The Shah's military spending became so rampant that under his rule Iran possessed the fifth largest army on earth. Other fortunes were squandered on worthless schemes, and while corruption made a small minority of Iranians very rich, rising inflation made the majority of them worse off. Recession then hit the world economy, sending oil prices spiraling downward and forcing the Shah to cancel planned social projects and reforms.

Resentment was rife and continued to build as the economy grew worse. In 1978, the Shah imposed martial law, resulting in the deaths of hundreds of demonstrators on the streets of Tehran, Tabriz, and the holy city of Qom. Whilst this was happening, Khomeini, now located just outside Paris, was plotting the Islamic Revolution with Abol Hasan Bani–Sadr. Increased internal resistance finally led to the Shah fleeing the country in 1979, taking with him some $20 billion of the Iranian people's money, which he stashed away in American banks. With the Shah gone, Khomeini returned to Iran to a rapturous reception and not long after took full control of the nation, bringing to an end 2,500 years of monarchy. Executions took place en masse after speedy and pointless trials, people went missing, and civil war looked a real possibility. The world's first Islamic state was set up after a hasty referendum, the results of which allegedly showed 98.2 percent of the country in its favor. Khomeini became Iran's supreme leader for life and got more than just a few places named after him as a result.

The bus station, or simply "terminal" as the locals called it, was at first a little on the confusing side. Here there were many different bus companies all going to the same places and all after your business. By the looks of the buses outside, it appeared that you could choose the price and quality of your ride accordingly. The buses ranged from sparkling modern "Volvos," as the locals called the nicer buses, to forty-year-old rust buckets with several cracked windows and worn-out, flat-looking tires. Fancying a bit of luxury, and safety, which I thought well-deserved after my extended hitching, I went into a bus company office that had a picture of a flashy modern "Volvo" in its window. I purchased a ticket for a coach, which left the next day at 6 AM, then headed off in search of food.

My rumbling stomach led me into a little kebab place on the high street, where I ordered a kebab in a crusty white roll and two ice-cold Iranian Zam Zam colas. Whilst waiting in line for my food, I experienced more stunning Iranian hospitality. A man standing with his wife introduced himself in perfect English as Kamran, and told me that he was a local English teacher. He was very friendly and not only insisted on paying for my food, but on hearing I was leaving Maku tomorrow, insisted that when I returned to the town, I should phone him, so he could show me the local sites and put me up. Although only one full day into my Iran trip, I was already witnessing something very different from what I had expected—namely, how hospitable Iranians could be to foreigners. I liked it very much, and after making a note of his details, agreed that if I returned to Maku, I would look him up.

Halfway through my meal, I panicked on seeing fresh blood all over the white roll. "Oh my God, it's raw!" I thought, convinced I'd soon be suffering from food poisoning.

Upon closer examination, I realized the blood wasn't coming from the meat. I wiped my hand across my lips and chin and realized the multiple cracks in my lips had all split open and were spilling blood like fresh operation stitches in a hot bath, not only on the bread but all around my mouth and chin. I must have looked a right old state, and I realized why the locals sitting nearby had been looking at me strangely.

I finished up and got straight down to the drug store. In a display of reassuring professionalism, the pharmacist behind the counter took one look at my bloody swollen lips and gave a loud audible "Urrrgh!"

Thanks, mate.

He gave me a big tube of jelly-like ointment for my troubles, the origins of which were unknown to me. Back at my hotel, I smeared on vast amounts of the stuff, which had a cool and pleasant soothing effect—especially when I put it on my lips.

CHAPTER FOUR

Disco Lake with Ferris Wheels

At the ungodly hour of five forty-five in the morning, the bus terminal was surprisingly busy. It was too early for me to function properly, though, and as I waited for my shiny modern bus to arrive, I slowly brought myself out of a dribbling semi-comatose state with a life-renewing sweet black tea.

The night before, I'd made the mistake of arranging a super-early wake-up knock on my door, but had been paranoid that the elderly man at reception, who'd seemed a little preoccupied when I'd asked him, would forget. As a result, I woke up several times during the night in a panic that I'd missed my bus. Since I didn't have a watch, I'd end up stumbling down to the lobby to check the clock hanging on the wall there, only to discover that it was still the middle of the frickin' night. It was a complete waste of time and I needn't have worried, as right at five thirty, there was a *tappity tap tap* on my door. I got up feeling not only tired but rather stupid.

When my bus finally rocked up, and I do mean rocked, I couldn't believe my eyes. It was modern, but only if this was the 1950s, and it didn't look like it had received a service since then. It was covered in rust, dented, missing both front and rear bumpers, and completely filthy. To complete the look were massive cracks to the windscreen and several of the side windows.

The "luggage" compartment was almost entirely filled with old car batteries and its floor covered in an oily sludge. I was far from pleased. On board was no better, with the springs on all the seats long gone and the once white seat covers now anything but. Taking a seat was an interesting organizational process of making sure no man or woman who weren't related sat next to each other. At every stop, this arrangement had to be rethought and the seating rearranged accordingly. Being new to all this, I kind of liked the novelty of it, but was well aware that had I to go through the process on a daily commute, the effect would soon wear off. I imagined the chaos there'd be at home were the same system to be implemented on London's hideously crowded buses and tube trains and wondered how on earth Iranians coped on the metro system in Tehran—a city with 15 million people.

I was placed toward the back and given a "window" seat, although part of the window was missing. The thick, broken glass was sharp to the touch, being anything but normal safety glass. It was a four hour journey to Tabriz, and although I was looking forward to checking out the landscape as we drove, the guy sitting next to me insisted on drawing the thick black curtain to block the sunlight from coming in. As a result, I saw nothing en route and arrived in the city of Tabriz delighted to finally have something to look at.

Tabriz is a thriving city of some 1.5 million people located in the northwest of the country and is the capital of Iran's East Azerbaijan Province. Although modern in the sense of infra-structure and amenities, Tabriz has a rich history dating back somewhere in the region of two thousand years. On numerous occasions in the past, it has been the country's capital and until the 1970s was the second largest city in Iran. Its history has seen many conquering empires come and go, including the Mongols, who under the leadership of Genghis Khan conquered the country, which they subsequently governed from Tabriz. Famous Venetian explorer Marco Polo traveled through and wrote of the place in the late thirteenth century, at a time when the Mongol Empire reached from Istanbul in western Turkey to Beijing in eastern China and controlled some 100 million people.

One of Tabriz's more disputed claims to fame is that residing nearby is the location for the biblical Garden of Eden. This theory was popularized by archaeologist David Rohl's book *Legend: The Genesis of Civilization*, in which he argues for a site to the south of the city near the beautiful Mount Sahand. As a result, you can now take tours to visit the supposed area where Adam and Eve first acquired their liking for juicy Golden Delicious.

Being a Westerner and carrying a huge backpack, I attracted a fair amount of attention as I walked, but when I stopped to look at my map, it was a different matter altogether. I was surrounded by a throbbing crowd in no time, none of whom spoke English past the basics of, "Hello," "What is your country?" and "David Beckham!" After that, they spoke at me in rapid–fire Farsi in the vain hope I'd suddenly twig and miraculously learn to speak in tongues and understand the language. I did my best to ignore this and stared at my map of the city, trying to work out where the hell I was. My concentration was interrupted by a kindly newcomer to the gathering.

"Can I help you?" he said, warmly introducing himself as Shahram.

Yes, he could help. I explained where I wanted to go, which was a nice–sounding place called the Hotel Azerbaijan, and asked how much a taxi there should cost.

Without further ado, Shahram ushered me away from the crowd, hailed a taxi, and motioned me to get in. I expected him to give instructions to the driver and leave it at that, but in he jumped also and paid for both of us up front. We hurtled off and with very little in the way of introductions, he asked me, in broken English, if I would join him and his wife in the evening so they could show me the sites of Tabriz and take me to a restaurant. I was a bit taken aback by his generosity and initially tried to wriggle out of it. He insisted in the nicest possible way, and then asked what time I would like to meet him.

I explained that, as I didn't have a watch, I wasn't sure of the time now, so maybe he should suggest the best time to meet. On hearing this, he immediately took off his own expensive-looking chunky metal wristwatch and handed it to me. I couldn't believe it, and tried strenuously to refuse many times, but he wasn't having any of it. He said that if I really wanted to return it to him then I could give the watch back when we met up later. I was touched by his generosity but determined to hand it back at the first opportunity.

We both got out of the taxi just down the road from the hotel and walked the last bit through the crowded streets together. Shahram insisted on carrying my backpack for this short stint but struggled with the weight of it. Instead of putting it on his back, he carried it from two flimsy straps attached to the front, which weren't designed to hold such a load. I could see his efforts ripping the fabric apart, but not wanting to sound ungrateful, I said nothing. I figured I could always sew it up later, which was preferable to pointing it out now and upsetting him after his astounding generosity.

I was face-to-face again with the obligatory picture of Khomeini, who stared out across the hotel's spacious and rather comfy lobby. Here, Shahram handed me his card and told me to phone him at four o'clock, at which point he would come over and collect me. He grabbed the number of the hotel and bade me goodbye. The girl behind reception, like most of the women I had seen thus far in Iran, was wearing the full traditional black chador, which leaves only the face uncovered. Her English was excellent and so was her steadfast refusal to negotiate on price.

I was happy to pay the asking price, though, as I particularly liked the sound of the room, with its own bathroom, television, and fridge.

I wasn't to be disappointed; the room was excellent. It was spotlessly clean with all of the aforementioned features as well as a marbled floor, a spy hole in the door, and a wonderfully comfortable bed. The bathroom toilet was of the "squat" variety but was clean and modern. I dumped all my gear, drank a load of cool water from the fridge, and headed outside into the blazing sunshine and the crowds.

Knowing that Shahram was going to give me the whole tourist trip later, I just strolled around getting a feel for the place. One of the first things I learnt here was just how hard it is to cross an Iranian road. None of the supposed crossings were observed in the slightest by the traffic, and as the traffic was constant, you just had to take a deep breath and sprint across. And forget about only looking left and right before stepping out. Check every conceivable angle of the compass and even throw in up and down for good measure. It was nerve–racking to say the least. Even on the pavement you weren't safe, with mopeds weaving in and out of the crowds and appearing from nowhere. I got a kind of formula down for crossing, which was to only do so when others did, but to make sure I was slightly farther down the road than them, so if things did go wrong, they'd get hit first.

Tabriz was teeming with life, and everywhere I looked was something insane to check out. I stopped by a crowd of men gathered around a television set outside a shop. Here, on screen, were two highly disabled men doing the most incredible break dancing. With stunted legs and arms, they looked like Thalid–omide sufferers, but both were as nimble as hell. Their crazy break–dance moves were well–received by the crowd and got a rapturous applause. I couldn't quite work out if I liked it or not. It would have been considered outrageous in England, but here it was perfectly acceptable and the DVD of it was selling like hot cakes.

I walked on down the road and was struck by another peculiarity, namely just how gender segregated Iran was. On the whole, women walked, sat, or talked with women and men did so with men. It was also something of a surprise to see a number of guys openly holding hands in what would definitely have signified a gay relationship at home. But here, I guess it was just a sign of friendship. After all, homosexuality is highly illegal in Iran and punishable by hundreds of lashes or even death, so it wouldn't have been a sensible thing to advertise.

There were many very inviting cake shops along the roads, one of which got the better of me and I popped inside. The cakes were all really cheap but of an exceptional quality and really attractive. I bought a whole bag of cream-filled cupcakes, which tasted delicious.

Another interesting place I tried was one of the many milk-shake shops. As well as the more traditional flavors, this place also did a fresh carrot milkshake. I tried one of these bright orange shakes, which was surprisingly good, as well as a fresh banana shake with big chunky grains of sugar in it.

Having lost myself for a good part of the day doing more wandering, tasting, and exploring, it came as something of a shock when I realized how late it was. Back at the hotel, I gave Shahram a call. He apologized that due to unforeseen circumstances at work, he'd now be about an hour late and would come and get me as soon as he could. This was fine by me, as it gave me a chance to recline on my bed and read up on Tabriz and Iran in general.

Two things in particular caught my attention on the same page of my guidebook. The first was under the heading "Marriage, although not until death do us part" and described a bizarre Iranian practice, unique to Shiite Islam, called *sigheh* or "temporary marriage." *Sigheh* allows horny singles to indulge in a bit of legal "slap and tickle" with full religious blessing, for anything from a few hours to a few months. Amazingly, *sigheh* is officially sanctioned in Iran, even though unmarried couples who simply date or hold hands can be arrested, fined, or in some cases flogged. Supporters of *sigheh* often defend the practice as a way for the widows of the Iran–Iraq War to still get a bit of action, although apparently many Iranians see it simply as legalized and sanctioned prostitution. I told myself that if the opportunity arose, I'd happily say "I do."

The second thing to catch my attention was a passage on Iranian social etiquette that mentioned a confusing practice known as *ta'arof*. This is where you might be offered something purely out of politeness, but it is not meant as a genuine offer to be taken literally and accepted. To tell if the offer is legit, what you must do is refuse three times, and if the offer is not then retracted, it can be assumed genuine and you can accept. I thought back to when Shahram had given me his watch, but that definitely hadn't been *ta'arof*, as I'd refused more than three times—in fact, it was probably closer to ten.

Shahram turned up and apologized repeatedly for being late. I tried to hand his watch back at once, but Shahram wouldn't hear of it and insisted I wore it "until we have seen a few places." The first stop on Shahram's guided tour was a place called Arg–e Tabriz or "the Ark."

This was a huge brick citadel built in the fourteenth century on the site of a massive mosque that had collapsed some five hundred years ago. There was construction work going on nearby on a mosque the size of a department store, which we needed to venture through in order to access the Ark. We asked the builders' permission before entering the site; they clearly had no concern for "health and safety," and waved us through without a second thought. We only had access to the rear of the Ark, which looked from here rather like an old, disused power station, but Shahram livened it up by recalling an interesting story from its past.

Its roof, he explained, had once been used to throw criminals to their nasty and rather squishy death in the ditch below. And, if legend was to be believed, one lucky woman cheated death through the parachute-like effect of her traditional chador. Whether they tossed her off a second time to finish the job he didn't know. Given the height of the thing, this ancient BASE jumper certainly wouldn't have been in a good state if she had survived, assuming the story was true. But there would, of course, have been a beckoning career as a disabled break-dancer ahead of her.

We left the Ark and walked on to the bazaar—a place I was looking forward to seeing. The bazaar in Tabriz is massive, totaling 2.1 miles in length and containing 7,350 shops and twenty-four separate *caravanserais* where the itinerant traders set up shop. It dates back a thousand years, although most of the buildings currently there are from the fifteenth century.

The inside of the bazaar made the streets outside seem empty and quiet. There were people everywhere trying to strike a deal, browsing, feeling the quality of goods, eating, drinking, smelling foods, working, chatting, and generally shopping until they dropped in this atmospheric labyrinth.

The bazaar was separated into five main areas specializing in gold, footwear, spices, general household items, and carpets. As well as these main sections, there was, to the north and across the Quri River, a section specializing in copperware and foods like honey, dates, cheese, and halvah. I couldn't help but walk around goggle-eyed. There were huge blocks of sugar being broken into more manageable pieces, mounds of brightly colored spices and dried foodstuffs, carpets being made and mended, bread being cooked, and many, many other intriguing sights and smells. But most impressive of all was the size of the place—it just went on and on forever.

Just when my brain was bursting with stimuli, Shahram led me to a little haven of tranquility in the form of a teahouse.

Here, seeking respite from the frantic activity outside, were men smoking huge *qalyans*, or water pipes, and sipping little glasses of black *chay* at small wooden tables. I was given a complimentary glass with several sugar cubes but no spoon. Shahram demonstrated for me the Iranian method of drinking tea. Grasping the especially hard sugar cube between your front teeth, you then suck the tea through it. A little sugar then disintegrates into your mouth with each sip and thus sweetens the tea. It seemed a lot of effort but I gave it a go. It was far from easy, as the whole cube kept falling apart in my mouth so I had to keep getting new cubes. Where I might have had one lump, I now ended up having seven or eight. Shahram was a master of this technique, though, and made it seem effortless. He was also a master of the pipe and got stuck into this whilst blowing out huge clouds of smoke like a dragon. I gave it a go but was far from impressive.

Even to a Brit, Iran is a nation of obsessive tea drinkers, and a whole set of social etiquette has developed around how you place your cup and saucer. If you place your cup upside down, you insult the person nearest to you. If you turn it on its side, you declare you're gay. And put the saucer over the cup, and you might as well yell out, "I'll take you all on!" as it's a slur to the whole teahouse. And watch how you smoke the pipe as well. One big faux pas is to ignite a cigarette on the pipe's embers, which can also lead to a spot of fisticuffs.

Shahram explained that he liked teahouses very much but tried not to go to them too often because he tried to stay in shape for his hobby, karate. By way of coincidence, there was a seventies martial arts flick playing on a small crackling television in the corner. It was dubbed abysmally in Farsi and featured a big, fat, bearded white guy taking on a group of lean, hard-ass-looking, and nimble Chinese. It wasn't the slightest bit convincing, as the bearded one was appallingly slow and moved about like the big fat white guy that he was. Seeing my interest in the movie, Shahram offered to take me to his karate class tomorrow. This was something I had to see, and the thought of getting involved in a punch-up, Iranian style, greatly appealed.

Three cups of tea and what seemed like a hundred sugar cubes later, we hit the street. Once outside, we were approached by a European-looking guy, the first I'd seen in Iran, apart from the one in my hotel mirror, who pointed at my guidebook and said, "I am tourist guide on page 205 of that book."

And indeed he was. His name was Nasser Khan and he ran the local governmental tourist board office directly above where we stood. He gave me his card and offered me a "Nescafé" in his office whenever I had some free time. Interestingly, in Iran, instant Nescafé is rated above ground coffee, as if the absolute pinnacle of coffee excellence. If you're offered Nescafé as opposed to just a coffee, then it's to stress the fact that it's not the cheap stuff. My dear mother, God bless her, would get on great with this social one-upmanship; whenever my folks have guests over for dinner, she slips in a discreet, "It's from Sainsbury's 'Taste the Difference' range," in an attempt to elicit an impressed and approving, "Oh, Mary."

Oh, Mother.

Finally, we arrived at a watch shop where Shahram bought a battery for a silver pocket watch. With all the excitement of the bazaar, I'd completely forgotten I was still wearing his wristwatch. I asked if I could now return it to him, and to my delight he said yes. I handed it over with great relief, but on doing so was immediately presented with another one—this time the silver pocket watch. Once again, my refusal was not allowed, despite my attempting it on more than three occasions.

It had a beautiful flowery pattern on one side, and on the other was the inscription, "World's Best Dad." He obviously couldn't read English as well as he spoke it, and said proudly, "English words." I was touched.

Poetry is big in Iran. Iranians take their poets very seriously, and poetry is without doubt the most important form of literature there. This is because poets often promoted Islam and the Persian language during periods of occupation. Not only do they have mausoleums named after them, but streets and squares as well–although probably not as many as Khomeini does.

Our next stop was to visit one such place called the Poet's Mausoleum, situated to the west of the bazaar in a quaint little park, which had been built after the death of a very popular local poet, Shahriah. The mausoleum was an odd-shaped monument consisting of several large hollow arched sections, which in totality formed a towering modern artistic structure that you could walk through. Situated around it were the statues of famous Iranian poets to whom it was a memorial.

One of Iran's favorite poets, Ferdosi, started an epic poem in the tenth century called *Shahnama* or "the Book of Kings," which he began at age forty and finished thirty years later. It was, as you might expect, a touch on the long side and contained no less than 50,000 couplets. This he presented to the Turkish king, who was less than impressed, as it contained no reference at all to the Turks. He rejected it and poor old Ferdosi died a penniless fellow. He is venerated now, though, and seen as the savior of Farsi, writing in this language when Persian culture was rapidly being Arabized. His writings record many details of Persian history, which, without him, might have been lost forever. Other famous and influential Iranian poets include Hafez, Sa'di, and Omar Khayyam.

Beneath the mausoleum was an underground exhibition hall displaying local photography. The photos were all of regional attractions, and one in particular caught my attention. It was an old stony castle situated on top of a rugged and very steep mountaintop, surrounded on all sides by forested hills. Its name was Babak Castle, and strangely it merited no mention in my guidebook. Shahram seemed to know it well but found it difficult to translate for me where it was or if it was possible to visit. I decided to make some further inquiries later with the tourist guide who'd offered me Nescafé.

Shahram was generous to a fault and had already bought me a notepad in the bazaar and was now approaching the till with a book. I suspected it was for me, and my suspicions were confirmed when he turned and presented it to me with a smile. It was a photography booklet of quality prints, including one of the mysterious castle. I thanked him many times over and wondered if all Iranians were this incredibly generous and hospitable to foreigners.

Not long after the sun set, I was introduced to Shahram's wife, whom we met up with at her office. Her name was Kimya, and as Shahram introduced me to her, I made the mistake of instinctively thrusting out my hand for her to shake before realizing it wasn't deemed appropriate. Once it was out, though, I couldn't retract it, so it just sort of hung there in the air for a second, whilst she pondered what to do. In desperation, she looked across to Shahram for guidance. He nodded that it was okay, and we shook. I hoped I wouldn't make that mistake again.

Kimya spoke much better English than Shahram, and it was good to talk to her without having to repeat myself several times as I'd been doing with Shahram. She went through all the standard Iranian icebreaker questions and seemed genuinely sorry and surprised to learn I wasn't married yet, as had Shahram when he had first asked me. "I hope you get married soon," was all she said before changing the subject tactfully, as if trying to save me the embarrassment of being single. Minutes later we left for another attraction.

We all piled into the back of a shared taxi, and on the way to our next stop, Kimya queried me repeatedly on what I knew of Islam. We talked religion together for a while and how Christianity, Islam, and Judaism are in fact very similar. Having read a bit about this, I managed to knock out a couple of quotes from the Koran to impress Kimya. I started with Surah 29, where Mohammed instructs his followers, "Do not dispute with the people of the book," (i.e., Jews and Christians), " . . . but tell them we believe in the Revelation which has come down to us and in that which came down to you; our Allah and your Allah is one." Kimya and Shahram were both very pleased and seemed impressed that I knew something of their religion.

Kimya then told me that when Mohammed entered Mecca in triumph, he ordered the destruction of all idols and images, but when he came across a picture of the Virgin Mary and infant Jesus, he covered it reverently with both hands and said that all other idols were to be destroyed, but the image of the Virgin and Child was to be looked upon as sacrosanct. We then talked about Jesus being a prophet to Muslims and that Mohammed had referred to Jesus as the "breath of God."

When we finally got to our destination, I tried to pay for the ride but gave up when Shahram seemed offended that I should try to do such an underhanded and despicable thing.

"You are our guest!" he said forcefully as he handed the money to the driver.

"Fair enough," I thought.

We had arrived at a magical place called King's Lake, which Kimya explained was now officially called People's Lake so as to have no reference to the ousted king of Iran, the Shah. It was a fair-sized lake with many multicolored illuminated fountains and a large restaurant built in the middle, which was accessible via a walkway. This, Shahram explained, had once been a disco when such things were allowed in Iran before the Islamic Revolution. Many people splashed around in little paddleboats, and everybody we passed seemed happy. Surrounding the lake was a park containing some fairground attractions, including a Ferris wheel lit up with twinkling colored lights.

We strolled leisurely along the outside path of the lake where other people were also walking, relaxing, eating candy floss, roller–skating, and generally enjoying the peaceful atmosphere. The limited visions I'd had of Iran before visiting had been of slightly worrisome street scenes where I'd have to keep my wits about me at all times, lest I be lynched by a mob of anti–Western fundamentalists. The farce of that misconceived image made me laugh now.

We ambled along in the balmy nighttime summer air to the walkway that led out to the restaurant. Here, I was treated to a yogurt and cucumber, then the finest Iranian style kebabs and rice with a big dollop of butter. We washed this down with cool beaded bottles of Sprite served with straws. It was strange to be in such an ambient restaurant without being able to order from a wine list and instead to be drinking through a straw. Over dinner, we talked about all manner of things, including our hobbies. They were both amazed to learn I skydived and got me to talk about this for a good fifteen minutes. They kept shaking their heads in astonishment. I promised to e–mail them a photo of me doing this, which both seemed genuinely excited about receiving.

When it was time to pay, I didn't really know what to do, but I decided to offer and did so three times. In the end, it was no good and I was overruled by the pair of them, but I felt better for trying.

Walking back through the park, we chatted about Iranian cinema, and I told them I had seen the Oscar–nominated Iranian film *Children of Heaven* (which, dear reader, if you haven't yet seen I'd highly recommend, as it is a delightful and touching piece of cinema). Kimya was most impressed by this and recommended another film for me by the same director, called *Color of Paradise*.

All in all, it was a splendid afternoon and evening, and when we got back to my hotel, they offered to put me up at their place the next night. I did the refuse three times routine then agreed on the fourth. Things were working out extremely well.

CHAPTER FIVE

German Pop Songs and
Chains of Misery

At the bottom of Shahram's apartment block was an area to leave your shoes before entering the block proper. We added ours to the pile of existing footwear, which belonged to everybody else who had a place here, and went on up in our socks to Shahram's third-floor apartment. Kimya was waiting for us, and although still wearing a hijab, she had lost the black chador she'd worn the night before and was now dressed in far more Western clothing.

I didn't make the mistake of trying to shake her hand this time but instead put my hand on my heart and gave a little bow. They had a nice but basic place with loads of furniture that was colored or painted gold. I got my first home-cooked Iranian meal, which was called *Ghorme Sabzi* and consisted of sautéed herbs mixed with black-eyed beans, dried limes, onions, and succulent lamb, all served with the softest melt-in-the-mouth rice, and a crusty sort of rice fritter. This was accompanied by an interesting Iranian drink of watery milk and dried mint called *doogh*. Shahram was the epitome of hospitality and kept piling the food on my plate, giving me far more than I could have possibly finished.

"What do you think of Arabs?" Shahram queried from out of nowhere.

"I don't really know any," I replied neutrally.

"They are just interested in money, don't you think?"

I remained neutral on this one and explained that actually a lot of people in the West mistakenly assume that Iranians are Arabs.

The color drained from his face in shock. This was not what he wanted to hear and was probably the equivalent of telling a Frenchman he's English or vice versa.

"Really?" asked his wife in disbelief. "Why would they think that?"

I did my best to explain that a lot of people, through ignorance, lump all of the Middle East together and don't have a particularly good sense of geography.

"What do people in England think of Iran?" she asked next. I could have lied and been diplomatic about this one but thought honesty was the best policy and explained that a lot of people, again, through ignorance, thought of Iran in George W. Bush's terms as a member of the Axis of Evil, full of dangerous terrorists, and that a lot of Western media portrayed the country in this way. I said some people were too shortsighted to differentiate between the people of Iran and its leaders, and told them that I had been warned on several occasions not to visit Iran, and even been told I'd probably get shot here. Both found this very funny at first but then expressed their sadness.

"Yes, I have heard in newspaper, they say we are terrorist," Shahram said thoughtfully. Things lightened up when Kimya asked what type of music I liked. She hadn't heard of any of my favorites and probably assumed Britain was years behind Iran on the international music scene. I asked what they liked.

"Michael Jackson, Pet Shop Boys, Chris de Burgh, David Hasselhoff, Ace of Base, and of course Modern Tacking."

"Modern who?"

"Modern Tacking!" she exclaimed.

"Tacking?"

"Yes, Modern Tacking, you must know!" It took a while before I realized she was saying "talking" but this was no help either. When I told them I'd never heard of a "Modern Talking" they honestly thought I was joking.

"But Modern Talking are the biggest rock group in the world," Kimya explained.

"Are they Iranian?" I asked.

"No, of course not, they are German!"

"Oh I see," I said and explained that German music wasn't particularly popular in Britain or the rest of the English-speaking world—thank God!

"But they sing in English!" she countered, incredulous that I hadn't heard of them. Shahram got up and returned to the table with a book. On the front cover were two cheesy-looking middle-aged jerks in full leather jackets and pants.

"It is English to Persian translation of the most beautiful songs of Modern Tacking," he explained.

Kimya chipped in with, "Yes, it is very beautiful words, like poetry, like our great poet Hafez."

I took a look at the book while Shahram slipped on a cassette tape. The lyrics were inspired, like Wordsworth, Keats, or Byron, but set to an eighties electro-pop disco beat. The words dripped with emotion and grace.

Think of something freaky in a crazy form
As long as I don't have to put my pants back on
She's the girl I never had; she's the girl of my dreams
A body like a Lamborghini covered in jeans

I couldn't believe they hadn't cracked the U.K. or U.S. market!

We left their apartment with Modern Talking ringing in our ears and set off on our second evening of sightseeing. Our first stop was the Tabriz museum on Imam Khomeini Ave. Immediately on walking in, I was drawn to a massive hunk of black volcanic glass called obsidian, which was on display just inside the entrance. Next to it were some arrowheads made of the same material. Having done a couple of flint knapping courses, I knew a bit about this and had the pleasure of sounding all scientific and knowledgeable for once.

"Obsidian," I stated for Shahram and Kimya in my best professor-like voice, "produces the sharpest edge known to man, which is some five hundred times sharper than the very sharpest steel scalpel."

In fact, surgeons have even made blades from it, as it will slice through human flesh far easier than a metal scalpel. It is so sharp that on a cellular level a blade made of obsidian is capable of slicing between cells as opposed to tearing them apart as a steel scalpel does. And the sharper the cut, the less the scarring, and the faster an incision will heal. I finished up by telling them that under high magnification the edge of a steel scalpel blade appears serrated, whereas an obsidian blade still looks smooth.

I felt all clever and learned as I recalled all this, and both looked suitably impressed. It was, however, the last exhibit I knew remotely anything about, so I read the English labels on all the rest. The museum had some interesting artifacts from regional excavations, including, amongst many other things, silverware from the Sassanid period (AD 224–637), drinking vessels from the Achaemenid period (550–330 BC), a vast collection of ancient coins, some beautiful bronzes from Iran's Lorestan province, and Shahram's clear favorite, a big collection of nasty-looking swords and daggers.

Also of interest were two skeletons called "the lovers" that had been excavated side by side. But the real highlight for me was an exhibition of the best sculptures I've ever seen in my life. They were made out of some sort of metallic material by a local, contemporary sculptor named Ahad Hosseini and were exceptionally striking. Most showed human figures in tormented states of one kind or another and were rather depressing, but all were hard-hitting.

The names of the sculptures included *Anxiety, Racial Discrimination, Chains of Misery, Population Growth, Hunger, Five Masters of Death, The Miserables, Autumn of Life,* and the worst and best of all, *Political Prisoners,* which depicted a group of men in a cage. One was partially beheaded, another was attached to a skewer hanging from the ceiling, while another was cramped into the fetal position inside a safe-like box with spikes protruding from inside, and yet another was screaming in sheer terror. It was scary as hell to think that these things actually happen. It was the antithesis of all the arty-farty impressionistic crap you see made by untalented modern art posers.

The next museum we visited was a little on the eccentric side. It was called Salmasi House, after its former wealthy owner, Mr. Salmasi, who'd traveled the world collecting things of interest as he went. Among the stranger exhibits protected behind thick security glass were some English scales from the 1950s, a collection of wooden school rulers, numerous heating meters, and my favorite, a whole load of speedometers.

Shahram and Kimya walked around listening intently to the curator in Farsi and translated for me in English. Both seemed genuinely fascinated by the displays, as was I but probably for different reasons. Among the exhibits were some more conventional purchases for a gentleman of leisure, which included opulent-looking Swiss clocks and watches, and some beautiful European furniture. But for me, the weirder stuff was what it was all about.

After finishing up here, Shahram and I split from Kimya to go to the karate class, while she got a shared taxi home. We stopped off first at the office where Shahram worked to pick up some things, where his two brothers and about seven of their friends were sitting and talking together in total darkness. I guess the electricity must have gone out, which made for an interesting few minutes. While Shahram pottered about in the dark looking for something, I sat with his brothers and friends answering the normal icebreaker questions in complete dark-ness. We left before the lights came on, so I didn't get to see what any of them looked like.

The karate class was held on the first floor of a crumbling old tower block, and the stale smell of sweat instantly transported me back to an old boxing gym I used to train at in South London. Although the smell would be repulsive to most people, it had a good association for me, and I couldn't help thinking back to all the great times I'd had there. We arrived just as a class was finishing and all the young guys were getting changed out of their white karate uniforms and packing up. Shahram got changed along with the guys waiting for the next class and said he'd ask the teacher if I could join in. I was of two minds about this; I quite liked the idea of getting stuck in with the locals but was also fairly tired after spending most of the morning at the bazaar, so the idea of sitting on my ass taking it easy also appealed.

The decision was taken out of my hands when no spare kit could be located. This was fine by me, and when it all began, I was extremely pleased to just be watching. The class consisted of stretching and frantic running around with the occasional flashy kick thrown in but precious little combat. All the running about looked exhausting, and in the state I was in, it would have killed me.

After about forty-five minutes, Shahram made his excuses and left early before the class was over. Before we left, Shahram gave his teacher a formal, martial arts–type bow. The teacher returned this to him, then put his hand on his heart and bowed to me in a more informal manner. I did the same in return.

On arrival back at Shahram's place, we were presented with a delicious spaghetti bolognese. It looked and smelt divine and was beautifully prepared. Shahram and Kimya seemed keen to smother all the flavor out of theirs with copious amounts of tomato ketchup, and it was a real effort to stop Shahram doing the same with mine. At first, I think he thought I was just trying to be polite and that surely I wanted some of the stuff. It wasn't easy to convince him that I didn't, but he eventually gave up.

I liked Shahram a lot but it has to be said, his table manners weren't the best in the world. Not only did he make loud intentional slurping sounds for effect, but he forced whole chunks of bread into his mouth, with his fingers pushing the bread into every available cheek crevice. It left him resembling a bloated puffer fish, which he thought most amusing. As well as eating like a pig, he was also keen to hear if I'd ever tasted pig and what it was like. Rather unfairly, I said it was without doubt the greatest tasting meat in the world—after all, you can't beat a good bacon sandwich. Kimya asked if I had tasted rabbit and explained that this was also forbidden by their religion. This was news to me.

Shahram took charge of dessert, which was a large green melon. He had an interesting way of serving it, which was to hold it in one hand and peel off all of the outside skin with a knife without putting in down once. Still grasping the whole peeled melon, he chopped it into little cubes then served it.

Being the better English speaker, Kimya had plenty of questions for me about life in Britain. Of particular shock to her was learning that unmarried friends of the opposite sex could share apartments together and that people didn't have to live with their parents up until marriage. She asked what I thought of the hijab scarf she wore and if girls in England would wear one. I let her know the lay of the land at home on this one and asked if women in Iran would wear it if they didn't have to. This provided a telling response from both of them.

"If women didn't have to wear the hijab, I think a lot of them wouldn't wear it," said Kimya.

Shahram chipped in and corrected her. "Er, no, I think they would still wear it."

"Oh yes," she now corrected herself, "Yes, I think they would still wear it."

They were both fascinated by my lifestyle and thought it very strange I had casually left a job to go traveling and just planned to find a new one when I returned.

"In Iran, you don't choose a job, the job chooses you," said Shahram.

I had as many questions for them as they had for me and got them talking about what they thought of their government. Shahram summed it up nicely with, "Government bad, people good."

"Like mine," I told him.

I wondered what they would think of a dose of Bush and Blair style "liberation." Both were absolutely appalled by the suggestion and said of the situation in Iraq, "It is terrible." I agreed. After we finished dinner, there was a knock on the door. Kimya went to answer while Shahram and I reclined on the sofa. She returned a minute later and explained that earlier on she had told her friends that they had a "tourist" staying with them and that now they had come around to, as she phrased it, "look at" me. And that's pretty much what they did.

In walked a guy of about thirty along with two girls in their early twenties who were dressed in light-colored bedsheet-like cloths, leaving only their faces visible. I shook the guy's hand and put my hand on my heart and bowed to the girls. Kimya explained, as if to put my mind at rest, that it was okay her friends were out together as they were brother and sisters. "Phew, thank goodness for that," I thought.

The girls seemed very shy and much less approachable than Kimya. Neither of them spoke English, so their limited questions were translated for me by Kimya. It was the normal stuff again: What was my job? What was my salary? How old was I? Was I married? Along with a couple of new questions like, "What is the main industry in England?" I struggled with this one and copped out by saying, "Banking." After this, they just sort of stared at me as if they'd never seen a funny-looking bastard before. Fifteen minutes later and they were gone.

I then got my first taste of Iranian state television, which was put on especially for me, when it was time for the nightly Iranian news broadcast in English. Ironically, the woman reading had a very strong American accent, which I thought strange considering the Iranian government's dislike of all things American. It was nearly all about the chaos in Iraq and filled with gruesome footage of civilian deaths. The news was followed by loads of patriotic war clips from the Iran–Iraq War, along with clips of Iranian flags fluttering in the wind.

We all hit the sack soon after, and despite my protests, they insisted I slept in their nice big double bed, while they slept on the floor of the television room. They were both exceptionally generous to give me their bed, and on it I slept like a log.

CHAPTER SIX

Rules of the Road

At the time of writing, there are 9,418 Iranian rials to every single U.S. dollar. Since the highest commonly available denomination in Iran is a 10,000 rial note, any exchanging of Western currency leaves you with one hell of a big bank roll.

Since Iran is essentially a cash economy where credit cards are just about nonexistent (not that I have a credit card, thanks to my declaration of bankruptcy a few years ago), I had to change a significant amount of money. In total, I had about $1,200, having blown around $150 to get here, so I figured $600 would be a good amount to convert. To help with the translations, Shahram had kindly accompanied me to the main bank in Tabriz, which looked like a bank from old Victorian London. There were no security screens and everything was done face-to-face. I handed over my thin sliver of hundred-dollar bills and waited for what seemed like an eternity while the guy behind the counter counted out my Iranian cash. He finished one pile, and then started on another. The first, it turned out, was only the small decimal change. The main bank "roll," which was so big I couldn't have rolled it, was ridiculous and must have been a good ten inches thick, containing roughly six hundred notes.

I felt a bit guilty at having changed such a vast sum in front of Shahram as the average annual income in Iran is around six thousand dollars, and one in seven Iranians earns less than a dollar a day.

Shahram and I bade each other goodbye outside the bank with a warm man–hug. I thanked him an embarrassing amount of times for his and Kimya's generous hospitality and promised to be back again to see them within the month. This was imperative because earlier in the morning, I had asked them if I could leave some of my camping gear behind as I was now lugging around far more stuff than I needed. My tent and camping equipment had been invaluable on the way to Iran but as I planned to stay in hotels from now on, they had become obsolete. Shahram had agreed to this without a second thought, and as a result, I had stripped everything down to the bare essentials. By the time I'd finished, my backpack was a fraction of its former weight.

* * *

A steaming black Nescafé was graciously passed my way in the Tabriz Tourist Office by multilingual Mr. Nasser Khan. He was a wealth of information, and after hearing my planned itinerary, suggested that I take a slightly different route around Iran and go to see Babak Castle when I returned to Tabriz.

His recommended route, he explained, would still include all the sights I wanted to see but would save me loads of time with connections. This was very important considering the staggering size of Iran, into which you could fit France, Germany, Britain, Holland, Belgium, Austria, Portugal, Switzerland, and the Czech Republic with over 15,440 square miles to spare.

After very little in the way of deliberations, I decided to go with his suggested route and now planned to leave this afternoon on an overnight bus for the town of Rasht near the Caspian sea, and from there to travel on to the scenic mountain village of Masuleh. Having time to kill until my bus left, I decided to pay a visit to a large, blue-colored mosque in the center of town, aptly named the Blue Mosque. The entrance portal was very attractive and decorated with hundreds of brilliant blue tiles repeating the name of Allah in different variations. It was incredibly intricate and completely unlike the mosques I'd seen in Turkey on the way here. The mosque dated from the fifteenth century and had suffered repeatedly from earthquakes, and as such was under extensive restoration. This made it a bit of a building site on the inside, but still well worth seeing. It had a massive central dome some fifty-five feet high and several large columns, again decorated with tiles. At the rear was a room that was once a little private mosque for the Shah. Here the walls were covered in marble and the vaults with shimmering gold and beautiful tile work. It also contained the tomb of Jahan Shah who ruled Persia in the seventeenth century.

I liked the place, but due to the building work and the fact that most of it wasn't tiled, I can't say I was bowled over by it. If it had been completely restored then I'm sure it would have been awesome. What was wonderful, though, was the coolness of the interior, which offered a very welcome respite from the blistering heat outside.

When I braved the sun again, it was to head back to the tourist office, where I met a young Swedish couple called Hannes and Malle. Hannes was six foot four with long fat blond dreadlocks and was wearing a vomit-color tie-dye hippie shirt with matching pants, while Malle was short, petite, and of Indian origin. They looked an interesting couple and would have stuck out like a sore thumb just about anywhere, but especially in

Iran. I got chatting to them and learned that this was indeed the case. They hadn't been in Iran long, but neither seemed particularly enamored by the place and Malle said she hated wearing the hijab. Both spoke fluent English, so it was nice to chat away at a normal speed for once. I fancied a spot of food, so asked them if they were hungry and wanted to join me at a café. Mr. Khan recommended a place around the corner for us, and whilst walking there, everybody, and I mean everybody, turned, pointed, and then laughed at Hannes and his blond dreads. The locals had never seen anything like it, and poor old Hannes didn't look happy to be the center of attention. I thought it was great, and most amusing.

Things didn't get much better for them in the café, where both ordered what they thought was vegetarian food only to be presented with a bowl of steaming meaty stew. They pointed this out to the guy working there who helpfully demonstrated how to remedy the problem, which he did by simply plucking out the pieces of meat with his bony fingers then returning the stew. Hannes and Malle handed their bowls over to yours truly and stuck instead to rice.

Malle explained that nobody would talk to her; all questions would be directed through Hannes. With a straight face I turned to Hannes and asked how Malle was coping with this.

In general, they both seemed very unhappy and said they were looking forward to leaving Iran for their next destination, which I think was Pakistan.

As soon as we stepped out of the café, Hannes was confronted with more pointing. Whilst working our way through the crowds, we spotted another backpacker and stopped to say hello. He was an extremely friendly Portuguese guy called Ricardo who was traveling overland all the way to Nepal, where he was going to do a load of trekking. I immediately hit it off with Ricardo, who was a soft-spoken polite guy of about my age.

Like me, he was new to Iran, and it turned out had been considering a very similar route around the country to my initial plans. I told him briefly of Mr. Khan's recommendations and how they could save him substantial time. This he was keen to hear more about, and since Malle and Hannes wanted a drink, I agreed to fill him in on all the details at a milkshake shop. Ricardo recommended a wonderful little place on Imam Khomeini Ave, which we all set off for.

Poor old Hannes got the same treatment the whole way there, with young and old gawping in astonishment and cars narrowly missing one another as their drivers stared at him. Hannes walked looking at the ground to avoid the prying eyes on the way. I can't say I felt sorry for him though, as I'd got my hair cut short and respectable to fit in before I left, and what's more I didn't dress like some lentil-munching soap dodger, so as far as I was concerned, his troubles were pretty much self-inflicted.

The milkshake shop was great, and we were greeted there with warm handshakes and smiles from the staff–all of us except Malle that is, who was ignored. After an animated sales pitch from me to Ricardo on the promised savings of Mr. Khan's recommended route, Ricardo changed his plans and decided to tag along to Masuleh with me. This was great news as it would be nice to have some English-speaking company for a bit.

Having failed to pay for just about anything over the last two days with Shahram, I gladly picked up the tab for everybody using a mere fraction of the obscene-sized bank roll I had in my pack.

A round of carrot shakes later and we made a move out onto the street. Here, I saw a small stall selling posters which were simply too good for me to pass by. I purchased one of a stern-looking Khomeini for my friend Nick, one of another bearded religious-looking chap for my friend Chris, and two posters of a big muscled Iranian wrestler hugging his minute little old mother, who was wrapped up in a full black chador and wearing big chunky spectacles. It was exceptional. Down at the bottom of the poster were smaller shots of him in different poses to show his various qualities: family man, philosopher, scholar, man of the people, philanthropist, and all-in bare-knuckle wrestler. I got one for my ex-girlfriend and one for my brother. I couldn't stop laughing at the thought of their reaction upon receiving them in the mail.

Unfortunately for Hannes, we now walked straight past a barber's shop. On spotting him, all the staff inside went crazy and rushed out, leaving their clients in the chairs. They were amazed at his dreadlocks and invited Hannes inside so they could study his hair. I was keen to go in, but there was no persuading Hannes. A couple of the barbers touched his hair out of real fascination. I know he was having a hard time of it, but I thought Hannes could have popped inside for a minute to satisfy their curiosity.

Ricardo and I bailed out on Hannes and Malle at this point and headed off on our own in search of a post office. Whilst walking around in circles, hopelessly lost, we were approached out of the blue by a young guy in his late teens, who said in English, "Can I help you?"

His name was Nima and he was very keen to practice English, so we forgot about the post office and went for a cola with him in a nearby café. He was a dentistry student, and wanted to meet up with us if and when we came back to Tabriz. He couldn't stay for long but passed on his details in case we returned. Before he left, he craftily went up and, under the pretext of speaking to the café owner, paid for our drinks. Iranians sure are generous people.

Ricardo still needed to book his bus ticket and get back to his hotel to pack all his gear up, so we quickly got down to the ticket office. After squaring up there, we started the long walk back to his hotel, where on the way we met the most amazing character imaginable.

He approached us like the student before from out of nowhere and with the same greeting: "Can I help you?" There was nothing we needed help with but it was a rhetorical question anyway. With manic enthusiasm, he fired off a volley of words at breakneck speed.

"I want my daughter be superstar!" he exclaimed. "She is singer very good, oh yes!"

"And your son?" Ricardo queried.

"He just be accountant."

"How old are they?" I asked.

"She is six; he is seven!"

"Are you married?" he asked me in a fraction of the time it would take a normal person to say three words. I told him I wasn't and was expecting the usual condolences but instead got, "You are very lucky man; it be far better to be single!"

This was a shock to me and to Ricardo who'd obviously already had the same treatment as I had for being single.

"But surely you are married if you have children," I said.

"Yes, but I do not like her," he said without a moment's hesitation, whilst shaking his head.

"I think maybe I do divorce."

He paused uncharacteristically now for a whole second. "But it is unfair for woman with children."

When I asked him why he didn't like her, he came out with a gem. "We have nothing in common. I like detective stories but she doesn't like them!"

Ricardo and I were in stitches. It sure would have made for some interesting marriage guidance counseling, maybe with him imploring her, "Darling, please, for the sake of our marriage, I beg you to at least try some Sherlock Holmes or Perry Mason. Is that too much to ask?"

Ricardo asked why he had married her if he didn't like her.

"I meet her twenty–four hours before and think, mmm why not!"

I could well imagine him thinking just that. Her family, he explained, were friends with his family so it had been an arranged marriage. This he said was normal. Whilst on the subject of marriage, I took the opportunity to ask him about the *sigheh* temporary marriages and if they were common.

"You need not worry, have sex with anyone you want and do not get the marriage. It is not a necessary!"

We were in stitches again. We continued down the road chatting and laughing with him all the way to Ricardo's hotel. Ricardo went inside to get things organized; I stayed outside with Mr. Enthusiastic. I suggested we sit on the sidewalk whilst waiting, but on looking at it he said, "It is dusty we will lean against car instead."

I queried the wisdom of this as I was wearing my backpack and didn't want to scratch a car.

"In England, do people mind you leaning on or scratching their cars?"

"Yes," I told him.

He laughed and said that no one minded in Iran, and to prove the point he started hitting a car parked next to us. I half–expected some burly Iranian car owner to come out and administer a swift serving of on–the–spot justice with a golf club. Luckily, none was forthcoming. It was all completely and utterly insane but I loved it. Iran was my kind of crazy place.

Ricardo took forever getting ready, and after a while, Mr. Enthusiastic said with a laugh, "Maybe they kill him inside!" Whilst waiting, he told me his dream in life was to one day visit neighboring Turkey and to be a tourist there. It made me feel very lucky to be able to live my dreams and go more or less where I wanted. I told him I hoped that one day he would get to visit Turkey. When Ricardo appeared again, he was told by

Mr. Enthusiastic, in a matter-of-fact, manly way, "You have very beautiful eyes." Mr. Enthusiastic turned to me for an endorsement. "Doesn't he have beautiful eyes?"

"Um, yes, very beautiful," I said.

Our new friend walked us to a spot where we could get a shared cab to the bus station. On the way, he had a business proposition for me—it went something like this: if I bought things in London and he bought things in Iran, could we swap and make lots of money? I didn't quite grasp the subtleties of how we made all the money and asked for clarification. He replied, "But I want to be rich; how can you help me?!"

Before we parted company, I asked him his views on the government. He didn't like it. "The people now think maybe they make mistake."

He also was of the opinion that the people were scared of the government and that the government used religion to "control the people."

He offered to hail a shared taxi for us and speak to the driver personally to make sure he charged us the correct price and didn't rip us off. "It is better. Maybe driver try hanky panky!"

We laughed again. He waved down a cab for us, had a brief chat to the driver, and said goodbye. Both Ricardo and I were sad to see this cheerful and just plain nutty guy go. Inside the cab, we were greeted by a suited Iranian man who warmly welcomed us to Iran and told us how much he hoped we'd enjoy his country.

Iran and the words "road safety" don't sit well together. The country has some 200,000 reported road accidents a year, and no doubt many more unreported ones, and roughly 28,000 road deaths per annum. This appalling figure crowns Iran with the unfortunate title of country with the highest rate of fatal road accidents in the world. My *Lonely Planet* had some interesting comments on the rules of the road, in particular stopping at red lights. Apparently, the willingness of a car stopping at a red light has less to do with road safety and more to do with the number of armed traffic cops the driver can see within rifle range. No shit.

We got to experience the full nightmare that is Iranian road travel on our bus to the Caspian. We were given seats at the front of the bus near the driver who drove like a psychotic, suicidal IndyCar racer on crack.

He pulled out without looking, overtook on blind corners next to jagged cliffs with no crash barriers, tailgated whatever vehicle was in front of him, and at one stage sped around a massive row of cars stuck behind a slow-moving farm truck by using a sort of imaginary middle lane–the type of thing you would only consider doing on a computer driving game, and even then you wouldn't be so reckless, unless you wanted to end your go. To the oncoming cars, he just honked his horn aggressively.

But most of all what scared me was the speed. He drove so fast it really was suicidal, and we missed oncoming cars by the narrowest of margins on several occasions. As a result, I found myself slamming my right foot down involuntarily onto an imaginary brake pedal. At the speed we went, it would have been game over permanently, no doubt about it.

Things got worse when the driver added his cell phone into the equation. He drove with his right hand, holding the phone with his left but to his right ear, and even started gesticulating at one stage with his steering arm. I watched in horror just waiting for the bump in the road that would turn the wheel and send us headfirst into the approaching vehicles. My late grandfather used to say, "It's better to be twenty minutes late in this world, than twenty years early in the next." Well, I was getting ready to meet up with him in the next, and prayed like the condemned man I knew I was.

At one stage, we approached some traffic cops by the side of the road, but somehow the driver managed to hit the brakes and avoided being pulled over. He glanced across at me as if to say,

"We showed them, didn't we?" I gave a nervous half grin back. They say that monkeys smile when they're scared to indicate non-aggression. Whether that's true or just a load of monkey piss, I don't know, but the smile I gave him was of the primate "scared and defenseless" kind.

Whilst he was still in view of the law it was a cautious, "Mirror, signal, turn—okay, slowly into first gear and ease on the accelerator . . . Now check your mirror, that's it and slowly into second."

He drove as cautiously as an eighty-year-old grandma with eyesight problems and bad nerves at the wheel of an economy Sunrise Mobility Scooter. If I thought this brush with the law would have a lasting effect on his driving then I was about to be sorely disappointed. As soon as we rounded the corner, he dropped the clutch—we were back at the Indianapolis 500 and now he was playing catch up. I gave in, held on tight, and just closed my eyes like a kid on a scary roller coaster.

I awoke from this prolonged nightmare when we finally arrived at our destination. We got to the city of Rasht, near the Caspian Sea, at sunrise. Before getting on another bus, Ricardo and I both needed a good stiff caffeine injection, so we scouted out a little *chay* shop and drained an ocean of the stuff. Whilst there, I read up on the place. Rasht had a population of 400,000, making it the biggest city in the Caspian region, and was the area's main industrial center. It was a popular holiday spot for people from Tehran, more as a base to visit the surrounding areas than for the place itself, which if my *Lonely Planet* was right, wasn't up to much.

The Russians didn't agree, though; they'd occupied the place on several occasions, most notably in 1668 when the forces of Cossack brigand chief Stenka Razin rather unfairly massacred the entire population. They'd also popped over for a visit in 1920 when the Bolsheviks gleefully smashed up most of the bazaar, leading the majority of the locals to flee as refugees. Perhaps more interestingly, though, I learned that when the poor Rashtis weren't on the receiving end of a dose of Russian rape and pillage, they were suffering the indignity of being made fun of by the rest of the country as the butt of national jokes. Much comedic value is derived from the lisping Rashti accent, but the real focus of the gags is on the popular perception that Rashti wives are unfaithful–the shameless Jezebels!

We didn't stick around in Rasht long and made our way to a small minibus station that, despite the time of day, was thriving. We caught a ridiculously cramped minibus to the town of Fuman, where we hoped to get a shared taxi all the way to Masuleh. Fuman, which is known as the "city of statues," was a cheerful-looking spot. The brightly colored plaster cast statues dotted around town depicted things like bow hunters or people handing out biscuits and, although they were of a tacky nature, I kind of liked them. The statues all looked really cheerful, and along with the multicolored traffic islands and leafy tree-lined boulevards, gave the place a sort of storybook appearance, which was so very unlike the pictures of Iran on Western TV.

Finding a shared cab going to Masuleh was no drama but the drive there was, especially for some poor chap we saw riding toward us on a motorbike. He made the understandable mistake of trying to ride one-handed along a potholed road whilst carrying a tray of bread and wearing no crash helmet–as I'm sure we've all done from time to time.

The predictable happened when he hit a bump and went flying. We all watched in horror as over the handlebars he went, sending the tray of crusty bread rolls spiraling helplessly into the air. As he hurtled toward the road, it looked for sure like he was going to smash his face and hard. But miraculously, at the last minute, he managed to arch his back and adopt a belly flop pose, landing instead with a bounce on his protruding chest. The rolls rained down around him and sadly didn't fare so well, getting squashed cruelly by our taxi's tires, creating a cloud of breadcrumbs all over the road.

I spun around and looked out of the rear window to see if he was okay. He staggered to his feet apparently unhurt and picked up his bike. He was very lucky—after all, it could have been a tray of cream cakes.

The rest of the journey to Masuleh was absolutely nothing like my imagined picture of the Iranian countryside. The landscape was lush and green with rice paddies, tea plantations, banana trees, and pretty thatched roof houses by the roadside, with dense forested mountains in the background. It was a hot and humid morning, and the surroundings looked more like Vietnam or Cambodia than the Middle East.

Everybody else in the cab except Ricardo and I disembarked before Masuleh, so we arrived there by ourselves. If the journey here had looked like Southeast Asia then Masuleh looked more like a slice of Italy or Switzerland. Set in a valley surrounded by forested mountains with ribbons of silvery water meandering down their slopes, the village was a stunning place.

The historic houses of the village were the real attraction, though, as they clung to the mountainside so steeply that to get to the top of the town you had to walk on the roofs of the houses themselves. It was breathtaking. Ricardo and I approached the only proper hotel and were greeted by the friendly manager, who on hearing I was English insisted on phoning a friend for me to talk to.

I expected an English speaker in another part of the village or a different part of Iran on the other end of the phone, but instead got a rather tired sounding Iranian man in Twickenham, West London! I couldn't believe it. After a few minutes of labored English, he asked if when I came back to London we could become friends.

"Yes," I said. "Best friends."

The poor chap had been woken up at five in the morning just to speak to me, and he did so happily and without irritation. Ricardo turned to me and said simply, "Iran is crazy!" I couldn't agree with him more. The hotel manager spoke little English, so negotiating a price was next to impossible. In fact, he didn't seem particularly interested in whether we stayed or not and seemed content just to sit with us at a table outside, whilst speaking at us in Farsi and munching on sesame seed biscuits.

Whilst talking to Ricardo, I mentioned a town on the coast called Ramsar. On hearing this, the hotel guy butted in and corrected my pronunciation, saying slowly, "Ramsar," which to me and Ricardo sounded identical to what I'd just said. I tried again with another "Ramsar" but got, "No, no, no" in return and a slow "Ramsar!" It still hadn't changed discernibly to my ear, so I gave it another go this time with a bit more "RRR–" but it elicited the same response from him.

Several more variations were attempted until the hotel manager had a brain wave. Off he went to the reception desk where he fetched a pen and paper. He returned outside and put his master plan into action. In completely illegible cursive Persian script, which meant less than nothing to me, he wrote down what I assume was the word "Ramsar." It was as if he was spelling out the syllables on the assumption that I could read Persian. He now said "Ramsar" again. I tried once more for the hell of it, and low and behold on this occasion I got it right. He was convinced it was due to his writing, so set about scribbling down a host of other Iranian place names for me. He read a few of them out, pointing to the script at the same time, and then handed me the paper smiling as if I'd have no problem from now on.

As we were sitting with him, another man approached who spoke a little English and offered us a place in his "home stay." We bade my Farsi teacher goodbye and left to check it out. It was a steep walk back and forth on the roofs of the houses to the very top of the village. The higher we went, the more spectacular the view became.

It was a charming little place, which wasn't really a "home stay" at all but a small studio. It had a little kitchen area, a clean tiled bathroom with a "squat" toilet and a small living room that doubled as the bedroom. Instead of beds, there were two big traditional floppy mattresses. It even had a small old television.

Ricardo and I were both delighted with the place and took it on the spot. After jumping in the shower, separately of course, we struck off for a mountain walk.

There were no properly established walking tracks in Masuleh so we just picked a mountain and headed on up. It was hard going and the lack of sleep from the night on the bus took its toll, but it was well worth the effort. The sun pounded away, so we took advantage of one of the many silvery mountain streams cascading down the slopes and sat and cooled off. As I plonked my tired feet in the delightfully cool and soothing water, Ricardo pointed out that technically, we were breaking the law, as our trouser legs were rolled up to just below the knee, showing what would be considered an obscene amount of flesh. Ricardo pretended to be shocked and called me a whore.

When we returned to the village, the serenity we'd experienced there in the morning had long disappeared. Loads of Iranian tourists had since turned up and were snapping away with cameras, picnicking, checking out the sites, trying to control their children, buying postcards, and doing all of the other normal touristy things. We were the only Westerners though, and attracted plenty of inquisitive good-natured stares.

For a spot of food, we went to a café whose terrace was located on the roofs of a number of houses below. We sat beneath a shady canopy made up of old Persian carpets, and both ordered Iranian Zam Zam colas and that other Iranian favorite–the kebab, this time of the chicken variety. These were served still dripping blood and had to be returned for a while longer in the flames.

After some more pottering around, we were approached by a pretty young Iranian girl who spoke perfect English in what I thought was an Australian accent. She was in fact an Iranian New Zealander. Her name was Leyla and she was here with her mother who also spoke English but not with a New Zealand accent. After a brief chat, they invited us to join them for *chay* at an open-air teahouse.

Leyla was nineteen years old and had grown up in New Zealand, where her family had moved not long after the Islamic Revolution. They had all moved back to Iran in the last couple of years and now lived in Tehran. It was great to talk to them, as not only did they have a foot in both Western and Iranian culture but could explain it to us—thanks to their flawless English. I bombarded them both with questions.

We discussed everything from human rights abuses to wild student parties in Tehran and much, much more. I was intrigued to learn of the students in Tehran, who sounded very Western in comparison to other parts of the country. Leyla said that there were even illegal raves and illegal parties where the drink flowed, drugs were taken, and sex was plentiful. This sounded like my kind of place and certainly worthy of further inves-tigation when I got there. She also said there was an unusu-ally high gay population in Iran, which was a byproduct of the forced gender segregation and the fact that it was illegal to have a boyfriend or girlfriend. I wondered if all the guys I'd seen holding hands in Tabriz had in fact been gay after all. "Of course they are!" she said. Her mother disagreed with her on this point and said that it was just a sign of friendship.

Either way, I found this all completely fascinating. I particu-larly liked the sound of the young people in Tehran and really hoped to experience a bit of their lifestyle. Kindly, Leyla offered to take Ricardo and me to an Iranian rock or rap concert when we made it to the capital. We accepted immediately. They were, Leyla warned us, terrible, and the musicians dressed up like the American gangster variety with baggy clothing and big chunky chains–it would probably be so bad we'd think it was great. I hoped so.

She also mentioned how Western music was officially banned in Iran because the songs were deemed to contain lyrics that were sexual, spoke of teenage rebellion, or were just plain meaningless and therefore inappropriate. However, the cassettes and CDs were freely available on the black market and every-body had them.

Leyla now enlightened me on the popularity of Chris de Burgh. He, amazingly, is the only foreign artist whose music isn't blocked under the official embargo. The reason, and I just love this, is that de Burgh's lyrics are considered educational by the Iranian government, particularly as one of his songs features the words, "There is only one God," which is the essence of Islamic belief whether Sunni or Shiite. I loved the irony. After all, if anyone's music should be banned then undoubtedly his cheesy crooning should be the first to go.

Where Leyla was a great insight into current young people's lives, her mother, having been in her twenties at the time of the revolution, was a great insight into how Iran had changed. Among other things, Ricardo and I discussed with her what she thought the future would hold for Iran and what level of support the government currently had. She said their support was, in general, very low and that most people hated them, but that the people were too afraid to do anything about it.

She told me a harrowing tale of a young girl of just sixteen who'd been arrested recently for having a boyfriend. In court, she'd been denied a lawyer and was forced to defend herself. She was sentenced to death by the judge, not for the alleged crime, but for answering him back. She was publicly hanged. It was very hard to get my head around just how nice all the people I had met here were, compared to just what a bunch of bastards their government was.

I asked why they had come back to Iran considering the terrible things that went on politically. Leyla's mother said that they would only stay for a few more years and that she wanted Leyla to experience some Iranian culture. Leyla was back off to New Zealand next year to go to university and said she would not return to Iran to live. I had to ask what they made of the whole "freedom" and "democracy" enterprise in neighboring Iraq and Afghanistan and if they thought the U.S. would invade Iran next.

Leyla's mother dismissed it by saying that as long as there were foreigners like Ricardo and me in Iran then it was a sure sign that they'd be safe from invasion. I wondered if she was right. She added, "If it is really about democracy and human rights then why aren't they going after their friends in Saudi Arabia and Uzbekistan where they boil people alive?" I couldn't have agreed more.

The four of us were hungry from all the talking and we all went for dinner together at an open-air restaurant. It was decided that Leyla and her mother would order some traditional Iranian food for us, and just after the food arrived, there was a power outage, throwing the whole village into darkness. It was wonderful as there was a clear night sky with a big silvery moon, which, along with the candles hastily supplied by the waiters, provided all the light we needed.

We had garlic soaked in vinegar, succulent meat-skewered kebabs, rice with butter, and for dessert a local specialty of soft, aromatic cinnamon biscuits. Whilst tucking in, I asked how difficult the obligatory dawn-till-dusk fasting was during the holy month of Ramadan, which, luckily for me, was occurring just after my visa expired. (Ramadan celebrates the period in which the Islamic holy book, the Koran, is believed to have been revealed to the prophet Mohammed.)

Leyla's mother's answer provided a real insight into Iranians. "Most Iranians are actually not particularly good Muslims, and won't hesitate to eat heartily behind closed doors. What is important to them is the perception by others that they are fasting."

I was so surprised and asked, "Really?"

"Yes, of course," she said. "Look at the mosques on Fridays; they are nearly all empty." Since Friday is the holy day for Muslims, this was in stark contrast to how we had perceived Iranians before our visit. Ricardo and I found this fascinating.

When it was time to pay, Ricardo and I tried to pick up the tab but were scolded like little schoolboys by Leyla's mother who said forcefully, "Sit down. I am older than you! You are our guests."

We did as we were told.

Before we parted company, Leyla gave us her cell number and told us to call her just as soon as we got to Tehran. We thanked them for the meal and for such a fascinating and enjoyable night and headed back to our room very satisfied.

"That was just brilliant, Jamie! Just brilliant!"

I agreed with Ricardo.

We were back at the room by ten and, after washing some clothes in the sink, were nearly ready for bed. At around ten thirty, just as I was yawning my way into bed, there was a knock on our front door. I went to open it, and standing there was a man carrying a cake. He apologized in broken English for disturbing us and explained that he'd heard there was an Englishman from London in the village, and so just had to come and see me. He asked if I was returning to London tomorrow. On hearing that I wasn't, he sighed with disappointment. "It is a shame," he said. "I have a friend in London and I would like you to take this cake to him."

Doing favors for strangers was clearly a way of life in Iran. Here was a man I'd only just met who wanted me to take a big, icing-topped, cream-filled cake, as hand luggage, to London, then travel across the vast city to deliver it, in person, to a guy I'd never met before. He apologized for the inconvenience, and I apologized that I couldn't help him. When I closed the door, I realized I'd been talking to him wearing just my boxers, which in Iran was hardly the done thing.

CHAPTER SEVEN

Mosquito Mayhem

The small antiquated television in the corner of the room displayed rather a strange spectacle. Here were loads of Iranians walking up a hill, and that, believe it or not, was the be all and end all of the program. This seemingly innocuous event got top billing and was jazzed up with funky music and dramatic zooming in and out with the camera. It went on for a good fifteen minutes, and for all I know much longer, as we had to leave before it finished.

On our way to pay the owner of our accommodation, we saw Leyla and her mother again, who were staying in another home stay a few doors down. We decided to have breakfast together at a café nearby. Over boiled eggs and bread served with real honeycomb and thick cream, I showed them the funny posters I'd bought in Tabriz, which, due to my not being able to find a post office, I was still carrying around. They thought they were hilarious, especially the ones of the wrestler, whom they now told me about.

His name was Gholamreza Takhti, and he was an extremely popular national hero who'd had a rags-to-riches life. He was raised in abject poverty but had succeeded in becoming the first Iranian wrestler to win a medal at an international tournament. He went on to become an Olympic champion, and began to attain a legendary status. He was seen by many Iranians as a sort of larger–than–life champion of good, a person Persians refer to affectionately as a *pahlavan*. Although there is no direct English equivalent, a *pahlavan* can roughly be described as an ethical, chivalrous, and heroic warrior fighting for good. Many Persian folklore stories tell of legendary *pahlavans* who stood up to unfair rulers to defend righteousness despite the dangers to themselves. And this is what Takhti did.

He was a staunch supporter of the popular democratic Iranian Prime Minister Mohammad Mossadegh who was ousted by a CIA and MI6 sponsored coup in 1953, which led to the Shah's twenty–six years of despotic reign. Because of this support for the former Prime Minister and Takhti's huge popularity, the Shah's secret police sought to diminish his status and began to watch his every move. Although he was well past his prime, the secret police purportedly arranged for him to compete in the 1964 Olympics and the 1966 World Championships in the hope that if he lost, the Iranian people's affection for him would wane. He was unsuccessful in these competitions, but the secret police's plan failed, and his popularity remained as high as ever. He died mysteriously a couple of years later, and although the official cause of death was recorded as suicide, the generally held opinion was that the secret police had assassinated him.

I felt a bit guilty at having found a poster of such a national hero so funny, but they agreed it was a naff picture and laughed at it also. Leyla's mother warned me that I might have trouble sending the Khomeini poster through the mail, as it might be deemed disrespectful, and so to be careful doing this. When it was time to get the bill, Ricardo and I asked Leyla's mother politely if we could pay and said it would make us very happy. She agreed.

We were all heading back to Rasht today, so Leyla and her mother asked if we'd like to share a private taxi with them. We parted company when Leyla and her mother got out at the main bus station to catch a coach back to Tehran. Leyla's mother kindly insisted on paying, not only for the fare from Masuleh but for the taxi to take Ricardo and me on to the local minibus station so we could catch a bus to our next stop, the coastal town of Ramsar.

On the way there, the driver put some thumping Western dance music on, and when he saw that Ricardo and I both approved he cranked it up and beat his fist enthusiastically into the air. We both laughed and then joined him as if at some crazy rave party. It was great fun.

We caught a minibus down the coast to Ramsar, which had been described in our identical guidebooks as one of Iran's most attractive seaside resorts with some of the best scenery anywhere along the Caspian coast.

It certainly didn't look it from the place the minibus dropped us, which was a crowded intersection called Imam Khomeini Square, on a busy street called Imam Khomeini Boulevard.

By way of a caveat, our *Lonely Planets* added,

It has to be said, though, that unrestrained development has started to spoil some of the erstwhile wonderful views. People here are very friendly and like to see foreigners, perhaps because they bring back memories of the boom years before the Islamic Revolution when women strolled around town in bikinis and blackjack was the game of choice in the casinos.

The thought of women in Iran wearing bikinis was something I found very hard to picture.

Our first priority was finding a place to stay where we could dump our backpacks, and pretty soon a local approached us with an offer of a home stay. Apparently, he had a place a few minutes away and offered to take one of us on the back of his little motorbike to check it out. Ricardo wasn't too keen on this, so it was decided I'd jump on, while Ricardo remained with the backpacks.

I clung on for dear life as we sped along, swerving in and out of cars to get there. It was in a nicer part of town near a big hotel, which apparently used to be Ramsar's main casino in the days before the revolution.

The apartment was a nice enough place, but he wanted far too much for it at IR300,000, about thirty bucks. I tried to negotiate but he could smell those tourist dollars and was reluctant to drop the price. We'd traveled a good couple of miles on his bike to get here, and as I didn't want to forfeit my ride back, I said I'd have to discuss it with Ricardo. The return journey was terrible, and I swear we nearly got hit twice. I got off the bike on shaky legs and gave Ricardo the news. We both agreed to look elsewhere. On seeing the deal slipping away from him, the owner miraculously dropped his price to IR70,000. Not only that, but he said he'd throw in a taxi ride, which he'd pay for, so both of us could get there. This was more like it, so we agreed and shook on the deal.

He hailed a taxi for us, which followed closely behind his bike. This time he led us along a different route and we turned onto a dead-end street in a different, shadier part of town. I turned to Ricardo and told him we weren't going the right way. He looked at me concerned and said, "This isn't good!" And it wasn't. We followed along behind the guy's bike twisting this way and that until we arrived at a dilapidated, half-built house at the end of the cul-de-sac. It looked very ghetto.

He tried to make out like it was all an honest mistake, but his English was too good for that excuse. I wasn't happy at getting scammed—and after looking at the interior of the place was even less so. It was filthy, even for someone used to sleeping on the side of the road, and contained just one horribly stained double bed. As much as I liked Ricardo, I wasn't snuggling up in the same bed with him. I let the guy on the bike know I was pissed off and told him that he'd wasted his time and ours, and that we weren't interested.

The taxi driver now demanded an extortionate payment, but the guy on the bike refused to pay anything despite his promise to the contrary. A bit of a stand off ensued. It would have been one thing if the taxi driver was just asking us for a normal fare, but it was clearly bumped up several hundred percent since we were foreigners. And what's more, biker boy had given us his word that he'd be paying for the taxi anyway, so we were being ripped off on both fronts.

Ricardo played the part of Switzerland and remained neutral. It all got a bit on the heated side, but I wasn't particularly bothered and was willing to stand my ground. Ricardo didn't share my enthusiasm for this approach and was clearly uncomfortable.

"Let's just tell them both to get lost and walk out of here," I said to Ricardo. He didn't like this option.

"Let's just pay them, Jamie," he said more intelligently. "Look at the area; it's not good." After a moment's further reflection, I conceded. It wasn't worth getting into any trouble over, which was of course the last thing we wanted in Iran. I thrust a note into the driver's hand and we started walking. Halfway back to the main road, the guy on the bike sped past and deliberately swerved toward us, scowling.

"What a prick," I thought.

So much for the guidebook's assertion that people in Ramsar are very friendly and like to see foreigners. Like to fleece foreigners more like it.

We walked to a hotel along the main road and got a wonderful, spotlessly clean and reasonably priced modern room with two single beds, a fridge, TV, and two chairs still covered in their factory plastic wrappings—something surprisingly common in Iran. The bathroom was a proper "wet room" with a high-powered shower and that rare luxury in this part of the world, a sit down toilet. We were both delighted. We threw our packs on the floor and flicked on the TV for the hell of it. On screen were more clips from the Iran–Iraq War just in case anybody was trying to forget about it.

We turned it off and went out. The beach and the Caspian Sea were calling our names, so we headed in their general direction. What we thought would be a quick five–minute stroll turned out to be a walk of a couple of miles and not a very scenic one at that. As we finally got closer to the Caspian, we passed row upon row of huge, opulent–looking houses, their gardens completely overgrown, and their outside walls made of nasty cement block. There was just no synergy to these homes; they looked expensive but at the same time cheap and unattractive.

When we got to the water, it was late afternoon. Although technically a lake, the Caspian looked for all the world like a sea, with fishermen lined along the front and boats going by just off shore. It would have been a nice spot, but it was covered with trash, both on the gravelly shore and in the water. We were both very disappointed. A nice–looking restaurant jutted out into the water like a tiny pier, which we thought a suitable enough place to grab a drink. Both of us ordered *chay*, but I was brought a large iced coffee instead.

We sat on the balcony looking out to sea as trash floated gracefully past. We both wished we hadn't wasted a whole day in coming here. As we sat chatting, I noticed a guy and a girl in their late teens discreetly stroking each other's thighs beneath their table. I couldn't help but look and wondered how difficult it must be to be a young person with such ridiculous restrictions on dating. My mind wandered and I probably stared too long, because the girl saw me looking their way. She stopped stroking her boyfriend's thigh immediately and looked very uncomfortable.

Ricardo started to read up on the Caspian in his guidebook and gave me the lowdown on the place. Apparently, the Caspian was the biggest lake in the world, covering over 140,000 square miles (larger than Germany) and measuring 752 miles from north to south and between 130 miles and 271 miles from east to west. It was five times larger than the next biggest lake, Lake Superior, and contained 44 percent of all the water in the world's lakes. Its water was salty, although only about a third as salty as the sea, and it had no outlet into the ocean. Five countries bordered the Caspian: Iran, Turkmenistan, Azerbaijan, Russia, and Kazakhstan.

The Caspian was in very poor health ecologically, although we didn't need to read about that—all we had to do was just look at the crap floating past. It was under threat from shipping, the development of ports, industrial chemical waste, oil and gas exploration, broken oil and gas pipelines, and severe over-fishing, particularly of its once huge caviar stocks. And perhaps most interesting of all, the oil and gas in the Caspian Basin is estimated to be worth an incredible 11 to 12 trillion dollars.

Cruising past us now was a fair-sized yacht whose occupants gave us a friendly wave. We returned the gesture and in doing so I remembered, and recalled for Ricardo, a time back in London when I'd been the one waving from a yacht but in a slightly different manner.

My brother Matt and I, along with my friend Mark and his friend Gary, had been sharing a well-earned post-work drink in a pub on London's River Thames, overlooking the permanently moored Second World War battleship HMS *Belfast*. Unusually, moored next to this was the biggest, most opulent yacht I've ever seen in my life. On the rear of this floating billionaire's palace was a small private party going on where glamorous-looking individuals sipped champagne whilst looking at the views of Tower Bridge and the Tower of London, and occasionally across toward us plebeians, enviously drinking our pints at the pub opposite.

After several bladders full of liquid courage, I suggested that we try to crash the party. Mark was up for the challenge. We were still wearing suits from work, so looked relatively smart despite being only nineteen and twenty at the time.

Leading to the yacht was a long gangplank where several of the boat's impeccably dressed staff were standing to meet and greet guests. "Let's just walk up and straight past them as if we own the thing," I said to Mark. He agreed.

We decided to button up our suit jackets as if this somehow made us look smarter and more successful, then strode confidently up the gangplank. Mark gave a little approving nod of the head to the guy who looked in charge, as if to say, "Well done, my man. Keep up the good work."

I was sure we were about to get rumbled, but the staff member gave a gracious nod in response. Before we knew it, we were on the yacht proper. We couldn't believe it, and by the looks on the faces of Matt and Gary, who were staring open-mouthed from the pub, neither could they.

We headed to the party. Once we were mingling with the great and the good, it was easy to gain further access to the yacht's interior. Inside was the height of opulence with ridiculously thick carpets, lavish furnishings, and private bars in all the rooms. On one floor, there was even a framed photo of the Queen with, presumably, the owner of the yacht. It was unlike any official photo I'd ever seen of the Queen, in that she wasn't just smiling but laughing like you would in a shot of you and your mates at the pub. She obviously knew the boat's owner pretty well.

After having a damn good mosey around the place, and considering raiding a few bottles of vintage brandy from the rooms, we headed up to the top floor to beckon Matt and Gary to join us. Within minutes, they'd likewise strolled past the staff and were standing with us on the deserted top deck.

As we stood facing the river, we spotted a red London Sightseeing boat packed with tourists approaching, and we quickly developed a plan. I undid my suit jacket, which I held casually over my shoulder whilst Matt and Gary did theirs up, hands clasped in front of them in typical bodyguard fashion. As the sightseeing boat approached, I gave the royal wave as if to my humble subjects below, whilst Matt and Mark scanned around with a hand to one ear as if maintaining radio contact with unseen operatives elsewhere on the yacht.

The boat erupted in excitement, as if someone on board had shouted, "Hey, isn't that Prince William?" with tourists pointing and shouting hysterically my way whilst firing off their cameras.

In a moment of genius, Matt now gestured first to the tourists and then my way before giving a little round of applause as if encouraging them to do likewise and pay homage to their sovereign. Mark and Gary did the same and amazingly all the tourists followed suit, clapping away enthusiastically. I continued the royal wave at my applauding subjects until they drifted by, at which point we all burst into fits of laughter.

Ricardo and I left the restaurant after dark and walked back to our hotel, hoping for better things tomorrow when we would be heading to the city of Qazvin, which we hoped to use as a base for a trip to a mountainous fort called the Castle of Assassins.

We had hoped to check out a local museum before getting on the road, but after oversleeping we were running late and decided to skip it. It was a shame as the museum sounded quite nice and had formerly been the summer palace for Reza Shah, the father of Iran's last Shah and the man who in 1934 officially changed the country's name from Persia to Iran. The palace was apparently very opulent and had been left exactly as it was back in his day. Interestingly, the bedroom was said to contain no bed as Reza Shah liked to sleep on the floor, a habit he apparently acquired from being a soldier. In the hallway was purportedly a copy of the edict issued by Khomeini in 1979 that authorized the confiscation of all of the last Shah's possessions, which included his father's Ramsar palace.

Before checking out of the hotel, I went to the main post office and bought four large envelopes that I brought back to our room. I put the relevant posters in these and sealed them here as opposed to doing it at the post office where everyone would be able to see me irreverently folding up Khomeini and sending him second class to England. I dropped them off and paid the relevant international rates, and as far as I know they didn't get opened, as they all arrived a month or so later to much amusement.

We caught a cramped and crowded little minibus back to Rasht and due to the lack of seats, Ricardo and I had to sit apart. Whereas Ricardo got a seat next to an interesting English speaker, I got one next to a stinky weirdo who just stared at me the whole journey like I was an exhibit in a freak show. It was swelteringly hot inside, and although there were plenty of little windows that could have been opened for fresh air, for some reason nobody sitting next to them did so. I was pleased when it all came to an end, and so was Ricardo, as the chap he'd sat next to insisted on paying for him—and for me as well.

At the bus station we were incredibly lucky and found a guy hollering out the destination "Tehran." Ricardo asked, "Qazvin?" which was on the way to Tehran.

"Yes, yes," the bus driver told us.

It was a modern air-conditioned vehicle with comfy seats, dark curtains, and a television. It sped off nearly as soon as we were on board and a few minutes later we were approached by the ticket guy who insisted that as the bus's final destination was Tehran, we should therefore pay for a seat all the way there. Ricardo and I weren't happy about this, but we were by now well outside the town, and the ticket guy said if we didn't like it then he'd drop us here. Needless to say, we paid up.

A rather interesting film started up on the television, which was turned up to maximum volume for all the bus to hear just in case someone wanted to sleep. It was a violent seventies Indian "revenge" film dubbed into Farsi whose basic premise, as far as I could tell, was that everyone on screen was going to die and in a rather nasty way because they bloody well deserved it. The special effects seemed to consist solely of a big bottle of ketchup spread liberally amongst the actors, but Ricardo and I were on our own being amused; the rest of the coach was riveted. For the grand finale, the bad guy (they all seemed bad) was thrown off a cliff. The genius was that they chucked off a shop front mannequin dressed up like the baddie instead. It fell all the way down in the same body position, and, I swear this is true, its wig came off in midair!

Ricardo and I laughed so much that it hurt. The rest of the coach burst into applause at this dramatic ending, while a few old women wiped tears of emotional exhaustion from their eyes.

The landscape we drove through looked far more "Iranian" than yesterday's had: dry, dusty, hot mountainous desert. After a few hours of driving, the bus abruptly stopped by the side of the freeway and the ticket guy came over and told Ricardo and me that we had to get off. We were incredulous as this sure as hell wasn't Qazvin but was instead a freeway exit for the city.

We had no option but to get out, as despite our strenuous protests, the driver was adamant he was going around and not through the city. We grabbed our bags and stood speechless on the side of the freeway as the bus took off. Before we had time to get really annoyed, a taxi approached and we both started waving frantically at it. Over he pulled and in we jumped.

The city was a welcome sight when we arrived. We drove along Imam Khomeini Street (just for a change) past the bazaar and onto Ayatollah Boulevard, which was heaving with people and vehicles. The main street was cheerfully decorated with colored lights lining the street and full-size illuminated plastic palm trees. I was familiar with these as they were identical to some that had been erected illegally outside a historic building converted into a Chinese restaurant near my parent's house. These were then torn down by the local council after numerous complaints, many of which came from my father. Great work, old man.

We asked the taxi driver to take us to the Hotel Iran but instead got dropped at the much more expensive and fully booked Hotel Alborz.

We consulted the guidebook map and started the walk back to the Hotel Iran, dodging through the crowds and taking in the sights as we went. Several people said "hello" or "bonjour" to us with a welcoming smile. On the way, we popped into a shop with the obligatory picture of Khomeini on the wall, accompanied this time by another bearded chap I didn't recognize. I pointed to it and tried to ask the shopkeeper what the bearded guy's name was. It got lost in translation and the shopkeeper pointed to Khomeini, cursed something-or-other in Farsi, and drew his finger across his neck at the picture in defiance. The meaning was clear. Ricardo and I did the same at the Khomeini picture, which the shopkeeper loved. He shook our hands warmly before we left.

The Hotel Iran was hidden away just off the main street and although it was recommended by the guidebook, we didn't think much of it. Not only that, it was full. The guidebook mentioned only one other place in our price range, the Khaksar Hotel. Whilst consulting our map, we got talking to a petite French girl in her twenties staying at the Hotel Iran. Her name was Sabine and she was traveling by herself. We were both impressed and asked if she had found it difficult to do so being a woman. She said that so far she hadn't had any trouble and that she had met many wonderful people. After a brief chat, we all agreed that as soon as Ricardo and I had booked into a hotel we would go to a restaurant called the Restoran-e Eqbali, which according to Sabine's guidebook, was considered one of Iran's finest restaurants. I wouldn't have gone that far.

We booked into the Khaksar Hotel without event and headed to the restaurant. I had some yogurt and cucumber then devoured some beef *khoresht*–a type of stew served with loads of rice. Over the meal, Sabine told us that she also wanted to visit the Castle of Assassins tomorrow and we all agreed to go together.

For one of Iran's finest eating establishments, the Restoran-e Eqbali was sorely lacking in the dessert department; all it had on offer was melon. We passed on dessert and whilst out strolling in the park got talking to a load of young Iranian guys hanging out together. They were exceptionally friendly, and wanted to talk to us about anything Western. First it was soccer, leading to a long discussion on the likes of David Beckham and Michael Owen before it moved onto music. A heated debate amongst the red-blooded lads of the group now erupted as to whether Jennifer Lopez or Christina Aguilera was the more delectable. Ricardo and I, although not Sabine, were asked for our input on this one, as if our opinion would conclusively settle the dispute. We both firmly joined the Aguilera camp.

One of the guys then asked if Sabine was my wife, and on hearing that she wasn't said, "She has very beautiful eyes." It was interesting that the guys all seemed too shy, or perhaps just mindful of Iranian social protocol, to address her directly. The same guy said, "I like her. Please tell her."

I did, even though Sabine had heard for herself, to which Sabine replied jokingly that she was probably old enough to be his mother. He then asked me to ask Sabine if she had a sister.

After the reaction to Khomeini from the shopkeeper, I was curious to ask them what they thought of their government and of the late Ayatollah. There was no dispute like the JLo and Christina debate; they all unanimously stated their hatred. Sabine seemed surprised at this and asked if their parents had similar views. They nodded and one guy said, "My father fucking hates him!" Without further prompting he then said, "I like Mr. George Bush very much." When we offered contrary opinions he replied, "Yes, George Bush is a bad man, but he is not as bad as Khomeini." We laughed.

When we bade them good night, they all wanted to shake hands although they wouldn't shake Sabine's. We walked Sabine back to her hotel and arranged for her to call on us tomorrow morning, where we would then charter a car or get a minibus to the castle. On our way back, Ricardo and I stopped off at a milk-shake shop where I had the best "milk banana" I've ever tasted. I finished the first and it was so good I had another. I don't know what the guy put in it, but it might have been crack it was so addictive. As soon as we got back to the hotel, we hit the sack.

Getting any sleep was another matter, though, as it was swelteringly hot and our room was full of mosquitoes. There was no screen on the window, but it was so hot we had little choice but to leave it wide open. The little bastards feasted on us for hours before it became too much, and at two in the morning, Ricardo turned to me and asked, "Jamie, are you awake?"

I was, and he didn't need to tell me what he was thinking. We jumped out of bed, turned on the light, shut the window, and set about a rampage of killing that made the Indian ketchup flick seem tame. One by one, we asserted our revenge. Halfway through the cull, I glanced across at Ricardo standing like me in nothing but his underpants, with a look of sheer intensity on his face. He looked as if on a life or death military operation. We both started to laugh. By the time we'd finished, there were probably some fifty bloody splat marks on the walls. The last few were the hardest to get, but when finally over, it was a tremendous relief and sleep was not far off.

CHAPTER EIGHT

The Assassins and the Smoking Car

By eight o'clock, Ricardo, Sabine, and I were chartering a taxi. The drive to the Castle of the Assassins was spectacular, taking us along meandering gravel roads through absolutely breathtaking mountain scenery.

The view from the car may have been great, but the car itself wasn't. It was in a terrible condition and felt very unstable, rocking from side to side like a skateboard with loose trucks. The driver pulled over at an isolated little roadside store to give the car a breather and its brakes a rest, which were smoking, and I mean that literally. I got out and took a photo of the billowing white fumes wafting up from the front wheel arches. It wasn't a reassuring sight considering the steep, curvy nature of the road and its many nasty vertical drops. We all popped into the roadside shop whilst waiting for the car to recover. Five minutes later and we were back on the road. The condition of the taxi was no reason for the driver not to put his foot down, though, and it was full speed all the way to the village of Alamut. Here the driver indicated that we should get out.

"What the hell's going on?" I thought. We still had thirteen miles to the castle, but the devious driver tried to make out that we'd only paid to get to this village, and if we wanted to go all the way to the castle then we'd have to come up with more money, to the tune of IR60,000. That was what we'd paid thus far and had traveled many times the distance from here to the castle. I told him that if he didn't stick to the normal deal, he'd get nothing (we hadn't paid him yet) and we'd hitch or catch another cab. Another annoying stand off set in with all of us determined not to give in first.

After about ten minutes of sitting around in the roasting sun, Ricardo and Sabine reluctantly agreed to give him a further IR10,000 to take us all the way there. He was very lucky to get this, as by now I was keen to tell him to take a long walk off a short pier. Our crafty driver dropped us in another village and pointed us in the direction of the castle, which he assured us was walkable from here. We took his word for it but were apprehensive since it would have been easy for him to stitch us up in revenge for the contretemps earlier.

We walked into the village past several mud-brick houses and inquired with an old woman who was beating an intricately designed Persian rug as to the whereabouts of the castle. She spoke no English but a young man nearby helped us out. Worry-ingly, he also informed us that the next bus back to Qazvin left not in the afternoon, as we'd assumed, but tomorrow morning. This was a problem as we were in the middle of nowhere in rural Iran and had no chance of finding a taxi out here.

Whoops.

I was convinced we could hitchhike back, but Ricardo and Sabine weren't too keen on the hitching option. We decided not to worry about it until we'd located the castle we'd come all this way to see.

It was a steep walk to the castle. We'd not hiked for more than a minute when a four-wheel-drive pickup truck came by and offered us a lift. This was what I loved about Iran: one minute you could be peeved with some crafty taxi driver for trying to rip you off, and the next some generous stranger was going out of his way to help you out. And go out of his way he did–not only did he give us a lift to the path just below the castle, but he also gave us some fresh figs and a frozen water bottle full of ice. The figs were fresh, not dried–green on the outside and fleshy red on the inside and unlike any I'd tried.

We thanked him, and cooled off for a minute by a clear stream before starting the steep trek to the top. It was a beautiful but tiring walk past a towering sand–colored rock face up to a little plateau. Here the track changed direction, hugging the rock face to our right, which led onto a series of steps winding up the cliff. The plateau was a great place to take a breather and take in the view. On our left were mountains of surprisingly varied colored rocks. There were shades of pink, yellow, green, and even purple, making them look like a vast pastels picture. Farther on from this was a little valley almost entirely enclosed by dramatic crusty layered rocks jutting up from the ground as if thrown skyward by some enormous force. Down in the valley was a flat piece of lush grassy ground almost in a perfect circle surrounded on its outside by proud, elegant, upright standing poplar trees, which were slowly swaying in the breeze. And in the distance, framing the whole picture, were the towering Alborz Mountains reaching to the huge endless blue sky above.

It was a great sight and one that only got better the farther up we went. When we reached the top, the castle came into view. The castle was called Alamut, which was one of several local fortresses known collectively as the Dezha–ye Hashishiyun or Castles of the Assassins. These once strongly fortified bases had been the hideouts for followers of a peculiar religious cult based, somewhat loosely, around the teachings of Ismailism.

The cult was founded in the eleventh century by a complete nutter by the name of Hasan Sabah, who recruited followers from as far afield as Khorasan province in eastern Iran and parts of Syria. His group were widely feared and for good reason, as they weren't adverse to a bit of beastly barbarity—their specialty being the murder of religious and political leaders. It's purported the assassins' crafty leaders would lure their followers into the castle's beautiful gardens where irresistible maidens would tend to their every need and get them hopelessly stoned out of their minds on hashish. Nothing wrong with that, but on the downside they would then be sent out to commit murder under the belief that their leader, Hasan Sabah, had the magical power to protect them from harm's way and that he could whisk them off to paradise.

Interestingly, the word "assassin" is derived from the word for the followers of the sect, the Hashishiyun. Alamut Castle is the only fortress of the Assassins that is easily accessible; the others, about twenty-three of them, require the likes of a guide and donkeys to get to. Alamut had been constructed in AD 860 but was captured in 1090 by the Assassins, who subsequently resided there until 1256 when it was captured by the Mongols, who consigned the Assassins to history.

The cult's existence was first brought to the attention of Europe by returning Crusaders, but the Assassins were made famous by English writer Dame Freya Stark's classic twentieth-century travel book *Valley of the Assassins*. Freya Stark was born in 1893 and after the First World War spent the majority of the rest of her life traveling, in total defiance of convention, alone in parts of the world where few men dared to venture. In Persia, she visited Alamut, Mazandaran, Hamadan, Qom, Esfahan, and Lorestan where she raided ancient graves in the hope of discovering valuable bronze artifacts. She was arrested there and told by the local governor, "No wonder that yours is a powerful nation. Your women do what our men are afraid to attempt." She died in 1993 aged one hundred.

There wasn't much left of the castle past the foundations and a few walls, which were in the process of being renovated and rebuilt. But it didn't matter, as the view was the main attraction and it was awe-inspiring. We took a group photo with Sabine's camera, which she propped up on a pile of rocks, then set the timer and ran in and joined the picture. We hung out together for a good while just talking and admiring the view until two other travelers turned up on the scene.

They were both guys from the Czech Republic and looked in their early thirties. One of them, Michel, spoke excellent English. He was a fascinating bloke, having visited to date a total of seventy-six countries. I asked him from all his travel experience how this place rated. He described the view with an English soccer analogy. He said it wasn't quite Premier League like the Himalayas, which were comparable to the likes of the Chelsea or Arsenal clubs, but it was a good solid First Division team with a strong chance at promotion, "Like Derby County or Ipswich." I laughed.

The five of us then discussed how we were going to get back to town, and the unanimous decision was to hitch a lift to Qazvin. Ricardo seemed skeptical we could get a ride this far (forty-five miles), but having hitched here from England I didn't doubt for a second that we could do it. Michel was equally confident. In the end, a pickup truck from the village took us to a nearby junction opposite some green fields and a small isolated mosque. Ten minutes later and we were riding along in the back of another truck, this time with loads of tools in the rear making the ride an uncomfortable but welcome one.

We were dropped in another small village and managed to persuade the driver of a beat-up old Land Rover to give us a lift, for a small fee, to the next town. He agreed and cleaned out the back of his vehicle first, which was filled with manure. He did this by spraying it down with a roadside hose. Michel and I grabbed the front seats, away from the smelly mess, and ended up getting the best views as well.

It was my first time in an old style Land Rover. Interestingly, you see a hell of a lot of these ancient Land Rovers in Iran, obviously dating back to before the revolution. In fact, you see an awful lot of three different types of automobile in Iran. The vast majority are old 1960s British Hillman Hunters, or "Paykans" as they are known in Iran. These were manufactured in Iran from 1967 up until as recently as 2005. From 1979 onward, the Paykan, which means "arrow" in Farsi, has been an Iranian model only, after the country purchased sole manufacturing rights. Other common vehicles are blue farming pickup trucks and finally the aforementioned ancient Land Rovers. Apart from these, you don't really see that many other types of cars. There are a few, of course, with Peugeots now being produced in Iran and increasing in numbers, but it will be a long time before the Paykan gives up the number–one spot. To combat this and add a bit of individuality, you see a lot of Hillman Hunters sporting other more salubrious foreign cars' badges, in particular the four rings of an Audi's badge. I don't suppose they fool many people though, as apart from that they're all identical.

The manure–smelling Land Rover dropped us by some hay stacks next to a bridge where we all reclined and waited in the now late afternoon sun. We must have been quite a strange sight for the locals out here. Our next ride took us all the way back to Qazvin, in the back of another blue pickup truck. It was a wonderful trip with the low orange sun creating huge curving shadows across the undulating hills, highlighting their natural pink and orange layers of strata.

Michel and I stood up the whole way holding onto the rear of the truck's roll bar. Our speed was so great that it physically hurt to get hit by a bug or a fly. It was bloody dangerous, but the view and the air rushing all around us justified the risk. Interestingly, as we sped along we could detect going through warm and cool patches of air that would last for maybe five or ten seconds before changing temperature again.

The journey back was great fun all round, except for poor Sabine who got stung by a bee on her bum toward the latter part of the ride, and who had also been sitting in the manure mess!

Tomorrow we were all going our separate ways. I was off to Hamadan, Ricardo was going to Tehran, and Sabine, Michel, and his friend, whose name I never got, were heading to different locations as well. I planned to see Tehran after Hamadan, so Ricardo and I arranged to catch up there and get in contact with Leyla, whom we had met in Masuleh. Before we all parted, Ricardo and I took everyone to the milkshake shop for an addictive "milk banana."

The special ingredient, I discovered, was not crack but a huge block of vanilla essence added to the mix. It tasted as good as the night before, and we all had two each. As we stood outside in the crowded street finishing off our milkshakes, we were joined by the owner of the shop and an English-speaking friend of his. In no time, we were surrounded by people asking us questions about our countries and wishing us a good stay in Iran. It was a nice end to a great day and a good place to say goodbye to Sabine, Michel, and his nameless friend.

CHAPTER NINE

Underworld Paradise

My coach pulled into Hamadan bus station at about midday. I consulted my map and started to walk through town toward my hotel. Hamadan was a fairly big place of 400,000 people, and like all the Iranian towns I'd seen, was full of life and interesting new sights, sounds, and aromas. It was strange to be on my own again after spending the last five days with Ricardo. I was kind of pleased to be solo though, as I was convinced I had a much better chance of getting to know locals when alone. And this, primarily, was what I wanted to do.

As I walked along the street, I was stopped and consulted by two guys debating something, who seemed to want the opinion of a foreigner. One held an electric drill, which he was trying to sell to the other guy. The seller pointed at the words, "Made in P.R.C," and said questioningly, and rather optimistically, "Germany?" I shook my head and said, "China" (People's Republic of). The potential buyer seemed disappointed, obviously hoping for a fine piece of reliable high-quality German engineering.

After some trouble, I located my hotel, the Hamadan Guest House, which was described in the guidebook as the most popular place and deservedly so. I will describe it in my book as "shit" and deservedly so. It was a complete dump with filthy beds, noisy rooms, and no atmosphere whatsoever. It was, however, central, being just off the main square, named, predict-ably, Imam Khomeini Square.

I checked in, and after quickly dropping off my pack, left for the bustle of the street outside. I went for a snack at a thriving little café to get orientated and read up on the place. Hamadan is steeped in history and was founded, according to legend, by the mystical King Jamshid. It has been inhabited for at least four thousand years and was the capital city for the Median Empire (750–550 BC). It was subsequently the summer capital of the Achaemenids (550–330 BC) and was known as Hagma-taneh or "the meeting place." In its heyday, Hamadan was one of the world's great cities, containing exquisite palaces decorated lavishly in precious metals. However, all this wealth caught the eye of numerous invaders, and with these its importance as a city slowly diminished.

It began its decline after the Arab conquest of the mid-seventh century, but was restored as the region's capital for sixty odd years under the Seljuks in the twelfth century. The Mongols weren't so good to the place and smashed it up good and proper in 1220, as did the Tamerlanes in 1386. After this, it regained some of its former affluence and enjoyed a period of stability until the eighteenth century when the Turks decided to invade.

Until recently, Hamadan had a large Jewish community, which had been in the city since the fifth century BC. This community, like the city itself, has declined dramatically and is now apparently down to no more than thirty-five people. Hamadan contains Iran's most significant Jewish pilgrimage site, which is a shrine said to hold the remains of Esther, the Jewish wife of Achaemenid King Xerxes I. The Old Testament Book of Esther is named after her, and, along with the books of Ezra, Nehemiah, and Daniel, paints a favorable picture of the relationship between the Jews and the ancient Persian Achaemenid Empire.

I was in Hamadan, like most Iranian tourists, to use it as a base to visit the famous Ali Sadr Caves some sixty miles from here. The caves sounded awesome and had only been discovered some forty years ago by a local shepherd wandering about in search of a lost goat. What the lucky chap stumbled upon was a spectacular series of caves containing vast clear lakes and rivers. It had been surveyed in 2001 by a joint German and British geological team who recorded a total of seven miles of chambers, but there are probably far more as of yet undiscovered.

I got down to the bus station but had no idea which bus to take, so asked a young guy by pointing to the Persian script for the caves in my guidebook. I needn't have bothered as he spoke good English and informed me that the next minibus to the caves left in forty-five minutes. But, being Iranian, he couldn't just leave it at that and insisted also on buying me a cool drink at a café nearby. We both had an orange Capri Sun–style drink in a foil carton. Instead of sticking the straw through the tiny, fiddly, purpose-made hole in the top, which from my experience nearly always leaks, my Iranian friend just turned the carton upside down, stabbed the straw through the base, and drank it this way. I did the same and it worked great.

Although it was just a small minibus, I got a great seat all to myself by the rear door where I could stretch out my legs and recline. I felt surprisingly fatigued in the heat, and drifted off not long after we hit the road. I awoke just before the Ali Sadr village. On the outside, the caves looked very commercial with souvenir shops, ticket booths, playgrounds, and a huge hall next to the entrance for the caves, the purpose of which I couldn't work out. Inside the hall was a huge grumpy-looking Khomeini picture. Despite all of the tourist infrastructure and a warning in my guidebook that the place could be crawling with Iranians and hundreds of screaming school kids, I found it virtually deserted.

I purchased a ticket and walked to the entrance of the cave. The blessed coolness of the air was the first thing that hit me as I walked down a gradual flight of steps into the opening chamber containing a massive underground lake. Here a long jetty-like platform hugged the water's edge and two paddleboats waited for passengers. This was clearly where the crowds must have queued on busy days but today, mercifully, there was just a single family and me. I couldn't believe my luck.

We all had to put on lifejackets, which for the family's little daughter of about four was nearly as big as she was. We got in the boat, which was connected with a rope to a paddleboat operated by a young guy of about fourteen. A guide joined our boat and slowly we moved off. The water was a shimmering green color, and the clearest I'd ever seen in my life. Looking over the boat's edge, I could see an immensely long way down into the water, which was as deep as forty-five feet. Strangely, nothing lives in the water or in the caves themselves. Even bats don't inhabit the place, and there is no evidence of human or animal activity in the caves over the centuries.

We slowly drifted past otherworldly rock formations, which our guide described in Farsi only, leaving me to ponder them myself without explanation. I preferred it that way. Hanging down from sections of the cave's stalactite-covered roof were labels for some of the larger formations, identifying them with appropriate titles such as "Statue of Liberty," etc. These were accompanied by separate placards containing quotes from the Koran. I was mesmerized as we drifted slowly along.

The lighting was just enough to reveal the cave's grandeur but not so bright as to illuminate every nook and cranny and take away any of its mystique. We glided gently past many interconnecting chambers, all filled with the same clear water. Some looked like mystical and holy grottos, others like the hidden underground lair for a James Bond criminal's secret submarine. We drifted along for about thirty minutes, passing only one other boat going the opposite way, before arriving at another little jetty where a walkway led into the center of the caves. Here we disembarked. I let the family go first, not out of good manners but to give them a few minutes head start so I could walk around in complete silence.

It was simply wonderful and I felt a reverence for the place. That is until I got to a little café playing music. I quickly skipped past this and came face-to-face with the most awe-inspiring chamber. It was 131 feet high and had a jagged boulder protruding from its roof. Strewn all around were the remains of many other boulders from partial collapses over the millennia. I stood in this cathedral-like inner chamber and truly felt as if I were in the center of the earth.

The trip back was just as good and as I climbed out of the swaying boat, I felt completely energized. I emerged, blinking, into the sunlight and baking heat with a big smile on my face. Here the family from the boat asked if they could take their photo with me, and after posing for a total of three shots, I headed toward one of the cafés.

It had the usual collection of water pipes for smoking tobacco, and carpeted platforms on which to recline. Three men sat here whiling away the afternoon in apparent bliss. I ordered a tea and got chatting to one of them who spoke English. He asked whether I liked the caves. "According to the government, they are officially the most beautiful nature in all the world," he told me. And I guess if the Iranian government officially says so then it must be true. When it was time to pay for my drink, I wasn't allowed, despite trying the usual three refusals.

I caught the minibus back to Hamadan and arrived just after the sun had disappeared. As I walked through the town in search of some food and an Internet café, the evocative sound of the calling to prayers emanated across the city from the mosques' speakers. The Internet café was overflowing with people, half of whom stood around sipping away at tea whilst giving advice on what to write to those at the keyboard. Interestingly, Iran has the fourth-largest blogging community in the world, which may very well account for the painfully slow speed of the Net in some places. This was the case here, where it took me the best part of half an hour to send two very short messages.

Not far down from the Internet café, situated along the thriving high street, was a Western-style fast food restaurant. It wasn't traditional local cuisine, but I didn't care as I really fancied a change from all the kebabs and rice.

I decided on a cheeseburger and fries.

Whilst ordering my food, I got talking to the cashier and asked him if I needed a calling card to make a call from a public phone booth to a cell phone. I wanted to get in touch with Leyla before I headed to Tehran tomorrow. The guy working the register went and got a girl in the restaurant to translate for him. She explained that the restaurant staff were happy for me to use their phone, if this was okay with me of course. This was more than okay.

I got through to Leyla, who was delighted to hear from me but had not yet heard from Ricardo as I'd hoped. She said to call her again when I got to Tehran and she'd come pick me up from my hotel in the evening.

The English-speaking girl joined me at my table while I ate. She came bearing gifts—a huge ice cream sundae complete with two crispy wafers, Jell-O, and sprinkles. I dropped a wobbly bit of ice cream clad Jell-O on my pants. The girl was a pretty twenty-year-old student from Tehran, although I didn't make a note of her name. Without my asking, she wrote down her e–mail address for me, seconds before her mother joined us at the table. The girl gestured to the piece of paper with her e–mail and said, "Secret, cannot tell." Mommy was a crone–like wretch with a face like a bulldog chewing a wasp, who eyed me and my table manners suspiciously.

Her mother spoke only a word or two of English, which was just as well, as her daughter asked my opinion on Khomeini, and I suspected for some reason that her mother was an admirer of his. The girl gestured to a framed portrait of the man in question on the restaurant's wall, which like every other shop in Iran has to have one. I had yet to meet a person who actually liked Khomeini, but on a hunch I asked her first what her mother thought of him. She translated the question to her old lady, who, as I suspected, expressed her admiration by putting a hand on her heart and bowing slightly toward the picture.

I told the girl that I wasn't a big fan of Khomeini, but for her sake, in front of her mother I would pretend that I was. I put my hand on my heart and bowed in a similar fashion at the picture. My reasoning must have got lost in translation as the girl seemed surprised and said quietly, "No, he is not good man!"

Interestingly, in none of the pictures you see of Khomeini is he ever smiling. His PR man didn't do a very good job; in all his photos he wasn't just a little on the grumpy side but downright angry. The girl's mother was the first, and in fact the only person, I met in Iran who openly expressed a liking for Khomeini. But if the information in my guidebook was correct then there were a substantial number of Iranians who not only liked the bloke but looked upon him as something of a saint. Since I encountered the opposite of this, I did wonder how accurate and up–to–date the book was in this regard. That said, Khomeini was definitely popular at the time of his funeral in 1989, which drew a phenomenal 10 million mourners. Not a bad turnout by anyone's standards.

The Khomeini–loving woman and her daughter left the burger bar a minute after my fake picture–bowing, but then the girl returned briefly on her own. She looked back to see if her mother was watching then held out her hand illicitly for me to shake. We shook hands, she smiled, and then left for good.

Before I left, two staff members came over and gave me a customer questionnaire. It was partially in English and listed categories like speed of service, quality of food, freshness of food, etc., alongside the ratings "good," "okay," and "bad," to circle where appropriate. I didn't pay too much attention to it and circled where I saw fit, but made sure to give the staff full marks. They took it away but returned a minute later looking most unhappy. The source of their contention was I'd only given the food an "okay."

"Why you not say food was good?" one asked.

They obviously took their customer questionnaires very seriously in Iran. I tried to explain that it was a nice enough cheeseburger as cheeseburgers go, but at the end of the day, it was, after all, just a cheeseburger, not fillet mignon served with a drizzle of truffle juice and half a bottle of the finest Chateau Latour '82. They weren't having any of this crap, and asked if I'd like to change my mind. I said I would and circled the good option instead. Everybody left happy.

I started to head back to my hotel but popped into a drugstore on the way to buy some toothpaste. For some reason, the man working behind the counter couldn't work out my mime for toothpaste and offered me cough lozenges instead. A young guy in the shop who spoke okay English helped out. He ordered on my behalf and before I could stop him had handed over the money for the toothpaste as well. He intro-duced himself as Pedram.

We got talking outside, where his cheerful plump friend, Behzad, was waiting. They were both students from Tehran and were just down in Hamadan for a couple of days visiting friends.

Not five minutes into our conversation and Pedram invited me to join them for *chay* in a nearby park. A few minutes later, we were squashed into the back of a nice modern car and speeding along with two of his other friends. The park was perched on a hill and had a great panoramic view of the city and all its sparkling lights below. Up here was an expensive-looking tearoom with several raised carpeted platforms outside.

We all had tea on one of the platforms and over our second cup, I was discreetly invited to join the lads back at their place for a drink of the alcoholic variety. This was an opportunity I couldn't resist but first, apparently, we needed mixers. Pedram and I were assigned this task and dropped the lads off at their apartment, which they'd rented for the weekend before heading out.

In the car, Pedram explained that he had to pick up a girl friend of his from the bus station and give her a lift to her aunt's place. As we drove, and chatted away, I was struck by how Western Pedram seemed when compared to other Iranians I'd met thus far. I couldn't quite put my finger on why but I got the distinct impression that he and his friends all came from well-off families.

I was left in the car while Pedram met his friend, who was a large but attractive girl of about twenty. After we dropped her off, Pedram told me that she had invited me to her sister's party when I came to Tehran. I was hugely excited at the prospect of going to an illegal gathering of drunken students, which I was sure few tourists would get to experience. Pedram said I could crash at their apartment tonight if I wanted, so we made a brief stop at my crummy hotel, where I grabbed my stuff, paid up, and got my passport back. Back at the apartment, the guys were all sitting around in shorts playing cards for money. The game was brought to a swift conclusion when Pedram and I turned up and they brought out what looked like an eight-pack of beer. On closer inspection, I discovered they were actually cans of whisky. I'd never seen whisky in cans before and asked the guys if this was normal. They'd never heard of whisky in bottles before.

We started the night off with a shot mixed with just a suggestion of cola. It was bloody strong and I knew I'd end up loaded before the night was out. A copied DVD was selected from a wallet full of illegal discs and slipped into the player. We all reclined on big cushions with another shot of whisky as the film began. It was *Basic Instinct* with the delectable Sharon Stone. We watched about fifteen minutes and just before the money shot, the DVD started to malfunction. A cry of horror went up from all around but it was no good, and despite Pedram's best efforts to right the problem, we had to admit defeat and were forced to abandon the film.

It has to be said, I was quite looking forward to the novel prospect of watching Sharon uncross her legs in Iran. I needn't have worried though, as this was fully compensated for by the next DVD selected by the lads, which contained acts that the lovely Miss Stone would be far too prudish to attempt on screen and which would have been of borderline legality in certain states of the U.S. until recently, let alone the Islamic Republic of Iran. I wondered what horrendous penalties there were if you were caught in possession of or watching such material whilst consuming vast quantities of hard liquor. I thought back to the television documentary I'd seen on human rights abuses in Iran, which had shown a man having his eye cut out for looking at "something immoral," and wondered if this Persian porn would count in that department. I knocked back a few more shots and no longer cared. It was a late night and by the time I passed out, I'd consumed a hell of a lot of booze.

I awoke feeling awful with a splitting headache and a desire to curl up into a ball and quietly die. It didn't look like I was the only one. I had planned to visit the Jewish shrine this morning before catching the bus to Tehran but that plan went out the window now. All I wanted to do was nothing.

I had to make a move though, and decided to push through it and get to the bus terminal. Pedram, who looked in a worse condition than me, offered to give me a lift there. Pedram's fat friend, Behzad, who looked surprisingly sprightly considering how much he'd drunk, said he'd tag along as well. As Behzad got dressed one of the guys, whose name I was in no state to remember or jot down, grabbed the poor guy's flabby breasts and said jokingly to me, "He is breast boy, no?" Even breast boy laughed at this one.

At the terminal, Pedram whisked me past all the sales guys shouting out their destinations to a bus company called Seir–o Safar. Pedram said it was the only bus company worth traveling with in Iran. He tried to pay for my ticket, but I put my foot down and handed over the money. What he did next was a great help. He phoned one of his friends in Tehran and arranged for him to meet me at the bus station when I arrived and to take me to a hotel. In a city of a staggering 15 million people this would be immensely useful. Pedram was going back to Tehran tomorrow along with Behzad, so he gave me his number and insisted I call him and stay at his parents' place when he got back. Things were going amazingly well.

The first thing you notice about Tehran as you approach it is the smog. It's situated in a natural valley surrounded by mountains, which lets the pollution build up and leaves the air a horrible brown hue. As we drove through the endless streets, I realized what luck it was to have a local waiting to help me at the bus station. It was one hell of a big sprawling city, and it would have been a nightmare to try to cope with it after a heavy night on the booze. A hangover is *not* a state most people are in when they first arrive in Tehran.

I got off the bus, collected my bags and within a minute was approached by two sharply dressed young guys in shades. One asked, "Jamie?" We shook hands and I was led toward their car, which like Pedram's was a modern European one. Neither spoke much English, so I just followed their lead. We drove through the most insane traffic and nearly crashed several times. The smooth two communicated that we were going to grab some food, and as I was hungry, this was just what I wanted to hear.

Along the highway, we passed two roadside murals in ornate frames depicting the infamous Abu Ghraib torture of Iraqis by U.S. forces. One was the well-known picture of the Iraqi with a leash around his neck, the other of the hooded man with the wires coming out of his fingers. The images contained some Persian text, which I subsequently discovered read something along the lines of, "Yesterday you were torturing Palestine; today you are torturing Iraq."

We stopped for lunch at a fast food restaurant called Apache, where my hosts ordered a mountain of burgers and fries along with some obligatory soft drinks. Despite my protests, and believe me I tried, the guys categorically insisted on paying, and I was literally physically forced to put my wallet back into my pocket. Over our food I got out my guidebook for them, and pointed to the hotels it recommended. They were adamant that these weren't up to much and wanted to take me elsewhere. As far as I was concerned, they were the bosses, as I had no idea where I was, and in a city this big it would have been a real mission to sort things out for myself.

Seated nearby were two young women sporting what looked like fresh Band-Aids across their noses. After a bit of miming to the guys, I managed to ascertain that these were nose job bandages, and that it was quite common. I later learnt that, amazingly, more plastic surgery is carried out in Tehran than in Los Angeles.

After feasting like kings, we got on the road again. We drove around and around for over an hour, passing a cinema showing Michael Moore's *Fahrenheit 9/11*, but for some reason we stopped at no hotels. It seemed the guys were no longer quite as confident about where to take me. They explained in their limited English that they were now taking me to a library instead.

"What the hell is going on?" I thought. I didn't want to sit down with a Harlequin novel–I wanted to get some accommodation sorted.

We turned up at a library nestled in a little park in the north of the city. Here the guys made hotel inquiries with one of the library assistants and not surprisingly came up with fuck all. I was grateful for their help but couldn't see why we were wasting time or why they were so adamant that the hotels in my guidebook were no good.

By chance, a professor who spoke better English than I did was also at the library. He sounded like an Oxford University don and was a charming fellow who was more than happy to translate. He told them to take me to my chosen hotel, which as far as he was aware, was an "awfully good little place," and said he didn't know what all the fuss had been about.

I thanked him, he gave me his card, and we set off again.

Tehran went on and on forever with very few prominent landmarks from which to get your bearings. The amount of people and traffic was something else; it seemed like all 15 million of the city's residents were out on the streets today. We stopped at three other hotels, all of which were full, before we got to the original one I'd selected. It was also full. This wasn't good news as it was now late afternoon, but the reception guy recommended a place around the corner. It was thirty-two dollars a night, which was by far the most expensive place thus far on my trip, but I paid it gladly and was just pleased to have a roof over my head. I thanked the guys for their help and headed up to my room. It was absolutely fantastic. It had a double bed, a TV with BBC World, a shower room with a proper toilet, a fridge, and to top it all off, the price included breakfast. I got on the phone to Leyla who arranged to pick me up in three hours, though she still hadn't heard from Ricardo. That gave me ample opportunity to shower and put my feet up and watch the BBC's *Hard Talk* program before indulging in a nap.

The phone jolted me back to reality from a deep sleep. Predictably, it was Leyla on the line, who told me to meet her in reception. The first thing she said when I turned up was, "This is not a good area."

Leyla told me there'd been antigovernment demonstrations near the hotel two days ago and that the police and the government's Basji Militia had tear gassed, beaten, and arrested loads of students. The demonstration had been inspired by an Iranian exile, Dr. Ahura Pirouz Khaleghi Yazdi, who had broadcast the call to protest from a satellite station based in the United States.

She expressed her relief that I hadn't arrived a couple of days earlier, but the journalist in me was genuinely gutted to have missed the opportunity to record the events and get some photographs.

Two of her friends were waiting in the car. The girl spoke good English but the boy spoke next to none. Both Leyla and her female friend looked very Western with makeup and jeans. Although wearing the compulsory hijab, they were of a light-weight material and covered only a fraction of their hair. We drove through the city, which was surprisingly quiet now that it was dark, and arrived at a little restaurant in the north of Tehran. It was an upmarket place and all of the customers looked very wealthy and Western in comparison to other parts of Iran, dressed in expensive-looking clothing, and the women wearing makeup and minute hijabs.

Leyla's friends were both twenty years old and were dating each other. Although it was officially not allowed, they said it was common for young people to be in relationships and to keep it from their parents. The girl, whose name I didn't make a note of, told me that her father had discovered her relationship and had gone crazy. He had told her to break up with her boyfriend but she had steadfastly refused. Surprisingly, she said, he had eventually come to accept it. Like Leyla, the girl had grown up abroad and had recently moved back to Iran when her parents returned (her boyfriend was Iranian). In Canada, her father had enrolled her in a Catholic boarding school, despite her being a Muslim, because he was determined to keep her away from boys.

I asked her if she would return to Canada when she got the chance after finishing her studies. I was surprised when she told me that she planned to stay in Iran forever. If she'd grown up here, I wouldn't have been surprised, but since she'd spent most of her life in an open society, I thought it odd she'd now happily live indefinitely in such a repressive one. She explained, rather unconvincingly to my mind, by saying that the state repression wasn't such a big deal to her personally and that she was Iranian and this was Iran.

Leyla was not in agreement with her and planned to be off within a year. Of the two, she seemed to be much more of a free spirit, and as a result I liked her far more.

It was very interesting to chat with them both and learn more about their lives and their attitude toward their government, which the Canadian girl said now just about everybody despised. I asked her then why she thought more people didn't rebel against the state. She put it down to the Iran–Iraq War having caused half a million Iranian deaths and people not wanting to cause any more bloodshed by rebelling. Leyla added that if you stepped out of line politically, you didn't just get reprimanded, you got killed or worse—which, of course, is a pretty effective deterrent.

When it was time to get the bill, it was no surprise that Leyla and friends wouldn't let me chip in. They insisted that I was their guest and that in Iran it was customary for them to pay for me. It was actually becoming hard to spend any money here at all due to the overwhelming generosity people were showing me.

On the way back in the car, we drove past a special jail that Leyla pointed out. It was specifically for people picked up off the street with either a boyfriend, girlfriend, or an inappropriate hijab. Leyla told me that the police did big swoops in certain areas and arrested loads of people all at once. She said that she knew of people who'd been there and that as jails go, it wasn't too bad, and that on the whole you just spent a night there for these offenses.

Near my hotel, Leyla spotted some cops on the side of the road. She got nervous, said once more, "This is a bad area," and pulled up her hijab conservatively. I asked what was wrong with the area and she said that a lot of people get arrested here for being with unrelated members of the opposite sex. When we pulled up, Leyla stayed in the car and said, "Hurry."

"Why?"

"I can't be with you," she said. "I could go to jail."

I got out and went inside.

Once in my room, I got really pissed off. I couldn't get my head around how she could have been arrested simply for being in a car with me, and I couldn't get my head around the apparent apathy of her Canadian friend who considered it no big deal. To me, it seemed a huge deal, especially when people were getting killed and tortured for simply stepping out of line. I went to bed highly annoyed.

CHAPTER TEN

All the Gear but No Idea

Pedram's car swerved recklessly across the main road, coming to a screeching stop outside my hotel. A moment later, his two library–loving friends did likewise in their car, drawing several hornblasts from agitated drivers behind. It was great to see Pedram again, and after warmly shaking hands, I jumped in the back of his car, which sped off at breakneck speed.

Our first stop was a pool hall in the center of the city where we met up with the ever–cheery Behzad and two more of Pedram's friends. Pedram explained that the party I had been invited to by his friend in Hamadan was scheduled for tomorrow night and that it should be a very good one indeed. I was delighted and couldn't wait to go along for another illegal Iranian gathering.

The pool hall was obviously one of their haunts; nearly all the young guys inside–and there were only guys inside–knew Pedram and his friends. I was the center of attention and introduced to all the locals, a couple of whom spoke good English. It was a typical pool hall with the same dark interior and laid back atmosphere as any establishment back home, minus the alcohol of course. We decided on a game of doubles, with Pedram and me versus Behzad and one of the other guys, whose name was Ali. It wasn't a convincing victory, but Pedram and I pulled off a win. Just when we were about to rack them up for a second game, over walked a confident-looking guy carrying his own personal cue case—always a dangerous sign—who challenged me to a singles match.

I accepted reluctantly. In no apparent hurry, and as if playing for the audience which had gathered to watch, Mr. Professional placed his cue box on the table and slowly flipped its briefcase-like locks. It popped open revealing a beautifully crafted piece of equipment. He screwed the two ends of the cue together with a quick twist of his hands, then held it to the light and looked along its length, checking for straightness.

What the fuck?

But this wasn't the end of his little ritual. Next, he got out a strange three-fingered glove, which he purposefully slipped onto his lead hand. His knuckles were then given a full crack, the cue was given a scientific application of chalk, and he was ready to begin.

I didn't fancy my chances.

Now I'm either a good player or a bad player, and one that improves with alcohol, which wasn't an option today, but by sheer luck I played a masterful game and beat Mr. "All the Gear but No Idea" hands down. He looked embarrassed. After this victory, everybody in the club wanted to challenge me. I even had the gratifying pleasure of pulling off a fluke victory against one of the best players in the club, or so I was told by Pedram. After everybody had had a chance to play me, we headed across the road to a little café where we all tucked in to buttered rice and lamb and tomato kebabs. Once again I was not allowed to pay.

Everyone now discussed where I should be taken next. The conversation was conducted in Farsi, so I had no idea what locations were thrown into the discussion, but I was expecting maybe a museum or historical site. Nothing of the sort. I was taken to a shopping mall dedicated to nothing but a load of Best Buy–style computer stores!

God knows what possessed this insane decision, and for the next hour and a half, I had to do my best to look interested in the latest laptop or PC monitor. The highlight of this bizarre outing, which predictably was not much of a highlight, was eating a takeaway sweet–corn snack from a polystyrene cup and drinking mandarin juice from a vending machine. I was pleased when it all came to an end and we got back on the road.

Thankfully, there were no more computer stores for us next, as it was unanimously agreed that we were all going to head over to Ali's place and use his swimming pool. En route to his place, we raced around the city with the windows down and music from a cassette blaring out from the stereo—music which without a shadow of a doubt would have been on the government's official list of prohibited tunes. It featured a woman breathing and moaning over a fast–paced techno track. Either she was panting after a brisk five–mile run in the fresh air or she was rather enjoying herself. A strange mix followed of rap, hardcore dance, and romantic ballads, which blared out at deafening volume. The guys all sang along enthusiastically and saw no contradiction between throwing up gang signs to rap songs one minute and then swaying to a slow, pensive rendition of Chris de Burgh's "Lady in Red" the next. I thought that was great.

Iranian driving reaches its zenith of insanity and chaos on the heaving streets of Tehran. It certainly isn't for the timid, and Pedram's approach was anything but, with him swerving in and out of traffic, yelling at other motorists, and constantly beeping his horn at he went. It requires a certain amount of skill just to get through the day there without hitting or being hit by another vehicle.

One thing you can't help but notice when driving around Tehran is the vast number of political murals dedicated to subjects such as Iran's war dead from the Iran–Iraq conflict or the murder of Palestinian children by the occupying Israeli forces. These are all over the city, painted on the sides of buildings and on huge billboards along the road. Nearly all of them are very artistic and skillfully done, and range from depictions of heroic military figures gazing pensively off into the distance against a backdrop of fluttering Iranian flags, to banners of Persian text scrawled across war scenes.

As we got closer to Ali's, we roared past a mullah, one of Iran's turban- and cloak-wearing religious leaders, and the lads discreetly muttered abuse at him under their breath. Pedram explained that they all hated the mullahs because, as he put it, "They have closed mind."

We came to a dramatic tire-screaming stop outside a salubrious apartment block in the wealthy northern suburbs. This was Pedram's parents' place. He insisted that from now on in Tehran I would stay here. They had a really nice spacious apartment, which must have cost a pretty penny—property in Tehran is far from cheap. Only his mother was in, who greeted us with a warm smile and was wearing the full, tablecloth-like chador showing only a fraction of her face. Pedram grabbed some swim trunks for me whilst I dropped off my backpack and gave Leyla a call. It was a pain to get the call to connect, but when it finally did, she gave me the good news that Ricardo had been in touch and that he was going to meet us this evening, along with her mother, at a traditional Iranian restaurant. With characteristic generosity, Pedram insisted that he would give me a lift to the restaurant. I couldn't have asked for more. Ricardo was apparently staying in a dirt-cheap hostel in the nasty southern suburbs. I smiled to myself and felt extremely fortunate to be staying with Pedram.

Pedram's place was nice but Ali's was in a different league altogether. Two huge security gates opened up for us revealing a palatial, ultramodern apartment building. A beautifully tiled driveway led past several floodlit fountains showering a vast pool, and down to an underground parking area. Inside, it was like a five-star hotel with a vast lobby decorated in marble and gold, and carpeted with an exquisite red Persian rug. In the basement, there was a full gym, communal swimming pool, steam room, and sauna, which we had all to ourselves, and it's just as well.

My leisurely swim went out the window as the order of the day was a load of wrestling, ducking, and bombing, swimming contests, and general larking about. Poor old Behzad got a lot of shit for his slack frame, and Ali thought it most amusing to get his cock out and close his legs around it to impersonate a woman. The lads thought this was hilarious. I retired to the sauna shortly after this for a much-needed bit of sanity. It didn't last long. Everybody piled in and began flinging water all over the place. Maybe it was because I was tired, maybe because I was older than them at nearly thirty, but I began to get really bored with all the messing around and would have given anything just to be able to sit in here and relax for a bit.

The festivities came to an abrupt end when Pedram looked at his watch and realized that Cinderella was going to be late for the ball with Ricardo, Leyla, and her mother. It was dark outside now and we drove like complete fruitcakes through the crowded streets all the way from northern to southern Tehran. The city was even more chaotic than normal and all lit up with sparkling colored lights and decorations to celebrate the birthday of Imam Mehdi.

Iranian Shiite Muslims acknowledge twelve Imams who they see as the direct successors to the Prophet Mohammed and the only people capable of infallibly interpreting the Koran.

The twelve Imams are venerated much like Christian saints and everybody seems to have their favorite. I saw their images everywhere, from the inside of shops to the backs of buses. Coincidentally, I also saw many buses and other vehicles with the English word "GOD" in capital letters on their windscreens. Imam Mehdi was the twelfth and last Imam, and the only one said to be still alive. It is claimed he simply vanished inside a cave beneath an Iraqi mosque when he was still young. Shiites also believe that at the end of the world, Imam Mehdi and Jesus will return together, as a sort of tag team special, to sort the world out and reestablish peace on earth.

To Shiite Muslims, an Imam is divinely appointed and infallible, whereas to Sunnis, he can be appointed by man and is seen more as a leader of the Muslim community. Although many places in Iran are officially named Imam Khomeini Street or Imam Khomeini Square, the title is an honorary one given to Khomeini after his death by the Shiite government in an attempt to venerate him. Many Iranians I spoke to find this offensive and refuse to refer to him with this title, instead using more colorful and choice ones of their own.

We arrived at the restaurant, which was hidden away at the bottom of an attractive little staircase. The lads remained in the cars outside while Pedram came in with me to give Leyla his address. The restaurant was decorated with ornately tiled vaulted ceilings and was packed with people smoking the water pipe, drinking *chay*, eating, and generally having a great time. Four guys provided live traditional music that filled the restaurant with a contagious vibrancy. Their Persian instruments included a pear-shaped traditional guitar called a tanbur, a chalice-shaped drum made of mulberry wood known as a tombak, and the Persian equivalent of a small cello called a kamancheh.

Nestled in a cozy corner in the very best spot were Ricardo, Leyla's mother, and Leyla herself. They all looked far smarter than I did making me wish I'd made more of an effort. Ricardo, the old smoothie, had even bought them a bunch of fresh roses. I greeted them all warmly with handshakes, which I figured was okay because they were friends and had spent so long in the West. Pedram passed on his address to Leyla whose mother invited him to join us. He declined the offer and explained his friends were waiting for him. After Pedram departed, Leyla said that he lived in a very expensive area of Tehran and that it was not too far from their place so we could all share a taxi at the end of the night.

It was great to see them again and we all settled down to what turned out to be a wonderful evening. We had a traditional Iranian meal called *abgusht* or *dizi*. This is a stew made from super-succulent mutton or beef, potatoes, onions, chickpeas, tomatoes, and a good dollop of fat, which is all served in a container called a *dizi*. With the *dizi*, you also receive a pestle and a separate bowl in which to pour off the red soupy liquid at the top of the stew. You either drink this with a spoon or mop it up with bread. Then comes the fun bit—you pound the living hell out of the remaining foodstuffs in the *dizi* with the pestle until they've been reduced to a thick tasty paste, which you then scoop out with additional bread.

Ricardo and I thought it was fantastic, and it sure made a welcome change from all the kebabs and rice. To accompany the *abgusht* we also had loads of dates, yogurt, and fresh fruit, of which cucumber is considered a variety. Leyla and her mother showed us how to eat the cucumber by sprinkling salt on its juicy inner core before eating. I found it surprisingly good, as the watery nature of the cucumber really complemented the salty taste. We did the same with slices of apple, but I didn't think it worked quite as well.

The music was great and there were lots of people clapping hands and clicking their fingers in time with the music. There are several ways Iranians click their fingers all of which I found very difficult. The most popular method is to put your hands together as if praying, then slightly raise your two forefingers and push one against the other in opposite directions to cause the one pushing down to "click" onto your fingers below. It wasn't easy, and after much perseverance, I only managed to get a very insignificant click. Leyla and her mother had it down to a tee and could produce the loudest of snaps this way. They showed Ricardo and me several other finger clicking methods, but those were even harder to do.

Leyla's mother explained that the music's lyrics, like most traditional Iranian songs, were very melancholy. It was a song of regret for a person loved but lost, and this, she said, was a recurring theme in many Iranian songs. On the more modern music front, Leyla said that she'd looked into a government-sanctioned rap or rock concert to take us both to, but Ricardo was flying out tomorrow for the historic city of Esfahan, so it was not possible. It made a hell of a lot of sense to fly considering the distances involved, and as Ricardo said it was fairly cheap, I decided to look into it myself.

After the meal, Ricardo and I gave the water pipe a go. The tobacco in the pipe had a fruity flavor, and predictably, Ricardo was far better at smoking the stuff than I was. I couldn't get the water to bubble and as a result breathed very little smoke, maybe a good thing.

We stayed in the restaurant until closing time and no prizes for guessing who insisted on paying. When we finally left, all the staff wished us good night and insisted on shaking hands with Ricardo and me.

In the cab heading to Ricardo's hotel in the south of the city, I had an interesting conversation with Leyla's mother. I asked her if there were many other traditional Iranian restaurants in Tehran like the one we'd been to tonight. She said there were only a few that were comparable, but one in particular she would never visit because of its location. It was called, I think, the Persian equivalent of Seventh Heaven. Very few people knew, she explained, that it was actually located beneath a prison used for torturing political prisoners. Quite understandably, she said that the thought of having a celebratory meal whilst people were being tortured upstairs was sick. She went on to tell me that on the rare occasions the prisoners were allowed a family visit, these were conducted nearby in what she described as a "Lunar Park," which I took to mean a fairground or theme park, purely to make it more traumatic for all involved.

Just around the corner from Ricardo's hotel was a huge square called . . . you guessed it, Imam Khomeini Square. In the center of the square along with lots of cheerfully colored lights was a large replica of the black cloth–covered cube–shaped shrine in Mecca, known as the Ka'ba. Rather at odds with this was a display around the edge of the square that contained a number of massive missiles complete with mobile truck launchers. They looked just like the Scuds I'd seen on television during the first Gulf War. Next to a couple of the missiles was a vast banner of Iran's current supreme religious leader, Ayatollah Ali Khamenei, who is the true holder of Iran's executive power, with the president ranking number two in the country's political hierarchy. The Iranian president's status is very different to that of a U.S. president. He is not the commander–in–chief of the country's armed forces, and does not have the authority to set policies which fall outside the parameters approved by the true rulers of the country, the ayatollahs.

Before dropping Ricardo off, Leyla and I arranged to come pick him up in the morning in a taxi and to go around the city's sprawling bazaar together.

It was well past midnight by the time we arrived at Pedram's place, so I ended up phoning him on Leyla's cell so as not to wake his parents. Predictably, the poor bugger sounded like I'd woken him up. Apologies flowed from me for being so late, but he didn't seem to mind and he showed me to his room where

Christian Church Qareh Kalisa, near Maku.

My taxi driver and a sheep.

Iranian bus, lower end of the market.

Tabriz street murals. *Photo by Ricardo Almeida.*

Market in Ramsar, near the Caspian Sea. *Photo by Ricardo Almeida.*

Sculpture depicting torture techniques including partial beheading, as seen in the bottom right hand corner.

Mountain village of Masuleh, located in the lush green north of Iran. *Photo by Ricardo Almeida.*

With Sabine and Ricardo at the Castle of Assassins.
Photo by Sabine Richard.

View on the climb up to the Castle of Assassins.
Photo by Michal Schula.

Rural mosque near Qazvin. *Photo by Michal Schula.*

Tehran with its profusion of people and Hillman Hunter cars.

Rolling hills on the journey hitchhiking back from Alamut.
Photo by Michal Schula.

God bless America, Tehran street scene.

The iconic Abu Ghraib torture pictures, displayed for all to see on one of Tehran's main highways.

Street art, Iranian style.

The evocative old city of Yazd at dusk. *Photo by Ricardo Almeida.*

Shiraz mosque at sunset. *Photo by Ricardo Almeida.*

Picnic with the Tehran lads after several surgical spirit
spritzers. (Note the bottle in front of me.)

Traditional bakery, Yazd. *Photo by Sabine Richard.*

One of Esfahan's many historic bridges. *Photo by Ricardo Almeida.*

With Ian and the "Canada Iran" lads.

Traditional Abgusht meal. *Photo by Sabine Richard.*

The Imam Mosque, Esfahan. *Photo by Ricardo Almeida.*

Bas–relief at the ancient palace of Persepolis.
Photo by Ricardo Almeida.

a spare bed was waiting for me. Before we hit the sack, I invited him to come along with us to the bazaar tomorrow. He gave me a slightly perplexed look and said that there was no need for us to get a cab because he'd drive us all there but that he thought the bazaar a very strange location for us to visit. He probably thought a lovely computer shop would be more appropriate for foreign visitors.

CHAPTER ELEVEN

Mullah Madness

"Jamie, we're gonna have to get a taxi instead," Leyla turned to me and said from the back of Pedram's car as we careened through the streets of northern Tehran.

Soon after setting off together for the bazaar, it had become apparent that there was something of a personality clash between Leyla and Pedram. This had boiled over into a heated discussion in Farsi culminating in Leyla's comment to me. I had no idea what was going on and felt somewhat caught in the middle. I was staying at Pedram's house and therefore felt obliged to spend time with him, but on the other hand had also promised to go out with Leyla and Ricardo, whose last day it was in Tehran.

Pedram pulled over, and as Leyla and I got out, he asked me to call him later in the day. As his car wheels spun off, disappearing into the torrent of traffic racing along the road, Leyla gave me her take on the situation. Pedram, she said, had wanted to go and pick up a CD at his friend's house in the north of the city and didn't really want to go to the bazaar with us but wouldn't admit it. She said that by the time we'd gone all the way to his friend's place it would be too late to see Ricardo. She added that she thought Pedram was an idiot.

Without further ado, we headed to a little taxicab office, which Leyla had a special prepaid taxi card for. When the driver asked our location, she said "Imam Khomeini Square." The driver turned around and said something in Farsi. She translated, saying that he'd told her not to call it Imam Khomeini Square as Khomeini was no Imam and had no right to use the title. He clearly didn't like Khomeini but told her this in a friendly enough way. We got down to the square, driving past the missiles and other displays we'd seen the night before.

After going around in circles for a bit, we managed to locate Ricardo's hotel, where he was waiting outside. With Ricardo on board, we headed for the bazaar. On the way there, our taxi approached a mullah, standing by the side of a the road. On approaching the mullah, the taxi driver slowed down and yelled something at him through the open window. Leyla began laughing herself silly and took a minute to compose herself before she managed to translate: "I hope all the shit in the world falls down on you and washes you away."

Ricardo and I were hugely surprised at the driver's audacity and apparent fearlessness in abusing the establishment. He then went on to say, Leyla translated for us, that his dream was to see all the mullahs hanging from the trees, and to one day see them walk naked through the streets. He continued and told us that mullahs find it very difficult to get a taxi in Tehran as none of the drivers will pick them up. He was a real character and told Leyla to tell Ricardo and me to inform everybody about this when we got back to our own countries. He shook our hands warmly with a huge beaming smile as we left the car for the sprawling bazaar.

Although our taxi driver was fervently against the government, there was, apparently, a lot of support for the establishment amongst the men running the Tehran Bazaar, which we were about to enter. These men are, on the whole, extremely wealthy, well-connected individuals who wield a massive collective political power, with the vast majority of them being ultraconservative in both religion and politics. Traditionally, the Tehran Bazaar is the Iranian equivalent of Wall Street, where staple commodity prices are fixed. Some estimates put Tehran's Bazaar in control of up to a third of the country's total trade and retail output. And many bazaar merchants, the *bazaris*, have access to foreign currency and can give loans just as easily as a bank. The Shah tried to reduce the enormous power held by the *bazaris* by creating new roads running through the bazaar, and providing subsidies to their competitors running supermarkets. He also formed state purchasing organizations to handle some of the products sold in the bazaar. Predictably, during the revolution the *bazaris* got their own back by shutting up shop, which caused chaos in the national economy.

The streets outside the bazaar were crowded, but inside it was several times worse. There was a sea of people, and if you stopped for a second, you got swept along with the current. It was a confusing labyrinth of interconnecting tunnels, which almost formed a city in its own right. It contained hotels, mosques, several banks, a church, and even its own fire station. We managed to escape the worst of the crowds and found a more secluded spot specializing in wonderful Persian carpets.

This was the first time I'd been out during the day with Leyla in the city, and I noticed now how much attention she drew from every single male she passed. Simply walking through the bazaar, she turned heads all over the place. I pointed this out to her and she said, "Iranians have a staring problem."

She told me that when she first came to Iran she found it difficult, but now she was used to it. It was interesting to see her deal with guys, who, perhaps like Pedram, assume she'll be all submissive and respectful to them. Instead she was a real haggler, confident, and took no crap from anyone. It was great to see. She gave Ricardo and me a tip when negotiating for anything in Iran, whether for goods in a bazaar or a hotel room, which was to make your first offer just under half of the asking price and then work from there.

We spent the next hour just wandering, browsing, and soaking up the place. We passed hundreds of people gathered around a speaker system clapping and jumping about enthusiastically. It looked great fun but even Leyla didn't have the faintest idea what was going on. We left the intensity of the bazaar for the streets outside and walked to a lovely little restaurant opposite the sprawling British embassy. The embassy was set in a huge enclosed parkland right in the center of Tehran. It looked far too big for such a small island nation and must have dated back to when Britain, or "the old fox" as it is referred to in Iran, was far more important and really was a superpower. In a moment of fantasy, I imagined popping inside the embassy for a nice cup of tea and a "good to see you, old boy" chat with the ambassador.

Instead, I settled for a large cola in the restaurant opposite–a charming place called Café Naderi, which Leyla said had once been the preserve of writers, artists, and intellectuals in the days before the revolution. The food was great and we all got stuck into a juicy steak with creamy mushroom sauce, served with chunky fries and carrots. Leyla struggled with hers, so I helped out and polished off the rest along with mine. By the time I'd finished, I was feeling very full, very fat, but very satisfied. When it came time to pay, Leyla tried to treat us but without the support of her mother or Iranian friends, she didn't have the necessary back up and gave in to my and Ricardo's insistence that we pick up the tab.

When we handed over our money to the waiter, he looked at it, then back at us and stated simply, "Tip!" whilst gesturing for us to cough up more. We'd already left the standard 10 percent but he wanted extra and justified this by telling Leyla that we'd caused him a lot of trouble–the lying prick. He got his extra tip though, as we all quite admired his cheek.

During the meal, Ricardo had been selling me on the idea of catching a flight south instead of getting the bus and, although it seemed at odds with all the hitching I'd done to get to Iran, I decided to go for it. With this in mind we all went down to a travel agency, and I booked a flight to the jewel of ancient Persia, the historic city of Esfahan, which for many visitors is the highlight of Iran, and then on from there, a couple of days later, to the city of Shiraz.

After some quick browsing around an old antiques shop, Ricardo had to leave to catch his flight. Leyla was sad to see him go, and so was I, but at least I'd get to see him again down south. After Ricardo's departure, Leyla and I went for a drink together and chatted away until I thought it time to give Pedram a call. Pedram, it turned out, was nearby and said he'd be with us in fifteen minutes. Leyla seemed slightly disappointed on hearing of his close proximity, so in an attempt to smooth things over between them, I invited her to join us when he turned up. She declined and told me straight that she didn't like him. Again I wondered what they'd said to each other in the car this morning. I also invited her to the illegal party tonight but she was even less keen on this, and told me to be careful as parties got raided all the time. I thanked her profusely for all her generosity, asked her to pass on my regards to her mother, and wished her all the best at University in New Zealand. We parted when Pedram arrived.

He turned up with Behzad and Ali and explained that after meeting up with the other lads, they were going to take me to see the Shah's former summer palace. The palace was located in northern Tehran and we drove all the way there only to discover it was closed. It was set in hilly parkland and contained two main palaces called the White Palace and the Green Palace, as well as several other specialist museums. In particular, I wanted to see the White Palace and the odd sight out front–two huge towering bronze boots, which are the only remnants of a giant statue of Reza Shah. Also on the "to see" list at the palace complex was a 1,539–square–foot carpet woven with 150 knots per square inch, making it one of the biggest carpets ever made.

The White Palace's recent history was also of great interest to me; it was the location where the Shah had hosted leading CIA agents when plotting the 1953 coup to remove the democratically elected government of prime minister, Mohammad Mossadegh, from power.

The coup was initially proposed to the CIA by Britain's secret intelligence service, MI6, in response to Mossadegh's proposal to nationalize Iran's vast oil wealth to better the lives of the Iranian people, as opposed to lining the pockets of the British. Iran's oil had up until then been controlled solely by the British through the only oil company operating in Iran, the Anglo Iranian Oil Company (later to become BP). Mossadegh stated at the time that the Iranian people "were opening a hidden treasure upon which lies a dragon."

Although originally a British proposal, in the end the coup turned out to be much more an American operation than an Anglo one. The coup plan, known as Operation Ajax by the Americans and Operation Boot by the British, was to manufacture huge internal unrest in Iran by carrying out a wave of CIA–led shootings, bombings, and attacks, which would then be blamed through gray propaganda on Mossadegh. Many of the manufactured "terrorist" attacks would target Iran's religious establishment in an attempt to turn the country's religious community against him. The Shah, who was in on the deal, would then issue royal decrees dismissing Mossadegh from power while a handpicked army general would spearhead the actual coup itself and take Mossadegh's place.

The CIA bombings went ahead, one of which targeted a cleric's home. Muslim leaders who opposed Mossadegh were threatened by CIA–hired thugs in order to tarnish his name and turn the people against him. Mosques were stoned and rocks hurled at priests. At the same time, the CIA arranged for leading newspapers to carry articles denouncing Mossadegh's supposed brutality, and one newspaper owner was granted a whopping personal loan of $45,000 to bring him on side.

But when pro–Shah soldiers were sent to arrest Mossadegh, they were themselves arrested, and one of the top generals who was in on the plot lost his nerve and fled. The Shah did the same the next day, leaving for Iraq without so much as packing a suitcase.

The coup looked to all intents and purposes to be over, but Mossadegh unknowingly played into the CIA's hands by dissolving parliament. The CIA responded by holding a "council of war" in the U.S. embassy compound with their prominent Iranian agents to discuss the situation. They decided that all was not lost. From the American embassy vaults came a million dollars with which to rent a mob and arrange for a leading cleric to quickly travel to the holy city of Qom and lead a call against Mossadegh.

The next day, a nine–hour bloody battle raged in Tehran between soldiers supporting Mossadegh and those in support of the Shah. Three hundred people lost their lives and many hundreds more were wounded before Mossadegh's forces were finally overcome. The Shah returned to Iran and took control of the country for the next twenty–six years.

With the Shah now in the driver's seat, a new oil deal was struck. The U.S. and Britain shared a 40 percent stake each in Iran's oil wealth with the rest going to other countries in a new international consortium. The Shah thanked the U.S. by letting them do as they pleased in Iran, and the country soon became dotted with U.S. military and intelligence sites. For their part, the Iranian people got abysmal poverty and the terrifying Iranian secret police, the SAVAK, who were tutored in the tactics of torture by the CIA, and established under their and Israeli guidance. Their appalling methods included the insertion of broken glass and boiling water into detainees' rectums.

The Shah's grip on power over the next quarter of a century was only possible with huge U.S. arms and support. A surprised Senator Hubert Humphrey stated, "Do you know what the head of the Iranian Army told one of our people? He said the Army was in good shape, thanks to U.S. aid–it was now capable of coping with the civilian population. The Army isn't going to fight the Russians. It's planning to fight the Iranian people."

The backlash to all this led in 1979 to the Islamic Revolution and massive anti–Americanism. This in turn led to the Iranian hostage crisis, where fifty–two U.S. embassy staff were held captive by students who stormed the embassy compound that had been used to orchestrate much of the 1953 coup. The students declared that they had unmasked a "nest of spies" that had been manipulating Iran for decades. The hostage crisis, along with the new regime's open hard–line hostility toward America, contributed greatly to the spread of Islamic militancy and Iran's pariah status in the West.

Although oil had been the coup's real motivating factor, the "textbook" Western justification for the CIA's action was that Mossadegh had to be removed to prevent a communist takeover of Iran since he was something of a communist sympathizer. Mossadegh was actually a rich feudal–minded Persian who had not only kept the ban on the Iranian Communist Party in place but had brutally crushed one of their demonstrations. He had also successfully campaigned against the lingering Soviet occupation of northern Iran after the Second World War, and had been instrumental in parliament's rejection of proposals to form a joint Soviet and Iranian oil company. In 1951, *Time* magazine described Mossadegh as "the Iranian George Washington" and named him "Man of the Year."

A classified CIA document obtained by the *New York Times* that details the secret history of the coup had the following to say about the day hundreds lost their lives, the CIA successfully destroyed democracy in Iran, and in its place was installed a barbaric police state: "It was a day that should never have ended, for it carried with it such a sense of excitement, of satisfaction and of jubilation that it is doubtful whether any other can come up to it."

CHAPTER TWELVE

Milan, Paris, London, Tehran: Party Time!

It is unlikely that Tehran will ever be added to Milan, Paris, London, and New York as a fashion capital of the world.

I got my first encounter with Iranian party wear when getting ready to go to tonight's illegal "knees up." I had been planning to go in fairly casual clothing, until, that is, Pedram, who was wearing a full suit with frilly shirt and tie, saw my outfit. He looked at me as if I was in dire need of a fashion transplant and politely suggested that I borrow some of his clothing. This proved impossible since he was shorter than me, so he quickly called Ali, who was suitably proportioned, and arranged for him to have an outfit waiting for me at his house.

On arrival there, I was presented with skintight black trousers that flared at the ankles, a frilly patterned blue shirt, and worst of all, a pair of very cheesy leather shoes with big long pointed ends. Not just slightly pointed, I stress, but reaching out past the functional part of the shoe by at least a third of the total length. Anywhere else in the world I'd look like a complete knob, but for Iran I was styling it!

I was all excited and slightly nervous at the thought of going to an illegal party that could get busted, and I wondered what the hell it was going to be like. We parked and rang the bell. The door was opened by the first hijab-free girl I had seen in Iran—this was promising. What I saw next wasn't what I expected, and by the look on Pedram's face, it wasn't what he expected either.

Sitting on chairs placed neatly against the walls of the apartment were similarly dressed, subdued-looking guests delicately selecting and eating pieces of fruit from plates on their laps. It was about as wild and exciting as a vicar's parish tea party for members of the local choral society—and that's at a push. Pedram and I were handed a plate of fruit, a glass of lemonade, and were shown to our specified seats, which had our names written on them on little labels—rock and roll!

I found it all quite funny, but poor Pedram looked mortified and like me had obviously been expecting something a bit more on the lively side. Even the party girl's family was here, including, by the looks of it, Gramps. The only hint of illicit behavior was that none of the girls wore their hijabs and a couple of them were dressed rather on the risky side, at least for Iran. Two had low cut tops, and one even sported a tattoo of a tiger on her ample left breast.

Very nice.

The party began proper when a guy with similar pointed shoes to mine put some Iranian pop music on the stereo. Everybody got up in unison and danced to this in the center of the room in the most bizarre manner I've ever seen. It looked like the sort of dancing fake Kazakhstani reporter Borat would do, and many of the guests had mustaches that he'd have been proud of as well. When the track was over, everybody sat down and politely applauded. This was repeated several times.

When everybody had indulged in several slices of melon and glasses of lemonade and was feeling really crazy, they all got up and did a joint conga–type dance around the room. This went on for ages, and it's got to be said, it was bloody boring and the initial novelty and amusement wore off pretty quick. Pedram and I sat these dances out, and just when I was thinking how much I wanted a drink, my prayers were answered and Pedram whispered that one of the guys had some whisky in the kitchen and asked if I'd like some.

Damn right I did.

We both took our leave from the "dance floor" and went into the kitchen. We were joined by the whisky owner, who was more than happy to share his stash. He poured us a couple of stiff shots from a can. It was lucky we got a few drinks down as when we returned to the wild debauchery of the sitting room, Pedram and I were cajoled into getting up and shaking our asses on the dance floor, whilst everybody else watched.

Apart from Pedram, there was only one other person at the "party" who spoke English, but Pedram was determined to get me to speak a bit of Farsi. He persuaded me to go up to the girl with the tattoo and her friend, and say in Farsi, *"Shoma khoshy-elly,"* which I learnt afterward means, "You are beautiful."

To tell two strangers at a party back home that they're beautiful would of course be considered lame to say the least, but here in Iran it was the height of sophistication. They loved it and both insisted on a dance with me–together! And who was I to disappoint such lovely ladies? I was expecting a rather conservative boogie but was pleasantly surprised to find myself sandwiched between them in a delightfully pleasing bump and grind. Everybody else formed a circle around us clapping. It was alas the only highlight in an otherwise very subdued and boring party, which seemed to go on and on forever. The irony is that this inoffensive gathering was still illegal, and on the way back to Pedram's place, he asked me not to mention it to his parents.

The next day was my last with Pedram and the boys, so it was decided we'd all go outside of the city to Fasham for a barbecue. We all went Dutch and each chipped in for the necessary foods, which included a load of diced chicken, tomatoes, olives, naan bread, colas, and much more. On the way there, both cars drove in a manner I was now getting used to, which was far too fast and bloody dangerous.

On our way there, Pedram told me that slightly farther along the road was a ski resort called Shemshak, where he skied regularly during the winter. Although most people outside of Iran are unaware of it, Iran has twenty ski resorts decked out with modern infrastructure, some of which rival the best the West has to offer, and all of which cost a fraction of the price you'd pay to ski in Europe or the U.S. If you doubt this, then check out the excellent YouTube short film "Skiing in Iran" about an English-speaking Malaysian family who visited the slopes.

It took us maybe an hour of speeding until we got well out of the city and reached a little dirt track next to a dried up stony riverbed. We arrived in the early afternoon, parked up, and got out on foot, carrying all the gear with us. We hiked along the riverbed, which was surrounded by lush green trees and would have been a stunning area except for all the piles of trash. It looked as if the culprits had come out here especially to have a meal in a natural environment but couldn't be bothered to try to keep it that way afterward.

We found a nice little grassy section on the banks of the river, shaded by several small trees. Here we stopped and rolled out a large carpet to sit on. Being a keen camper and survival enthusiast, I located the perfect place for our cooking fire, which was nearby, and, crucially, on a mound of bare earth. This not only makes it easier to clean up afterward but, more importantly, prevents the fire from spreading or setting the ground alight, which can sometimes flare up weeks later. Everybody rejected my location, and I was encouraged just to sit back, relax, and have a drink, whilst Ali, the firemaster, did the hard work. I thought "what the hell" and let them get on with it.

They selected a place in the riverbed and surrounded it with river rocks to place the skewers on top of and cook the meat. I tried explaining that they didn't want to use river rocks, as they can explode when heated because of the moisture in them, but my warning fell on deaf ears. They laid out the fire in the most haphazard way imaginable and failed repeatedly to get it going, even with loads of paper and cigarette lighters. I decided not to get involved, but this was easier said than done, as on a couple of occasions I've taught classes on survival skills, which have included how to light a fire by friction and, believe it or not, how to get a fire going from a can of Coke and a bar of chocolate.

"Say what?" I hear you cry from your comfy armchair. For those of you now scratching your head, I'll elaborate. You take a cold can of Coke and carefully pour its contents into a glass containing ice and a thick slice of lemon. Be extra careful not to lose any cola from bubbles fizzing up past the rim of the glass. Now, take a long, well-earned drink. Mmmm. That was refreshing wasn't it?

Okay now for the fire bit. On the bottom of a Coke can, or indeed the bottom of any drink can, is a small concaved area of exposed aluminum with a slightly rough matte finish. What you need to do is turn this rough area into a polished reflector so as to harness and magnify the sun's rays onto whatever surface you wish to light (best not to try this on a four-foot-thick log, so I suggest a small highly combustible material like char cloth).

This is where the chocolate comes in. Since it is slightly abrasive, you can use the chocolate as a polish to buff up the rough concaved surface to the point where it has a mirror finish and you can see your face in it, which if you've bought this book is no doubt a highly attractive face—and even more so if you recommend it to a friend or give it five stars on Amazon.com. It's important to note here that you should never eat the chocolate after you've used it, for it will contain tiny fragments of aluminum from the can, which can make you very ill.

This polishing will probably take the best part of thirty minutes to complete. All you need now is some sunshine, and you'll be as happy as a dog with two dicks.

When you can get a fire going this way or from rubbing two sticks together, it makes using a lighter or matches child's play—not that you'd want to give a child a lighter or matches to play with, but I digress.

After watching the Tehran lads try unsuccessfully to light their fire for the best part of ten minutes, I could stand no more and forcibly took control of the situation. I should have started from scratch and relaid the whole fire, but I didn't want to get filthy taking off all the charcoal they'd already placed on top. Instead, I stuffed loads of the paper into all the available spaces and built a small teepee of pencil thickness twigs around it. It got going first time.

Everybody congratulated me as if I'd performed some incredible feat, and I was now assigned the task of manning the fire and getting it good and hot. Whilst I took charge of this, Pedram told me he was going off to buy some alcohol nearby. I wondered where on earth he could get it out here in the countryside, as surely it was the sort of thing you needed contacts to acquire. I didn't ask questions though, and fifteen minutes later, when the barbecue was in full swing, he returned with a couple of bottles of vodka. We all sat around and got stuck into succulent chicken and tomato kebabs served in soft folded naan bread. It was wonderful food, and although I couldn't communicate much with the guys, it was still great to be sharing their company and this meal together.

When we finished the first round of kebabs, Pedram poured out a round of huge shots of vodka into little plastic cups, which he then mixed with cherry juice. Three of the guys abstained, and after smelling it, I could well understand why. Its aroma was totally overpowering and sent an involuntary shiver up my spine. I wondered what the quality of the stuff was like, but didn't have long to ponder this, as on the count of three, we knocked it back.

As soon as I swallowed, I was grabbing my throat and gasping for breath. I'd never tasted anything so strong. It was horrendously powerful and as harsh as hell on the gullet. I wasn't the only one making wincing expressions, and Behzad in particular looked in a bad way. I turned to Pedram and asked in a croaking voice where on earth he'd got the vodka. He answered simply that he had bought it at a shop.

This was weird. I asked how it could possibly be the case, as surely vodka was highly illegal. "No," he said, and continued, struggling a bit with the translation, "you can buy for medical purpose to put on . . . how you say, cuts."

Fuck me! I was drinking a first aid kit! My eyes nearly popped out when I now looked at the bottle for the first time and saw that it was not vodka, but said on the label in big capital letters ETHANOL. It was a staggering 96 percent alcohol. I was speechless and couldn't believe I'd just drunk surgical spirit. I explained to Pedram that only an alcoholic living on the street would consider drinking such stuff back home. He thought this was very funny, as did the other guys whom he translated for, and explained that it was a normal beverage in Tehran.

I was roped into having a further three shots, and by the time I'd finished these, I was feeling suitably drunk. After loads more food to soak the booze up, Ali and I staggered back to his nearby car for a much-needed lie down. The rest of the lads remained behind crashing out on the carpet. They all returned just as it was getting dark, carrying the carpet, the mats, the skewers, and a few other bits and pieces but none of the plastic bottles, plastic trays, cups, or anything else disposable we'd used.

I might have been drunk, but the day I leave a load of trash knowingly out in nature is the day I die. I'm of the opinion that you should not only leave an area as you find it but try to leave it better, so this went completely against my principles. I asked Pedram where all the trash was and he said not to worry as they'd left it in "the place where you leave rubbish."

"Like hell you have," I thought, and told them I'd go and fetch it. They all tried to persuade me not to bother. I was determined to get it, but also wanted them to help me out, after all it was all our stuff so we should all go and get it. I tried to explain this but I wasn't getting anywhere, so I decided to try a different approach and lied by saying, "It is a sin for a Christian to leave trash. It is a very bad sin for me to do this." Surprisingly, or perhaps not, they all respected this and agreed to help me out now. We went back to the "place where you leave rubbish," which turned out to be in the middle of the dried up riverbed. Interestingly all of the rubbish was bagged up, so they'd gone to the effort of doing this, but for some reason hadn't brought it back to the car.

Not only did we clear our stuff up, but Ali even picked up a couple of bottles from nearby that weren't ours. We dumped it all in the trunk of the car, and I felt much better. Before we left, it was decided there was time to finish off the ethanol with a further two rounds, this time served with lemonade. From now on, things all got a bit hazy, and I have no idea how Pedram or Ali managed to drive after so much raw booze. But drive they did, or at least they sped and raced each other like a couple of maniacs with a death wish. They zigzagged in and out of traffic on the darkened motorway and seemed to get more and more fired up as the music pumped away at a deafening volume. This time it was dance music, including t.A.T.u.'s "All the Things She Said" in Russian–class!

In my intoxicated state, I simply didn't care about the driving and was singing away in the back to the music like a total idiot.

Things got really crazy when at high speed both cars pulled up alongside each other on the crowded highway so we could all give high fives to the other car's occupants. It was total madness, and had I been sober it would have been a completely different story but after several surgical spirit spritzers, I was loving it.

When we sped past an army barracks, everyone, including myself, yelled drunken abuse at it out of the window. And the lads had good reason to do so as they'd all soon become much better acquainted with the army when they finished their studies and started compulsory military service. The irony is that if Iran is ever invaded then Pedram, Ali, Behzad, and my other friends will all be called up to defend their country, and if they die they'll be written off in the West as expendable "legiti-mate military targets," not civilian deaths. With the way Iran is constantly demonized in the media, I fear this may become the case. For just like the American and British lies over Iraq's supposed weapons of mass destruction, much the same is now happening to Iran over its alleged "nuclear ambitions," despite the fact that inspectors from the International Atomic Energy Agency (IAEA) have found zero evidence that Iran is trying to obtain a nuclear weapon.

Under the terms of the nuclear Non-Proliferation Treaty (NPT), Iran has every right to enrich uranium for peaceful civilian purposes, and according to the IAEA, there is no evidence what-soever that Iran has ever deviated from this. The organization's head, Dr. ElBaradei, has reiterated this fact repeatedly and stated that his inspectors have for the most part been allowed to "go anywhere and see anything." Pakistan, India, and Israel all devel-oped their nuclear arsenals clandestinely and refuse to sign the NPT, but since their governments are buddies with the U.S. and Britain, no one makes much of a fuss. Such double standards are not lost on the Iranian people.

What the U.S. and Israel craftily demand of Iran is to somehow *prove* it is not in any way violating nuclear agreements, which is of course impossible. And since you can't prove a negative, the IAEA inspectors are obviously incapable of giving a 100 percent assurance that somehow, somewhere in Iran there isn't the faintest possibility that a nuclear weapons program exists. But this is no more evidence for one existing than to say that because I can't categorically prove Bertrand Russell's famous ironic suggestion that there is a celestial teapot orbiting the earth to be false, then, in fact, there must be one up there doing just that.

Even the CIA itself has admitted that Iran has no nuclear weapons program, by noting that Iran is ten years away from developing nuclear weapons. The importance of this timeframe cannot be overstated, for it means Iran has no such program whatsoever, or, as former UN weapons inspector Scott Ritter put it in a recent speech, "Ten years, ladies and gentleman, in this modern day and age, means Iran is not doing anything! Any nation in the world today is ten years away from developing nuclear weapons!" In 2007, much the same was concluded when America's collective intelligence agencies produced an authoritative National Intelligence Estimate (NIE) on the current state of Iran's "nuclear intentions and capabilities." This report rubbished claims that Iran is trying to obtain a nuclear weapon and concluded with "high confidence" that as of 2003 Iran had abandoned its nuclear weapons program and had not restarted it.

Another oft repeated distortion used to demonize Iran is that the country's president, Mahmoud Ahmadinejad, has stated that he wants to "wipe Israel off the map." My personal opinion of President Ahmadinejad is that he's an odious little twat, but when translated correctly, his alleged remark, which took place during a controversial speech in 2005, actually says something very different. According to American professor of modern Middle Eastern history, Juan Cole, as well as other Farsi language analysts, the correct literal translation of the remark is, "The Imam said this regime occupying Jerusalem must vanish from the pages of time." No reference to "Israel" or to a "map." And a regime is very different to the landmass of a country and its people.

In Farsi, the remark is *"Imam ghoft een rezhim-e ishghalgar-e qods bayad az safheh-ye ruzgar mahv shaved,"* which I put here not for the benefit of those who can understand it, but due to the significance of the fourth word in, *"rezhim-e."* This is the "regime" bit, which is pretty much pronounced the same way as the English version but with a bit of a throaty "eh" at its end. Ahmadinejad had actually been quoting from a speech given by the late Ayatollah Khomeini back in the early 1980s, so the words attributed to him are not even his original prose. Khomeini's earlier remarks had expressed a hope that one day the Israeli regime mistreating the Palestinians would be replaced with a fairer, more equitable one.

Also generally unknown is that Ahmadinejad compared the downfall of the regime occupying Jerusalem to the demise of the Shah in Iran. Jonathon Steele makes the following observation in an article for one of Britain's leading newspapers, the *Guardian*:

> The fact that he compared his desired option–the elimination of "the regime occupying Jerusalem"–with the fall of the Shah's regime in Iran makes it crystal clear that he is talking about regime change, not the end of Israel. As a schoolboy opponent of the Shah in the 1970s, he surely did not favour Iran's removal from the page of time. He just wanted the Shah out.

When Pedram, the lads, and I arrived back in Tehran there was a street carnival of some sort kicking off in the north of the city. After weaving our way through the hectic traffic and animated revelers, we headed over to Pedram's place. This would be the last time I'd get to see them, because I was leaving for Esfahan first thing in the morning. We all embraced and shook hands vigorously as we wished each other well. I was gonna miss these crazy bastards.

Once inside, Pedram and I had the unfortunate prospect of trying to act completely sober in front of his parents and not just in passing, but over a meal that they had prepared for me. The fact that Iranians eat their evening meals very late was our saving grace, as we managed to get a full two hours sleep before dinnertime. The snooze did the trick, and we both managed to hold it together, although it wasn't easy.

At the meal were both his parents, his sister, and his brother-in-law, who had come over especially to eat with me. His mother put on a wonderful spread, which was a mixture of traditional Iranian foods, like kebabs and crispy rice cake fritters, along with more Western culinary delights, like fried chicken. After being asked what I thought of Bush and Blair, I asked my hosts the same question, to which Pedram's brother-in-law came up with a novel reason, and possibly the only reason, to like the prime minister. "I like Mr. Tony Blair," he said. "He wear nice suits." When I asked them what they thought of their government, they were restrained and seemed reluctant to answer.

After dinner, Pedram presented me with an English translation of the poems of Hafez. "In Iran, there is a saying that every house should have two books, first the Koran and second Hafez." And from my experience, I might add a third—an English-to-Persian translation of the lyrics of German rock gods, Modern Talking.

Since I would be visiting Shiraz soon, which is home to Hafez's tomb, Pedram asked me to visit it and read some of the book there. I thanked him for the gift and his parents for the meal and their hospitality. Before going to bed, Pedram and I sat up with his father and drank several cups of sweet tea together as a sort of goodbye gesture. As a result, I awoke in the middle of the night in dire need of the bathroom.

Before getting out of bed, I recalled something Ricardo had told me about the reaction of a middle-aged Iranian man to his Turkish travel book. The man had casually thumbed through its pages until he came across a picture of a man in swim trunks on the beach. On seeing this, he looked embarrassed and gave the book back in a hasty way, as if handling illicit contraband. With this in mind, I considered putting my pants on in case I bumped into Pedram's parents in the hallway and they were similarly appalled by my unshapely hairy legs and knobbly knees. But as it was about three in the morning, I just couldn't be bothered; surely they were both tucked up in bed and away with the fairies.

I quietly got up and started the long dark walk to the bathroom, wearing nothing but my "smalls." I stalked across the creaking floorboards as if on some covert Special Forces op, trying to detect the slightest sound or stirring coming from Pedram's parents' room. All was clear on the western front. I reached the toilet door with a sigh of relief, and slowly began to open it whilst continuing my reconnaissance behind me, looking back in the direction of their room. I got the fright of my life when I now turned around and looked into the bathroom itself, where to my horror was Pedram's father, not a foot away, with his pants around his ankles taking a dump on the squat toilet. I quickly slammed the door with an, "Oh my goodness, I'm awfully sorry!" and made a tactical retreat back to Pedram's room.

Thank God it hadn't been his mother was all I could think. I lay in the darkness straining to hear his father return to his room. I heard him leave the bathroom and breathed a sigh of relief, but it was short-lived; just to make matters even more embarrassing, he came into Pedram's room and started to apologize repeatedly for not locking the door. I didn't want to have a drawn-out discussion on this one, so apologized back in the hope he'd leave it at that and we could just forget all about it. It took a while, but eventually, after several more cringe-worthy apologies, he left. I waited for a tense ten minutes or more before I tried to go back to the bathroom again.

I was far more agitated this time, and on reaching the toilet door, I cupped my ear against it to check it was vacant. After a fraught moment, I made the decision it was clear and quickly slipped inside. After taking a leak, I got myself ready for the journey back again but as I opened the door to leave, I had the fright of my life as there in the hallway in a tablecloth–like veil was Pedram's mother. I quickly shut the door again, my veins now awash with adrenaline.

I prayed fervently that this conservative Muslim woman hadn't seen me in my underwear. This was total madness, and I couldn't get my head around what the hell they were both doing up wandering around the house at this hour. I didn't dare exit for another fifteen minutes. In the end, I took a deep breath, turned off the bathroom light, then quickly opened the door and sprinted for Pedram's room. Next time, I decided I'd sure as hell be wearing my pants, a shirt, and if need be a tie as well.

CHAPTER THIRTEEN

Traveling in Style with the Single-Handed Man

Pedram and I awoke at six o'clock sharp when his alarm went off. We were greeted by a delicious breakfast prepared by his wonderful mother who must have got up especially early to make it before I left. I was quite touched at her generosity. After breakfast, Pedram phoned a cab and then had a word with the driver in Farsi, telling me the correct price to pay so I didn't get ripped off. We hugged, wished each other well, and parted.

The taxi was driven by a kindly old chap who spoke good English. He explained that the office had given him the job because Pedram had mentioned when he phoned that the lift was for an Englishman. As he was the only English speaker in the office they gave it to him, so I would have someone to talk to.

"How nice," I thought.

On hearing I was going to Esfahan, he recommended that I not only visit Esfahan's famous mosques but also the wonderful churches there and, in particular, Vank Cathedral. I said I would, and mentioned my visit to the Church of St. Thaddeus near Maku. He told me he'd been there as well. I asked him then if he was a Christian, and his answer was very interesting: "I am Muslim, but when I pray, I pray to Jesus to help me."

He went on to tell me that he thought all religions were the same in that they all said essentially the same thing, namely to "be good person, help others, and believe and pray to God. The lamps are different but the light is the same."

He told me he'd read a good book about this by an American woman, which had been translated into Persian. He struggled to remember the title and said it was called something like "Come into the Light." I immediately knew the book he meant, and asked if it was *Embraced by the Light*. "Yes, that's it!" he exclaimed. Having read the book myself, I double-checked it was the same one by describing it in detail. I told him I'd cried reading the last chapter of the book and he told me he had too. Call me anything you want, but I really believe we were meant to meet each other that morning.

One story he shared with me was a real testament to his faith and character. After the revolution, he had been arrested and accused of being a supporter of the Shah, but he told me this was untrue—he liked neither the Shah nor the current regime. He had been imprisoned, held in solitary confinement, and tortured for years. During this time, his torturers tried to get him to sign false confessions and admit to being against the government and for the Shah. He never did this and said it was his faith that got him through it. After a number of terribly hard years inside, he reached his breaking point. That night he got onto his knees and prayed like never before for four hours straight for God to help him. When he finally got to sleep, he had a dream in which a tremendous peace descended all around him and God spoke to him. He was told not to worry, that God would look after him and that soon he would be released—two weeks later he was. Goose bumps popped up all over me as he told me this, and writing it down many months later, I'm experiencing the same thing. I can't begin to imagine what hardships this courageous guy must have been through. I thought he was a real inspiration.

He went on to discuss the government's general lack of support among Iranians, and he said the problem was that if ten people dissented then the government could just kill all ten of them—therefore, no one dared do anything. However, he said that the people arrested at the recent demonstration that Leyla had mentioned would probably not be killed. "There is a lot of attention on the government at the moment and they wouldn't take any unnecessary risks," he said.

We reached the airport as the sun was breaking the horizon. I told him what a pleasure it had been to meet him, and he said it was a pleasure for him as well. We shook hands, and I gave him a tip several times the fare, which he tried to refuse but I insisted. I stepped out into the glorious morning sun and headed to the terminal.

It felt very strange to board an airplane after all the hitching and overland travel but it was far from unpleasant; in fact, it was fantastic. I got a window seat and the view was superb with rolling desert and rugged mountains below, which looked to me now quintessentially Iranian. I took a break from the sightseeing when breakfast was handed out. Whilst I tucked into my food, one of the staff kindly brought me an Iranian–English language newspaper, which was a strange read to say the least. It had the predictable anti–American rhetoric although it wasn't as bad as I thought it would be. But what I found really interesting and weird was a section described simply as "Anecdote," which told a tale called "The Single–Handed Man." It went as follows:

He lived in a city wherein the hands of thieves were cut. Since he was a single–handed man, all thought he was a thief! But he had stolen nothing. He was just a man with one hand! He decided to go to another city. While traveling, there came a whirlwind and his eye went blind. But he had reached a city wherein the eyes of thieves were blinded. Everybody called him a bandit, though he had not had a hand in a robbery. So he was forced to leave that city as well! On his way, while crossing a river, his leg was stuck between rocks and was broken. The doctors had to amputate one of his legs because of infection. But he had got to a city wherein the legs of murderers were cut! Upon seeing him, the people started whispering. The poor man could take no more and decided to go to a city wherein no guilty person is punished! But to his surprise, he was caught and guillotined in that city! You know why? Because there, they beheaded those who did not have a hand, an eye and a leg!

And the moral of the story . . . ? Your guess is as good as mine.

Whilst waiting for a taxi at the airport, I met a French guy, and after a brief chat we decided to share a cab to the center of Esfahan. He was visiting Iran as a tourist for a staggeringly brief three days and was in the city only until this evening when he flew back to Tehran. I initially thought this a little stupid but then he explained that his girlfriend was an air hostess and periodically offered him strange and quirky free flights. A few days ago, he had been in Paris when she had offered him a three–day trip to Iran. He took it, and under the circumstances, I'd have done exactly the same.

I got off at the Amir Kabir Hostel, which was the most popular hotel for backpackers and where I'd arranged to meet Ricardo. The guy behind the reception spoke good English and I asked about the price of a single room. He said there were none available until someone checked out but I could pay now and reserve one. I decided to go for this and we settled on IR60,000, which I didn't have exact change for, so handed over IR70,000, along with my passport. He didn't have change either, so he agreed to give me the money in a few minutes time.

When Ricardo turned up, we went through the whole long lost buddies routine with handshakes and back pats. I asked Ricardo if I could dump my pack in his room so we could go out and make the most of the day. He said that there wasn't really any space in his room for my backpack. I thought this was a tad far-fetched, but when we went up a few minutes later I saw he was right.

It was literally a windowless closet with a bed squeezed inside. On top of the bed lay his backpack, clothing, and other bits and pieces, leaving no space whatsoever for anything else. It was minuscule. Forget about not being able to swing a cat in there—you couldn't even swing a dwarf mouse. I decided there and then that no way was I staying here. As we walked back to reception, Ricardo added that the room's single feature, the bed, had a rather unfortunate aromatic stain on it.

I demanded my passport and money back at reception. The guy there capitulated immediately and said quietly, "I give you double room instead, but please, you no tell anybody." He passed me a key so I could look at it, and off Ricardo and I went to check it out. It was perfect, with two beds overlooking an internal courtyard. Ricardo couldn't believe he'd been fobbed off with such a terrible room for the last couple of nights, but if you don't complain you don't gain.

I left my gear, locked up, and headed down to collect the change that I still hadn't received. The crafty geezer now tried to explain that he was charging me more for this because it was a double room. I just couldn't be bothered to argue the point as it was still a good deal. I did, however, state that I thought he was very crafty. He smiled and took it as a compliment.

Ricardo and I went outside into the sunshine where he told me about Esfahan and I taught him the limited Farsi I had picked up from the lads in Tehran. Having already been in Esfahan for a few days, Ricardo had seen most of the more obvious tourist sites, so suggested we go to the more obscure ones and that I then go to the others after he'd left. We consulted the map and worked out a plan.

The main highlights of Esfahan are without doubt its elaborate blue-tiled mosques, which are masterpieces of architecture and craftsmanship and some of the finest, if not the very finest, in the Islamic world. The best of these are situated around the Imam Khomeini Square, known to the locals by its original name of Naghsh-e Jahan Square, meaning "image of the world," which contains the Imam Mosque and the Sheikh Lotfollah Mosque. Ricardo had seen the Imam Mosque but not the Sheikh Lotfollah, so we decided to start off here.

The walk to the square was through bustling and crowded streets that seemed nearly as busy as the ones in Tehran. The square itself was an oasis of calm, measuring a whopping 1,640 feet by 520 feet, making it the world's second-biggest square after China's Tiananmen Square in Beijing. It was far more peaceful than the chaos we passed through to get there, and in its center lay a grassy park containing a huge tranquil pool. Running around the exterior of the square were hundreds of beautiful archways leading to cool and shady shops. But the jewels in the crown of the square were three spectacular buildings. These were the two mosques with their huge exquisite tiled domes, and a strange six-story building with a vast elevated terrace and wooden roof, called the Ali Qapu Palace.

The palace dated from the seventeenth century, and had originally been constructed as a colossal gateway leading to the royal palaces situated behind the square in grassy parklands. It was used later on as a seat of government where the Shah hosted and greeted notables and ambassadors. It was unlike any building I'd ever seen. Its unusual wooden roof supported by huge external wooden columns brought to mind a Chinese or Tibetan temple, and it had a distinctly East Asian feel.

We paid a minimal entrance fee and climbed up to the palace's highlight, its terrace. The first thing you notice as you walk up the small stairway to the upper terrace is the devastation caused to many of the mosaics and murals lining the walls, which were heavily vandalized during the Oajar period (1779–1925) and more recently after the Islamic Revolution. It's a real shame, as from what little remains it's clear they must have been spectacular. This slight downer was quickly transformed into a feeling of awe as we stepped out onto the magnificent terraced area on the third floor. This was a fantastic vantage point from which to observe the whole square and in particular the huge dome of the Imam Mosque. And the view straight up at the roof was just as good. The roof, along with its supporting columns, was crafted to perfection out of wood and decorated with stunning intricate patterns. The terrace area was used by the Shah and his entourage to watch races and an ancient form of polo below.

We stood for a good while taking in the scene with several Iranian tourists, and clicked off a good number of photos. Access to the floor above was closed off for some reason, so we didn't get to see the "music room," which apparently had a decorative ceiling covered with the shapes of vases, elegant bottles, and other ornate household containers. It was said to be one of the greatest remaining examples of secular Persian art.

We walked next across the square's central park to the historic Sheikh Lotfollah Mosque, which was constructed between 1602 and 1691. The first thing that struck me about the mosque was its wonderful dome. Unlike the Imam Mosque, which was decorated with intense turquoise tiles, the Sheikh Lotfollah Mosque was decorated predominantly in shades of pale cream. Its tiles change color during the day and go from cream in the full sun, which we saw now, to a wonderfully rich pink at dusk. It was much smaller when compared to the massive Imam Mosque, but it was still one hell of a big structure.

Unusually for such a large mosque, it had no towering minarets or open courtyard, and had steps leading toward its entrance. The entrance was enchanting and its tiles of brilliant blues and vibrant yellows were in stark contrast to its creamy dome. The tiles were so intricate, detailed, and complex they defied belief. I stood marveling at the swirling floral designs and craned my neck up at the entrance portal. This was tiled in the same wonderful patterns and crafted into strange obscure shapes, some of which hung down like stalactites and all of which were a sight to behold. After burning a load more photos, Ricardo and I stepped into the mosque's cool and peaceful interior.

We walked along a winding hallway leading to the main attraction, the central prayer hall and its incredible dome. I was bowled over by it and as on so many other occasions on this crazy trip of mine, I felt so very privileged to be exactly where I was at this moment in time. I sat on the stone floor and just accepted the majesty of the whole. It was decorated in its entirety with extravagant patterns which got more condensed the closer they got to the center of the dome and thus drew and focused your attention. To what man created, nature added her finishing touches with shafts of hazy sunlight filtering through the elevated lattice windows adding a golden, ethereal quality to the kaleidoscope of mosaics and tiled calligraphy.

Ricardo and I had it to ourselves for a good long while before a couple of Iranian tourists turned up. With their arrival, we headed off into the furnace–like weather outside. We walked through a lush manicured green park and along the main road leading south toward the Zayandeh River, where several historic bridges spanned its width. We crossed the Si–o–She Bridge into the Armenian quarter of the city.

The bridge had been built in the seventeenth century and had thirty-three arches running its length of 524 feet. It was closed to cars and was teeming with people gathered around lively animated characters selling posters, cassette tapes, and the like.

On the other side, three girls passed us and said a giggly, "Hello, Mr." Without a moment's hesitation I replied, *"Salaam hoobi?"* They all looked very surprised and replied, *"Oh, salaam hoobi?"* This was exactly what I wanted, and I answered *"Khoobam, no karetam,"* in the same boisterous manner as the lads from Tehran had taught me. What the literal translation of this was I never managed to ascertain, but I think it was the Farsi equivalent of answering, "Yeah, not too bad, me old mate," when asked, "How are you?"

The girls were all stunned and Ricardo was well impressed. They began to talk to us in English after quickly discovering that this was the limit of my Farsi. Out of the blue, a grumpy middle-aged man walked past and said something to the girls, which by his mannerisms Ricardo and I took to be something along the lines of, "Don't talk to those foreign boys, you despicable girls!" Encouragingly, the girls gave him a sort of get lost look and turned back to us. Ricardo now tried out the line I'd taught him earlier this morning.

"Shoma khoshgelly," he said, or in English, "You are beautiful."

It worked a treat, and they were so flattered that if he could have proposed in Farsi too then I'm sure they would have accepted on the spot. We bade them goodbye and headed to Jolfa, or the Armenian quarter.

Christians had been in this part of Esfahan since the time of Shah Abbas the Great, who came to power in the 1500s. He was responsible for making Esfahan a great city and for establishing a Christian community here, which has existed in the city ever since. He did this by simply transporting all the existing Armenian Christians down from the northern border city of Jolfa in a huge diaspora, and then renaming the area he allocated for them "New Jolfa." The Armenian Christians were talented merchants and entrepreneurs, and although barred from the Islamic centers of Esfahan, their skills and religious freedoms were well respected. At the time of the Afghan invasion, a century later, there were 60,000 Christians in New Jolfa. Today there are thirteen Armenian churches and an old Christian graveyard.

The first church we located was called Kelisa–ye Maryam or the Maryam Church. Unfortunately, it was all locked up, but I thought there was a good chance we could get someone to open up the place for us. Inside the courtyard, we discovered the necessary individual, who retrieved a huge clanking set of keys from a room nearby and did the honors. The church's interior was lavishly covered by colorful frescos depicting biblical scenes and venerated saints. We didn't get more than a snapshot of the place before the janitor indicated he wanted to lock up again, so we thanked him and headed off.

The next one, Kelisa–ye Bethlehem or the Church of Bethlehem, was closed also, and even though we located the janitor and pleaded with him, he wouldn't open it. It was beginning to look like a bit of a wasted walk–a long and a hot one at that. Not far from here was Vank Cathedral, the church recommended to me by my taxi driver in Tehran. Mercifully, it was open. We had to pay quite a large admission fee to get in, which was justified by an English sign explaining that as they weren't an Islamic site, they received no government funding and so had to charge to cover the upkeep and restoration costs. That seemed fair enough to me.

From the outside, the church looked rather mosque–like with a rounded dome and several Islamic-style arches, but the inside was anything but. It was decorated with frescos, some of which depicted the more traditional Christian scenes like the birth of Christ and the last supper, whilst others were of a more hellfire and brimstone variety, depicting hell itself and the torture of St. Gregory. Hell was represented, predictably, by a hoard of tormented souls burning away in the flames and looking none too pleased to be there. But just in case being in the center of a raging inferno wasn't enough to ruin their day, a few were given the added irritation of having their guts pulled out and twisted neatly around a little stick. And poor old St. Gregory wasn't having the best of times either. He was shown having his eyes plucked out and boiling oil poured down a purpose-made tube into his backside. This was all very interesting in a macabre sort of way but not particularly conducive to fostering a feeling of worship, at least not in me.

In the courtyard outside was a bell tower and a museum dedicated to the Armenians. The museum contained hundreds of ancient hand written books and among these were several very early Bibles and Korans, as well as the first book ever printed in Iran. But the real attraction was an exhibit of women's hair, which to fully appreciate you had to view through a microscope. An incredibly dexterous Armenian had somehow managed to write on the stuff. Why? I have no idea, but it was damned impressive. Other examples of minute writing were on display including what is reportedly the world's smallest book, which weighs in at only 0.7 grams and is said to contain the Lord's Prayer in seven different languages. Also of interest was a small sketch of a bearded man by Rembrandt and a display dedicated to the Armenian Holocaust, something which, I'm embarrassed to say, I'd never even heard of until the museum enlightened me.

The Armenian Holocaust (also known as the Armenian Genocide) was carried out by the Ottoman Turkish authorities during the First World War. It is estimated that 1.5 million Armenians were systematically killed, out of a total of 2 million living in Turkey–close to 80 percent of the entire population. Methodical massacre, torture, abduction, mass rape, and forced starvation occurred. To save ammunition, victims were often killed with hammers, axes, knives, and swords. Women and children were killed in mass drowning operations. Thousands were burnt alive. The Armenians were removed from their homes by Ottoman Turkish forces and marched into the Syrian Desert to die of thirst and hunger in the burning sun. Others, who numbered in the thousands, were driven into caves where bonfires were lit in front to cause death by asphyxiation. As renowned journalist and Middle Eastern historian Robert Fisk points out, "The caves were the world's first gas chambers."

When Hitler wanted to convince his generals that a massacre of the Jews would be tolerated in the West, he invoked the Armenian Genocide, saying, "Who, after all, speaks today of the annihilation of the Armenians?" Churchill wrote of their slaughter describing it as a "holocaust" and referred to the Turks as war criminals.

In a chilling parallel to the words later used by Himmler when instructing the SS, Talaat Pasha, the Turkish Interior Minister, sent instructions to a subordinate on what to do with the thousands of Armenians in the town of Aleppo, stating, "You have already been informed that the government . . . has decided to destroy completely all the indicated persons living in Turkey. . . . Their existence must be terminated, however tragic the measures taken may be, and no regard must be paid to either age or sex, or any scruples of conscience."

There were a number of photos on display in the museum, which graphically showed some of what had happened. They were far worse than the depiction of hell in the church. It left me feeling numb.

After a good look around the museum at some of its less depressing displays, Ricardo and I went outside in search of a taxi. There was only one parked opposite the church, which proudly sported an Audi badge despite being a clapped out Hillman Hunter. I tried joking with the driver about this in the hope of building a bit of rapport and cutting a good deal. He quoted an astronomical price knowing full well he had a monopoly and could charge whatever he liked. Ricardo turned to me and said with a grin, "Try telling him he's beautiful."

"*Shoma khoshgelly*," I said.

He burst out laughing as did Ricardo and I, but it was still no good and in the end we crossed his palm with far too much silver and paid the full fare.

Back at the hotel, Ricardo and I said goodbye for the final time. He was flying to Shiraz, which was my next destination, but would be leaving for the former historic city of Bam—devastated not too long ago by an earthquake which killed 40,000 people—before I arrived. From Bam, Ricardo would travel overland to Pakistan and then all the way to Nepal. We promised to keep in touch.

CHAPTER FOURTEEN

The Jewel of Esfahan

One of the quirky things about Iran is all of the items for sale that were discontinued in the West decades ago but are still produced here and presented as modern and cutting-edge. A case in point is the 1960s Hillman Hunter automobile, which until as recently as April of 2005 still rolled off the Iranian production lines.

En route to visiting Esfahan's historic bridges, I noticed a large appliance shop with row upon row of seventies-style fridges in avocado and harvest gold. They were brand-spanking-new and gleamed as if they'd just come out of the factory, which of course they had. At home, these styles were all old and decrepit, so looking at them in such perfect condition was a bit like going back in time. I spent a good while browsing around the shop, much to the amusement of the staff, who realized I obviously wasn't going to buy one and stick it in my backpack.

Making my way to the city's historic bridges, I also noticed the proliferation of shops selling embroidered pictures of Jesus alongside ones of Imam Mehdi and Our Lady—something I

THE JEWEL OF ESFAHAN

certainly wouldn't have expected to see for sale in an Islamic Republic.

I finally reached the Chubi Bridge, which was built in 1665 to help irrigate nearby palace gardens via a canal. It was lovely, with twenty-one arches, and had great views both up- and downstream. I didn't cross since I was heading farther down the river; instead, I just sat on the bank and took in its splendor and that of the river and distant mountains.

Further downstream, I reached Esfahan's star bridge, the Khaju Bridge. It was built by Shah Abbas II in 1650 and had twenty-three huge arches and terraces constructed on two levels running along its 433-foot length. On the bridge was a large central pavilion, the remains of a number of period paintings and tiles, as well as some old stone seats used personally by the Shah to take in the view.

The Khaju Bridge also serves as a dam and contains locks on the lower terraces, which regulate the flow of the river, but more importantly it also contains tea shops. I stopped on the bridge for a slow cuppa and sat with many locals doing the same. It was a sunny day, the views were great, and the tea was plentiful–this was the life.

After my beverage stop, I started the long walk to the Golestan-e Shohda or The Rose Garden of Martyrs–a sprawling cemetery for the Iranians killed in the Iran-Iraq War. Here thousands upon thousands of graves, all accompanied with photos, were located. I took off my hat and began a respectful walk around, looking at the pictures of those that had died.

The sheer amount of graves and the fact that I was looking into the eyes of the dead made it all the more poignant a demonstration of just what a terrible waste of human life the war had been. A woman close by bent down and placed a flower on a grave, reminding me that for every picture there were grieving family members suffering unimaginable loss. And what a loss the war had been.

It began in 1980 when Iraq's president and then U.S. and British lapdog Saddam Hussein tried to take advantage of Iran's post-revolution domestic chaos by making an opportunistic invasion of the oil-rich Khuzestan province. This was encouraged by the then-head of the CIA, George Bush Senior. It was a huge tactical miscalculation and served only to strengthen the Islamic Revolution by giving the government an enemy against whom to rally the people and an opportunity to spread the revolution by armed force. Iraq had better military equipment but was much smaller than Iran. The Iranians were therefore able to use their numerical superiority to push the Iraqis back to the border. This was achieved by 1982. By this time, Iran had a more ambitious agenda and wanted to seize the holy cities of Karbala and Najaf in Iraq.

The Western powers backed Saddam, although America happily sold weapons to both sides. The U.S. also provided satellite images to Saddam so he could gas the Iranians on the al-Fao Peninsula, and U.S. warships assisted by destroying Iranian oil platforms in the Persian Gulf.

The war continued until 1988 when a cease-fire was finally declared. It finished with neither side achieving anything except a staggering death toll. Nearly three thousand Iranian villages and eighty-seven Iranian cites were bombed, causing roughly 5 million Iranians to lose their homes and livelihoods and forcing 1.2 million to flee eastward. Half a million people died on each side and the war is estimated to have cost a staggering 1 trillion U.S. dollars. The war officially ended in August 1990, just before Iraq was again devastated in the first Gulf War. In this, they lost a further 250,000 men, women, and children as a direct result of the war. A further half million children died as a result of the U.S. and British led sanctions (a policy described by the UN's humanitarian coordinator in Iraq as "genocidal"), and 1.8 million people were made homeless. The latest figures (as of 2009) for the second Iraq war, Operation Iraqi Freedom (sic), are 1.3 million dead Iraqis and 4 million Iraqi refugees (see JustForeignPolicy.org/Iraq).

As I looked at the endless photographs in front of me, I thought of former British Defense Minister Alan Clark's well-publicized comment that, "The interests of the West were best served by Iran and Iraq fighting each other, and the longer the better."

It wasn't better for all the youngsters in front of me now that had their lives and bodies obliterated, Mr. Clark. Looking into the faces of all the dead made it impossible not to think of the current chaos just across the border in Iraq, where these photos were repeating themselves thanks to the cowardly actions of Bush and Blair. But it was all too easy for me to get annoyed at politicians.

I'd been fifteen at the time of the first Gulf War, and every morning on my paper route I'd read all the propaganda in the papers before I delivered them. Not knowing then that the CIA had installed the Ba'ath Party from which Saddam Hussein emerged (described by the CIA man responsible as "my favorite coup"), or anything of the support Saddam received from the West when it was in "our" interest, led me to conclude that it was a simple case of good against evil. I had no idea at the time that anthrax was supplied to Iraq by the British government's Porton Down laboratories, or that the ingredients for biological weapons, including botulism, were transferred to Iraq from a company in Maryland in the United States, which was fully licensed by the U.S. Commerce Department and approved by the State Department—all documented in a 1994 senate report. Or that on July 25, 1990, Saddam asked U.S. Ambassador April Glaspie what America's response to an invasion of Kuwait would be. Saddam was told, "We have no opinion on the Arab–Arab conflicts like your border disagreement with Kuwait. . . . The issue is not associated with America. [Secretary of State] James Baker has directed our official spokesman to emphasize this instruction."

I continued walking around the cemetery and found that, after a while, all the faces seemed to merge into one another, and in a way they no longer appeared as individuals with lives, families, hopes, or dreams but more like a gray mass–a statistic. It was a horrible thought, but the scale of death was hard to take in, that is until I reached a photo of a toddler. Whether this was a photo of a baby killed in the war or a photo of a soldier as a baby I don't know. But the cold reality hit me that every one of the people in the photos, whether tough–looking soldiers or not, was once someone's baby–a cliché for sure, but true. I looked up from the picture to the ocean of other photos, and no longer wanted to stick around.

A few miles outside of the center of Esfahan is a rather strange attraction called the Shaking Minarets. These are two minarets on the tomb of a revered fourteenth century dervish that wobble and shake back and forth when leaned against. On arrival there, I discovered that I'd just missed the official shaking, so had an hour to kill until the next performance. This was easily spent reclining on a carpeted platform at a nearby café where I sipped an ice–cold pomegranate juice.

By the time the minarets were due for their next shake a crowd of Iranian tourists had gathered in the courtyard to watch. An official shaker climbed up each minaret, called on Allah for assistance, then gave the towers a bloody good wobble.

It took a fair while for the shakers to build up the necessary momentum before the towers shook back and forth but when they did it was surprisingly dramatic. The surprise was when only *one* tower was shaken, it caused the second minaret to shake also. This was demonstrated with the use of a bell on one tower, which would ring when the opposite minaret shook.

Neither of them looked in the slightest bit stable when rocking back and forth and I wondered how long they'd last. The scientific theory behind why they shake is that the type of sandstone used in their construction was of an inferior quality and contained feldspar, which, over the years, dissolved, making the stone slightly flexible. To others, it's a more miraculous occurrence and is simply the will of Allah. Proponents of the divine intervention theory point out that other buildings in Esfahan are made of the same material but don't shake.

It was all over pretty quick, so I caught a bus back to town full of giggling school girls, all of whom said "Hello" to me repeatedly but nothing else, that is until I got up to leave and then they all said a giggling "Goodbye" many times. I did the same but without the giggles.

I next headed into the city's 1,300-year-old rabbit warren-like bazaar. Esfahan's bazaar is one of the largest in the country and stretched for several miles. It had a mysterious atmosphere accentuated by lightsaber-like beams of light filtering down through holes cut into the high domed vaulted ceiling. I walked along, trailing my hand through the light beams and stopped to check out a store filled with colorful aromatic spices. Here I was greeted warmly by the owner, who spoke good English and invited me inside to look around. He pointed out all the different spices and got me to smell the ginger and the nutmeg before kindly taking me out the back to show me how they were all ground up. He showed me a huge and very old stone grinding wheel. It was mechanically operated, but the shop-keeper explained that in days gone by, it would have been attached by rope to a camel who'd walk round and round in circles to rotate it.

Not only did he grind and sell spices but he also made natural coloring. I was amazed at the ingredients he used, which included crushed up dried pomegranate skin and straw for the color yellow, and the shells of walnuts for brown. He introduced me to a desert plant called Chu Bear that he used to make powdered soap. He said it was as good as any modern detergent. The plant is dried and then ground up on the wheel into a very fine powder and used with water. He kindly gave me a bit of the dried plant to take away with me.

Since we'd been getting on well, the shopkeeper now took me up a couple of flights of stairs to the flat roof of a carpet shop, which was slightly higher than the domed roof of the bazaar and provided a panoramic view of Imam Khomeini Square. Up on the roof were several carpets, drying in the sun after being washed. He pointed out distant mosques and mountain ranges and the straw and mud covering of the bazaar's roof. He took me next to a nearby section of the bazaar where carpets were being mended by a team of young men. Some were nailing carpets to the floor for washing, while others were mending gaping holes in damaged rugs. A few snapshots later and we headed downstairs again.

On the way, my charming guide inadvertently walked into an air conditioning system, which was sticking out dangerously at head height from the wall. He took a nasty knock, and his forehead began to bleed. It looked bad, but he assured me it was nothing and used his handkerchief to stem the flow. He apologized to me for being so careless and asked if I would like to join him for a drink. The answer was yes.

He must have been quite well off, as he took me into a second shop he owned, which this time sold carpets made exclusively by Iranian nomads. He had two staff in there working away, one of whom fetched our drinks. The owner showed me a collection of the tools used by the nomads and photographs of them on the job so to speak. He pointed to a picture of the nomad's migration routes and told me that it was possible to visit them on organized tours where you went out to see them and their way of life. The photos from the tours did look a bit on the touristy side, and I wondered how authentic these particular "nomads" actually were. After a good chat, I thanked him for his hospitality and headed out of the bazaar and over to Esfahan's crown jewel, the Imam Mosque.

My *Lonely Planet* described it as "one of the most beautiful mosques in the world." Even from a distance, this seventeenth-century building was exceptional. Its size dominated the whole square, and I found as I walked toward its massive entrance portal and two towering minarets that I had butterflies of anticipation.

The portal was gigantic, reaching one hundred feet up and was decorated with deep vibrant turquoise and blue tiles. These were in swirling geometric designs, mosaic calligraphy, and intricate floral patterns. The portal, like the Sheikh Lotfollah Mosque, had an intricate honeycombed front with sections hanging down like stalactites. Each of these sections was decorated with its own pattern, but all with the same incredible detail. I walked inside to the spacious courtyard where a group of Iranian tourists stood in awe.

The courtyard was situated before the looming main sanctuary and dome. In the courtyard's center was a vast pool used for ritual ablutions, and all around the surrounding walls were sunken porches in mosaics of yellow and blue. The porches led onto vaulted sanctuaries all as awe-inspiring and detailed as the next. Every patch of the place was smothered with the most intensely colored patterned tiles. I slowly walked around investigating the more hidden areas before entering the main sanctuary itself.

Here I stood open mouthed at the sheer size and beauty of its truly massive dome. It reached a whopping 120 feet high on the inside and 167 feet on the exterior thanks to a double-layered construction. The patterns of the dome were as intense as the rest of the mosque, and no detail had been spared despite its height. I was standing, looking up at the dome in a silent respectful manner, when two locals came in and clapped their hands and shouted to test the echoes. Clearly silence wasn't a big deal so I gave it a go too. The echo was most impressive.

Despite the mosque's perfection as a whole, it contained many deliberate mistakes in the symmetry of the tile work in order to symbolize the craftsman's humility and his insignificance when compared to Allah. I liked this very much and it reminded me of a similar practice by Native American tribes who leave deliberate flaws in everything they make to remind them that nothing created by man is perfect, as only the Creator is so. I spent a long time in the mosque sitting, staring, taking photos, daydreaming, and even knocking out the occasional prayer. It was a real man-made wonder of the world.

I'd heard from the guy at reception that it could be very difficult to get a place to stay in Shiraz, and I didn't fancy the hassle of turning up there tonight and wandering around from place to place. He phoned a hotel for me and did the honors in Farsi.

At the reception desk, I got talking to an Australian girl who was also staying at the hotel and who was traveling to Shiraz tomorrow. We got on well so we went for a snack together in a shop a couple of doors down. Her name was Verity and she was traveling all around the Middle East by herself. I was very impressed. After Iran, she was heading to Syria, Lebanon, and then Jordan. She showed me her guidebook, and after studying the maps and reading how amazing these locations were supposed to be, I began to flirt with the idea of continuing on after my Iranian visa ran out.

Verity was a good laugh and had gone off traveling on the spur of the moment, much to the surprise and worry of her friends and family, who thought her crazy for wanting to go to Iran. She'd got annoyed with life in Australia, so freed up some inheritance left to her and then simply got moving. She had a sophisticated sense of humor, which was evident by the fact she actually laughed at my jokes. As much as we could have chatted for the rest of the afternoon, my plane's departure time was not far off, so I had to get moving. Verity was planning to stay in the same hotel as me in Shiraz, so we'd probably bump into each other again.

I grabbed my backpack and hailed a cab to take me to the airport. It was just beginning to get dark as I walked to the airport terminal but was a lovely warm and balmy evening. After what seemed like forever, we boarded and I got a window seat next to a middle-aged German couple who spoke excellent English and introduced themselves to me. The man was called Albert, but I failed to make a note of his wife's name, so I'll call her Gertrude. I told them about my travels, and they told me about the family they had in England and their investments in Iran's infrastructure. They had heavily invested in the country's ports and transport.

We talked at length and laughed about how many people in the West have no idea how friendly and safe a country Iran is to visit and about all the misconceptions there are about the place. Neither Albert nor Gertrude wanted their in-flight food or drink, so I was the lucky recipient of three meals. I put the third in a paper vomit bag to take with me.

They were both heading into the center of Shiraz, as was I, so when we landed, I asked if they'd like to share a taxi. They apologized and explained that they were being picked up by the tour company they'd booked with. I thought nothing more of it and bade them goodbye.

While watching all the luggage go round on the conveyer belt, I daydreamed about what I'd do to earn cash when I got home. Just as I was thinking how much I hoped things worked out for me back in England, Gertrude approached and held out her hand for me to shake. It was full of bank notes. I tried to refuse but she insisted, saying that she and Albert wanted to pay for my taxi. She stepped back into the crowd and said goodbye. I called out a thank-you after her. Wow.

If I had this sort of luck at home then I'd have nothing to worry about. I hoped it was an omen. While I was thinking this very thought, she returned once again and thrust a load more notes, this time big green 20,000s, into the vomit bag with the in-flight meal that I was carrying. Both my hands were full so I had no way of refusing. She gave me a motherly kiss on both cheeks and said, "We thought you might like a little more," and left with a smile. This was absolutely incredible! I thought back to when I'd been hitching through Bulgaria and had met a woman called Maria who'd kindly put me up for the night in her home. Maria had traveled a bit herself and told me that whenever she was on the road, she seemed to have tremendous luck and always felt looked after somehow. That was exactly how I felt now, and very happy, too.

I didn't count the money until I'd booked into my hotel room. It totaled IR210,000 or about forty dollars, which in Iran is a lot and certainly enough for a good couple of night's accommodation. I drifted off into a contented sleep.

CHAPTER FIFTEEN

Mr. Private Jet's Gate of All Nations

("I no want to make cock with you.")

I was in Shiraz, like most tourists who visit the place, not so much for the city itself, although it has some nice attractions to be sure, but to use it as a base to visit one of Iran's main attractions, the ancient city of Persepolis. Everywhere I'd been in Iran, I'd seen pictures of this place and was excited to finally be going there myself.

Persepolis is a massive ancient palace and city complex that once stood at the heart of the great Achaemenid Empire, which dated from 550–300 BC and was the biggest and most powerful in the ancient world. It spanned 3 million square miles and stretched from northern Africa to the Indus Valley and from central Asia to the Persian Gulf. In its heyday, the city of Persepolis covered an area of 1,345,500 square feet and, although what remains today is a mere fraction of its former splendor, it is still exceptional, with vast ancient statues, bas-reliefs, fire temples, huge stone staircases, stone columns, and much more. I couldn't wait.

I asked at the hotel's reception about how to get there and was offered an organized tour of the area. This had a very rigid itinerary, which didn't appeal in the slightest. I made up my mind to make my own way there instead, and after grabbing a bag full of cakes from a nearby shop for breakfast, I hailed a cab and got down to the local minibus station.

I couldn't get a bus direct to Persepolis, so I got one going to a small town nearby called Marvadasht. From Marvadasht, I caught a taxi to Persepolis some seven miles away. The taxi stopped far back from the ruins at a traffic barrier. The city's walls and huge stone columns loomed ominously in the distance, framed by a rugged desert mountain range. Every cell in my being tingled with excitement at the sight of it, to the point where I almost felt like running toward the ruins in a frenzy. The furnace-like heat put a stop to that idea, and instead I walked at a brisk pace all the way up to a ticket office at the foot of a huge stone staircase that led into the ancient city.

When I got there, I discovered it was no ticket office at all but simply a place where you were meant to hand in your pre-purchased ticket. The place to buy a ticket, I now learnt, was all the way back where the taxi had dropped me. By the looks of it, I wasn't the only one who'd made the same unfortunate discovery after walking all the way up here; on the way I'd passed several other tourists traipsing back in the opposite direction with disgruntled looks on their faces. I traipsed back myself now, but without the disgruntled look, and bought a ticket. A few minutes later, I was climbing the imposing stone staircase leading into the mysterious Persepolis.

As I reached the top of the stairs, the scale and magnificence of the site came into view for the first time. It stretched across a vast area and was full of huge ancient statues, the remains of grandiose buildings, spectacular bas-reliefs, massive stone pillars, and crusty aristocratic British pensioners. The British blue hair brigade were on a private tour and had all congregated at the top of the stairs near two giant stone statues.

"I say, is everyone ready to begin, what?" called out an old chap who looked like his mother had married her brother and then given birth to him. He looked like the plastic surgery mutant Liza Minnelli married but with a slightly British aristocratic bent, sporting terrible gap-ridden goofy teeth and as much hair flaring from his nostrils as he had on his flaky head. He finished the look with a thick smothering of sun block, which was intermingling with a bath of sweat and dripping down his face. The poor chap was suffering big-time in the heat, and I'm not surprised, as today was by far my hottest yet in Iran and rather stupidly he wasn't wearing a hat. What he was wearing was a small day sack on his back with a large badge that announced proudly, and I kid you not, EXPLORER II, EXPEDITION TO THE WORLD'S LOST CITIES BY PRIVATE JET. Very nice, too, although I'm not quite sure sipping a gin and tonic in a Learjet really counts as an "expedition." The old-timers obviously weren't short of a buck or two.

All the toffs nodded their willingness to begin, and after a quick "Oh, good-oh!" Mr. Private Jet introduced their tour guide. The guide was an Iranian chap who spoke excellent English and seemed to know his stuff, so I decided to tag along with my fellow countrymen and women and listen to what he had to say. He started off by telling us about the stone staircase we'd entered the city by. It was, he said, carved purposely with shallow steps in order to allow Persians wearing their traditional elegant robes to ascend gracefully to the top.

At the top of the stairs would have been a group of trumpeters who belted out a quick number to announce the arrival of important foreign delegates coming to meet the king. These dignitaries would then be led by servants of the king through a monumental gate and into a palace, the remains of which were nearby. The guide led the group over to the gateway. It was very impressive and consisted of two massive stone creatures whose heads were partially missing. To me, they looked like either powerful horses or stylized bulls. I was pleased to hear the guide confirm a second later that they were indeed meant to be bulls.

The gateway was called the Gate of All Nations and the bulls gracing it were apparently reminiscent of the statues of Assyria, not that I'd have known this, of course, but a few of the group seemed to be familiar and stated knowingly, "Oh, yes indeed." In fact, they all seemed to know their stuff, as evidenced by the complex historical questions they kept asking the guide. One tiny woman in particular, who was straight out of a period drama, really knew what she was on about and gave a lengthy explanation to the group on the type of roof the palace would once have had.

"Of course, it was common practice to pop across to Lebanon and cut a good quantity of cedars for the roofing. Ideal tree—grows long and straight, of course."

"Yes, quite so," agreed one of the group.

The guide explained that the gate was inscribed in Persian, Babylonian, Elamite, and good old English—the latter being graffiti left by British soldiers stationed here in the nineteenth and early twentieth centuries. For graffiti, though, it was pretty damn good and skillfully executed in beautiful script complete with the date, and in some instances a regimental badge. Some were so good they must have been done by a stonemason amongst the soldiers. The oldest English one I saw was from 1810 and had a skull and crossbones above the words OR GLORY, for a regiment called the 17th L.D. Other interesting ones were from a regiment called the Central India Horse and one by Colonel Malcolm J. Meade. Beneath Malc's name he'd carved, or more likely got his manservant to carve for him, H.B.M CONSUL GENERAL 1898. Next to it was added by way of a footnote, & MRS. MEADE. I liked that.

One horsy-looking woman in the group piped up in a cut glass accent, "I say, Malcolm Mead should have known better!"

The guide explained that the original, much older inscriptions read, as my guidebook confirmed, "I am Xerxes, Great King, King of Kings, King of Lands, king of many races . . . son of Darius the King, the Achaemenid. . . . Many other beautiful things were constructed in Persia. I constructed them and my father constructed them."

We moved on through the gate toward two magnificent griffin-like statues. The guide explained that these had been discovered buried deep underground and that nobody knew for sure why they had been there. One theory was that they were buried near a hidden underground burial chamber, the other that they were simply of a shoddy quality and therefore buried out of sight by embarrassed craftsmen. They looked pretty damn good to me, so I had my doubts about the second theory.

As we moved on to the next section, I was approached by the horsy woman, who asked bluntly, "I say, you do realize this is a private tour?"

I lied through my teeth and turned on the silver spoon with an accent as poncy as hers. "I'm awfully sorry," I said. "I had no idea. I thought it was simply an English tour and that the one behind was a French one." I gestured to two French tourists walking behind us who clearly weren't on a special tour, but what the hell.

"Would you like me to leave? I really am awfully sorry," I said in the same stupid overblown prep school voice.

"No, of course not, I didn't realize you were one of . . . erm . . . No, please, feel free to stay, but maybe stand at the back of the group."

I wondered if I'd have received the same response had I put on the accent of a cockney "geezer" instead. Probably not. I got talking to Mrs. Horsy and asked her about the tour she and the rest of the group were on. She told me it was specifically for people with an interest in archaeology (and apparently a big wallet), and that it used to be affiliated with the British Museum but was now independent. I asked if she and the rest of the Jilly Cooper crowd were archaeologists.

"Well, not exactly, but Mrs. Fortescue–Cholmondley–Carruthers–Smithe–Rowel–Tomkinson is from the British Museum and an absolute expert." She pointed to the tiny period drama lady. "As is our quaint little Iranian guide, but the rest of us do possess a good background knowledge," she said—or words to that effect.

Our next stop was the "Palace of 100 Columns." This was the biggest of the Persepolis palaces, and it was here that representatives of subject nations came to pledge their loyalty and pay tribute to the king and the Achaemenid Empire. This was done in ritual procession past special lamps placed in alcoves along the walls. All around here were massive gateways, stone carvings, exquisitely crafted bas–reliefs and the remains of the palace itself. We all marveled at these for a good while before heading on to our next stop and the highlight of Persepolis, the Apadana Staircase.

Its splendid bas–reliefs are among the greatest of Iran's historical sights, and although it is over two thousand years old, many of the bas–reliefs looked brand new, such was their excellent condition. The staircase was in three sections—northern, central, and southern. The bas–reliefs of the northern section depicted Persians in long robes and feathered headgear along with Medes in round caps and shorter robes. Also shown were imperial guards with lances, and the horses of the Elamite king.

The staircase's central panel was dedicated to symbols of the deity Ahura Mazda of the ancient Persian religion Zoroastrianism, and carried an inscription imploring God to protect the palace from famine, lies, and earthquakes. This panel also contained large dramatic bas-reliefs of a lion biting into the rump of a rather distressed-looking bull. This image is repeated all over Persepolis, owing to the bull being a symbol of worship during the festival of Noruz, or Iranian New Year, which was the specific time of year Persepolis is thought to have been used. At other times of year, the city is believed to have been deserted.

The southern panel, considered to be the finest, showed twenty-three delegations bringing gifts to the Achaemenid king. Apart from being extremely beautiful, it is also a very important record of the nations of the time. It shows, amongst others, Indians, Ethiopians, Cappadocians, Thracians, Parthians, Medes, Elamites, and Arabs all coming to pay tribute to the all-powerful king. It was my favorite bit of the staircase by far. One of the depictions was of a small giraffe being led into the royal court, which caused quite a bit of discussion amongst the group. The Iranian guide said that he was unsure of the reasons why a giraffe would have been presented as a gift. The period drama lady from the British Museum interjected. "I think you'll find it was a sign of status to have a zoological park, just like the Assyrians."

"Quite so, quite so," I concurred as if a professor of ancient history. The group now split in two, with the Iranian guide explaining a section of the staircase to half of them, and the woman from the British Museum doing the same with the others. I initially attached myself to the Iranian guide's group.

"Why are some of the representatives allowed to carry swords inside the royal court?" asked someone pointing to the relevant bas-relief.

"A very good question," responded the guide, whose explanation was that the people depicted were Persians who were not subjects of the king but had a treaty of peace with him and were therefore allowed to carry their weapons.

"Fair enough," I thought and wandered back to the other group to see what they were discussing. A minute later and we had shuffled along to the same spot with the sword–wielding figures. I stood and marveled again at their exceptional designs, as well as at the spectacular nostril hair of Mr. Private Jet, who stood next to me. The woman from the British Museum was now asked the same question about the sword–wielding characters and gave a completely different explanation. She said they were not Persians but Assyrians and were lacking their normal bows and arrows, which wouldn't have been allowed in the royal court and so had swords instead.

"Well, whoop–de–do," I thought and wondered how much any of their assertions about the site were correct and how much they were just conjecture. I was about to have my moment of glory and correct Mrs. British Museum with, "I think you'll find they are in fact Persians who aren't actually subjects of the king but have a treaty of peace with him . . . " etc., but before I got the chance they'd moved on to another section. I decided to stick to my guidebook, which was probably more reliable, and go it alone.

I walked around by myself looking at the splendors of the site, whilst trying to imagine what the city would once have looked like at the height of its glory. It must have been simply amazing. Interestingly, the site had only been discovered relatively recently; for centuries it had been totally covered by sand and dust. Proper excavations only began in the 1930s, when the full grandeur of the site was revealed once again.

Although the city of Persepolis stood at the heart of the Achaemenid Empire, it features extremely rarely in foreign records, leading some archaeologists to believe that its existence and exact location were purposefully hidden from the wider world. The records that still exist focus instead on the other Achaemenid cities at Baghdad and Shush.

Persepolis had originally been called Parsa, but after its devastation by Alexander the Great's army (or Alexander the Vandal, as he is known in Persian history), it became known by the Greek name Persepolis, which means "city of Parsa" (Persia) and "destroyer of cities." Alexander's mob had burned Persepolis to the ground when he came to visit in 330 BC, which many believe was retribution for Achaemenid King Xerxes's ransacking of Athens some 150 years earlier.

Above the city, partially up a hill, were the spectacular tombs of Achaemenid kings Artaxcrxes II and Artaxerxes III. I climbed up to get a better look at them. They were carved directly into the cliff and must have been a good forty to fifty feet high. Not only were the tombs themselves excellent, but the panoramic view of the rest of Persepolis from their hill was breathtaking. The tombs' frontage consisted of a palatial doorway, large stylized rock face pillars, and grandiose carvings depicting Zoroastrian symbols, all of which were hewn out of the cliff.

The Iranian religion of Zoroastrianism probably dates back as far as 1500 BC when it was founded by the prophet Zoroaster who was born in either Iran or neighboring Afghanistan. Zoroastrianism is the first religion to embrace the concept of a single supreme God. Its theology has had a huge impact on Judaism, Christianity, and other later religions, in particular its beliefs surrounding God and the devil, heaven and hell, free will, the soul, resurrection, and the final judgment.

The main thrust of Zoroaster's teaching was his emphasis on an individualized form of religion, and his belief that everybody has a personal responsibility to choose between good and evil. It is by how we use our free will that Zoroaster believed we would be judged in the next life. If your good exceeds your bad, you will enter heaven, and if your bad exceeds your good, you will go to hell.

The natural elements are seen as holy by Zoroastrians, and fire in particular is a sacred symbol to them and used in their temples where they maintain "eternal" fires burning. Zoroaster taught that God, known as Ahura Mazda, is the creator of all that is good, which includes mankind and all of the natural and spiritual worlds. Evil, on the other hand, comes from the violent spirit Angra Mainyu—which is where the English word "anger" is derived from. Angra Mainyu is seen as the creator of all that is bad, and has been in eternal opposition to God.

Zoroaster saw the world as a battlefield between the forces of good and evil, and believed that the earth and mankind had been created in order to assist in this fight between opposing forces. He taught that although the earth is generally a good and decent place, it has been corrupted by evil. Zoroaster believed that this fight against evil would one day reach a peak, at which time good would be victorious over evil, and once again the earth could revert to its intrinsic state of perfection. It would be then that we'd be judged. The evil would be cast into hell, and the virtuous would live with God in heaven forevermore.

Zoroaster was initially attacked for his teaching but finally won the support of the king. Zoroastrianism became the official state religion of a number of Persian empires until the seventh century, when the Arab conquest brought Islam to Persia. There are thought to be about 150,000 Zoroastrians today, of which roughly 30,000 live in the city of Yazd in Iran. India also has a large Zoroastrian community, which was established by refugees who were driven into exile from Persia when Islam arrived.

Zoroastrianism is also referred to as Mazdaism, relating to the Zoroastrian name for God, Ahura Mazda. It is also known as Magism, which is derived from the name for its priests, the magi—which is where the English word "magic" comes from. The magi played a significant role in spreading the religion, and were a priestly tribe who accompanied state delegations on both diplomatic and military assignments. As a result, they traveled widely and resided in settlements spread out across many parts of the Persian Empire. They are the same magi mentioned in the Christian Gospel of Matthew, who refers to magi (wise men) journeying to visit the newborn Jesus. The subsequent assertion that they were kings is incorrect. Although generally considered to be three magi, the Gospel makes no reference to their number, mentioning instead the three different types of gifts that were presented to the infant Jesus. This led to the general presumption that there was one magus for every type of gift given, but there is no historical certainty on this, with some traditions favoring more, or even less, magi. The earliest Christian art is inconclusive also, some depicts two, some three, others four, and a vase in the Kircher Museum shows eight magi.

I left the Zoroastrian tombs and went down to the main site again. I spent a further couple of hours exploring at my leisure, then headed out, thoroughly satisfied, to the taxis. I struck an excellent deal with a driver who agreed to take me all the way back to Shiraz via two other historical sites nearby.

The two sites that were thrown into the taxi driver's deal were Naqsh-e Rajab and Naqsh-e Rostam. The first of these was only a couple of miles away and consisted of an enclosed rocky area where yet more amazing bas-reliefs had been hewn out of the rocks. These depicted various scenes, including two coronations where the Zoroastrian God, Ahura Mazda, was shown handing over the ring of kingship to the monarch. They were all beautiful and merited a good investment of time, but my taxi driver was impatient to get moving, so it ended up being a stop of no more than five minutes. We drove onto our next site, which dominated the surroundings and came into view long before we arrived there.

Cut into a dramatic sprawling rock face high above ground level were a number of huge cross-shaped Zoroastrian tombs. They were magnificent and brought to mind the pictures I'd seen of the famous rock temple at Petra in Jordan. We pulled up and I got out to go and explore, whilst the taxi driver stayed in his car. There were lots of other tourists here, nearly all of them Iranians from a couple of coach parties. In some respects, I found these temples even more impressive than Persepolis. Their condition was so excellent, you didn't have to picture in your mind's eye what they would have once looked like, as you do with Persepolis.

Although no one knows for sure, the tombs are thought to be the resting place for the bones of Achaemenid kings Darius I, Xerxes I, Artaxerxes I, and Darius II. I say "bones" as opposed to remains, because the Zoroastrian tradition was to place the dead on "towers of silence" where vultures would devour the flesh. The reason behind this seemingly macabre practice is that Zoroastrians consider the earth and the elements sacred and so do not wish to pollute them. A burial is seen as polluting the earth and a cremation as polluting the sky. The tradition was for the bodies to be arranged in a seated posture on top of an open-roofed tower and to be accompanied by a magus who would sit nearby and observe which eye was plucked out first by the birds. It was said that if the right eye was the first to go then all was well for the lucky soul and no doubt a land of milk and honey awaited. However, if the left eye was gobbled first then things weren't so rosy. The practice has now all but died out, with modern day followers of the faith preferring a burial in a concrete enclosed grave, which is seen as not polluting the earth.

I had a good look around the site, which also included more stunning bas-reliefs and a fire temple, before giving in to my taxi driver who came looking for me. We arrived back in Shiraz in the late afternoon.

Back at my hotel, I found a note on my door addressed to "The World's Best Dad." It was from Verity, who I'd previously shown my Iranian pocket watch to, and who, according to the note, was staying in a room down the hallway. I popped down the hall to say a quick hello. Being in her room, Verity wasn't wearing her hijab, which shouldn't have surprised me, but seeing any woman in Iran without one on took a bit of getting used to and just seemed a bit strange.

We both filled each other in on what we'd been doing, which in Verity's case consisted mainly of sitting on a cramped bus all day. I was very pleased that I'd flown and saved so much time. Verity had arrived earlier in the afternoon and was staying in Shiraz for the next few days before going on to the city of Yazd, which was also my next destination. She was keen for a bite to eat, and since I could force down a bit more food, we decided to go out somewhere together and consulted her guidebook for a suitable place. We selected a restaurant called the Shiraz Eram Hotel and headed out in search of it.

It took us forever to find the place, but when we finally did, it was well worth the wait as the food was excellent–or more accurately, my food was excellent. I went for a succulent chicken schnitzel with all the trimmings. Verity opted instead for a reverse macrobiotic, unleaded, candida–free, detoxifying anti–Atkins option, or something like that, which consisted of a few limp green leaves and a dribble of salad dressing. It didn't look up to much, but Verity seemed quite content to nibble away like a rabbit and was adamant it was "good for a detox"–it looked good for a compost heap!

Over her feast, she told me a funny story about an Iranian guy who had been talking to her in Esfahan, and to impress upon her that his intentions were honorable had said with utter sincerity, "I no want to make cock with you."

Verity had burst out laughing at the time as I did now on hearing it. We had a great time over dinner and Verity made me laugh with her repertoire of jokes including, "What's an Austral–ian's idea of foreplay?" Answer: "How about it, Sheila?" which Verity accompanied with a mimed elbow in the ribs as if to awaken a sleeping partner.

Verity and I also had a giggle at her poor mother who was so concerned about Verity's well–being in Iran that she'd got her local prayer group working regularly on her case and had even had a mass said for her, such was her worry. Verity had sent her mother numerous e-mails to let her know how safe it was, but there was no convincing her. As far as she was concerned, Iran was full of dangerous cutthroat terrorists and that was that.

I was leaving Shiraz tomorrow night, so we both agreed to go to some of its main attractions together during the day, including the tombs of renowned Iranian poets Hafez and Sa'di.

CHAPTER SIXTEEN

"Super Film" with Celine Dion and Eminem

In the center of Shiraz is a most remarkable building. Standing timelessly amongst the city's bustling streets is a vast sand-colored ancient citadel called Arg-e Karim Khani. It's not the sort of thing you expect to see in a city center and looks instead as if it should be situated amongst rolling sand dunes being used as a desert stronghold. Constructed in a vast high-walled square, its basic but imposing structure is beautifully accentuated on each of its four corners by forty-five-foot high circular towers embellished with decorative patterned bricks. On its southeastern side, the fortress's tower has an interesting architectural anomaly, in that it leans over at an insanely sloping angle, reminiscent of the Leaning Tower of Pisa. It is said, although I'm not sure I believe it, that experts from the more famous leaning tower once visited Shiraz to offer their expertise to help correct it, but after a thorough examination, the Pisa boys admitted defeat as the slope was just too great for them. It was the first site that Verity and I stopped off to visit together.

Inside the fortress was a sign announcing, THE EXALTED STATURE OF KARIM KHANI CITADEL AMUSES EVERY NEW TRAVELER FOR A LONG TIME WHO ARRIVES IN SHIRAZ. The structure had previously been used as both a prison and part of the royal courtyard, although not at the same time. I quite liked the idea of its dual use, and whilst walking around imagined a similar scheme in Britain, where maybe the royal family could use the exercise area of Wormwood Scrubs Prison as a courtyard at weekends and a group of inmates could go stay at Buckingham Palace–something I'd be all in favor of.

Although the citadel contained little of interest within, its vast internal courtyard was a welcome sanctuary away from the bustle of the streets outside and had many attractive exotic plant displays. After a good gander at these and around the building, Verity and I got a cab to the Aramgah–e Sa'di or Tomb of Sa'di.

This was a lovely place dedicated to renowned Iranian poet Sa'di that contained a charming mausoleum set in a picturesque and peaceful garden. It had a relaxed and very reverent atmos-phere despite the fact that it was crawling with Iranian tourists. Sa'di's marble tomb was attractive, as was the building it was housed in, but it was more a place to come to relax and soak up the atmosphere rather than stand in awe at the architecture.

It had a nice selection of books on Iran at a little kiosk, which Verity and I browsed through before heading into what for me was the star attraction of the place, a little underground tea shop. This was beautifully decorated and had a delightful fishpond in the center. Its interior was wonderfully cool, which was more than welcome as today was blisteringly hot. I had a cool pomegranate juice whilst Verity indulged in a very strange Persian dessert. It consisted of that classic combination–ice cream, Jell-O, and soft squidgy savory noodles. I gave it a try but didn't like it one bit. But taste, or lack of it, was no reason to eat or abstain from something as far as Verity was concerned.

So long as it had a cleansing effect on her negative toxins, she was happy to tuck right in.

After two juices for me and more strange culinary combinations for Verity, we headed to the coach station so I could pre-book a ticket to Yazd. I would have flown, but according to my guidebook there was no airport in Yazd (or so I thought until I got there and discovered one had been built since the book's publication).

The bus terminal was heaving with people, and as I walked through its crowded interior, loads of bus operators tried to steer me in the direction of their particular company's travel counter. I wasn't having any of it and was determined for a bit of luxury on this trip so went straight for the Rolls Royce of Iranian bus companies and over to the Seir-o Safar counter. The helpful man there was dressed up like an airline pilot and spoke good English. He was the bearer of bad news, though, and informed me that all his coaches to Yazd were fully booked tonight.

This wasn't what I wanted to hear; the last thing I fancied was spending the night on some death trap of a bus for such a long and arduous journey. He recommended another operator and said that their coaches were "okay," although obviously not up to the superior quality of his. I wasn't going to take his word on it, and before booking the ticket, I got the guy behind the recommended counter to confirm for me that the bus I'd be getting was the same as the nice modern Volvo pictured on the wall behind him. I repeated the question three times to be on the safe side. He was so determined to convince me he was legit and that I'd be getting a Volvo, that he got up from behind the counter and walked me out to where the coaches were parked. He pointed out the relevant one and said, "Volvo, yes?" It was indeed. I booked a ticket with him a moment later. With this in hand, Verity and I got on the move again.

We strolled to the town center via the city's ancient bazaar, which was full of weird and wonderful sights. I particularly liked the shops selling sugar, which had chunks of the stuff purposefully solidified into phallic objects that looked for all the world like big sugar lump dildos.

We stopped by a man with a huge silver urn selling tea so Verity could get herself one. Never one to pass on a *chay* myself, I indulged again and handed over the money to the man with the urn. I was amazed at the lack of change I received from my substantial note and was sure I'd been ripped off. Verity was likewise convinced and said to watch closely when the next Iranian paid for a cup, to see how much they were charged. A group of three turned up and ordered tea, but before they had the chance to dip into their pockets, the tea man muttered something to them in Farsi. I was very suspicious of this, and even more so when the three seemed to give me a slight appreciative nod of the head. It was as if he'd said, "Don't worry about this one, lads. The foreigner has paid for all of you and the rest of the bazaar." There was no way of proving this, though, and in dollars or British pounds, the cost didn't amount to much, so we ambled on our way.

Not far on, we popped into a bookshop for a browse around. On the spur of the moment, I said to the shop assistant, "Modern Tacking!" and was led to a huge section of the store dedicated to Germany's answer to the Beatles. There was an array of Modern Talking material on offer, ranging from quality hardback books to cheap photocopied pamphlets with terrible spellings and rather dubious translations of their lyrics. These were hilarious and had vast sections edited out, presumably because they were deemed inappropriate. One song's title had even received a seeing to and only "My ****, **** *****" remained. It must have been a racy number, because nearly the entire track was blanked out as well, making it almost indecipherable. Verity and I flicked through a couple of these pamphlets and were in stitches at some of the lyrics.

I wanna freak you here, I wanna freak you there
I wanna run my fingers through your freaking hair

I couldn't control myself and bought one of these and one of their sturdier Persian-to-English translation books. They were both outstanding.

I took this literature, along with my copy of Hafez that Pedram had given to me, to the tomb of the great man. Like the tomb of Sa'di, Hafez's resting place was situated in a lovely garden that had a very tranquil atmosphere. His mausoleum was more modest in size and was an octagonal pavilion structure with an internally tiled decorative dome in a kaleidoscope of patterns and colors. The most amazing thing about the place was the absolute reverence with which people treated his tomb. It was as if a revered saint were buried here, not simply a poet who had strung a few ditties together. People would walk up and bow their heads, touch their hearts, and reverently place their hands on the tomb. Iranians sure do take their poetry seriously.

We both sat down in the park, and to fully appreciate Hafez's work, we had a look at his book together. Now I mean no disrespect to my Iranian friends, and maybe the translation of the book was incorrect, but the verses seemed to all rhyme in a very similar fashion to Modern Talking's lyrics. To test this theory, Verity and I selected a passage from each book, which we read aloud for the other to guess which one it was from without looking. It wasn't easy. Perhaps this accounted for the huge popularity of Germany's finest in Iran. And I wondered if, in years to come, Iran would have a mausoleum dedicated to Modern Talking, where thousands of pilgrims would flock to pay their respects and sit and read their lyrics. It wouldn't surprise me, and I'll bet good money on there being one for Chris de Burgh just as soon as he snuffs it.

It is said that if you want to know your destiny, you should open a copy of Hafez and it will be revealed to you. I tried it with Hafez and with Modern Talking. This is what I got, and I'm not saying which is which:

Arabian gold
For your gangster love
Arabian gold
For the last albatross

Of my gipsy?
Was she happy? Was she well?
Was she tipsy?

In a quest to find a good eating establishment, Verity dipped into her guidebook, wherein she discovered a fascinating-sounding location called the Restaurant Mir Mohanna. Here it was apparently possible to get a shark kebab served by identical twins dressed rather eccentrically as indistinguishable sailors. This sounded my kind of place, so I lobbied hard with Verity for this option. She wasn't convinced and favored a more traditional upmarket place called the Soofie Traditional Restaurant. In the end, though, I won through and off we went to go see the salty sailors. It took a while to get there and turned out to be a complete waste of time, as according to a kindly old chap we met there, the restaurant had been closed for years.

We got in a cab and went to Verity's option instead. Or to be more accurate, we went to a restaurant that sounded vaguely similar to the one we'd asked the taxi driver to take us to.

It might not have been the place we selected but it was nice enough and the food was okay, if a little on the raw side–my chicken kebab sported a few splatterings of blood. Verity of course went for the funny herbivore option. It was strange to again be in a nice restaurant and unable to order a bottle of wine, especially as we were in Shiraz, home of the famous Shiraz grapes used around the world for wine of the same name. We made do with an Iranian Zam Zam cola instead.

Since we were both heading to the same city next and had had a good laugh together, we agreed to meet up again in Yazd, at the most popular hostel there, the Silk Road Hotel. After our meal, we spent the rest of the day window-shopping along the main street, where we discovered a rather interesting baseball cap for sale depicting an Australian flag but with the word PORTUGAL emblazoned across it. I didn't buy one, but I wish now that I had, as it would have made a great present for one of my Aussie friends. When it was time to go, I said a quick "Adios" to Verity, grabbed my gear, and got a cab down to the bus terminal.

It was dark by now, but it was another tantalizingly hot and sticky Middle Eastern evening. I went to the counter where I'd bought my ticket from and inquired which bay I needed. The man I'd spoken to earlier was now no longer here, and a colleague of his pointed me in the direction of the correct bay. On arrival there, I was astonished to see not a shiny new modern "Volvo," as promised, but a beat-up old rust bucket that didn't look like it could make it to the other end of the terminal, let alone a few hundred miles. I couldn't believe it and was just about to go voice my discontent when it reversed out of the bay and in its place pulled up a shiny new "Volvo." This was more like it.

Whilst waiting to board I was approached by a friendly man who spoke good but extremely fast and slightly quirky English.

"Ah, you are Englishman from England. I like the Englishman very much!" he said. "I once have English gentleman stay with my family. His name Mr. Montgomery Fielding; he is frightfully frightfully!"

I laughed.

I didn't get the guy's name, but he was a real character and introduced me to his son called Reza, who was twenty years old and catching the same bus as me.

"You will sit next to my son on bus and stay at my home in Yazd as my guest," he stated simply, as if it was totally normal to offer accommodation to complete strangers met at the local bus station only moments before.

Being fully aware of the refuse three times rule of Iranian social etiquette, I did so to check if the offer was genuine—it was. In many ways, this typified the unbelievable hospitality shown by Iranians toward foreigners, and although I was initially surprised at his generosity, I really shouldn't have been. His son, he explained, was a student and spoke only a little English, so it would be good for him to practice with me. He assured me that Reza would be more than happy to look after me in Yazd and show me around the place. He apologized for not being able to do this himself and explained that he wasn't catching the bus but staying in Shiraz for a week on business.

One of the destinations in Yazd he said Reza would take me to was a Zoroastrian fire temple. I asked him if he was a Zoroastrian. He said he was and then told me a little bit about the religion's beliefs, in particular about the earth, the trees, and the water being sacred. I liked that and him very much.

Reza and I both sat at the front of the bus and, although his English wasn't great, we just about managed to communicate. After some labored conversation, he pulled out his DVD collection, which was contained in a little zip-up wallet. With a mischievous grin, he pointed to one of the disks and said, "Super film!"

At first I didn't understand what was on the disk, but after a while I managed to ascertain that a "super film" was in fact a porn movie. I asked what the penalty for having this would be. He struggled with the words but answered with exactly the right ones, saying, "You put in cage for maybe two or three year." That was quite a risk to take for a bit of porn, no matter how super it was. Although I'd planned to sleep on the bus, it didn't really work out like that as we talked, or struggled to talk, to each other most of the way.

We arrived in Yazd much earlier than the bus was due and got to the terminal at about two in the morning instead of four. Reza gave his older brother a quick call, who came to pick us up in a beat-up old Land Rover. Even at this hour, his brother didn't seem in the slightest bit tired and was very enthusiastic to meet me. He introduced himself as Ashkan. Ashkan's English was far better than his younger brother's, and on the journey over to their house we both chatted away nonstop.

When we arrived there, I was asked to be as quiet as possible, as the rest of the family was asleep. They led me inside the front room, where about eight people were all lying on thin mattresses on the floor. I assumed I would be doing the same, but Iranian hospitality being what it is, I was shown instead to an empty room that I had all to myself. I didn't want to try to refuse their generosity and risk waking someone up, and what's more, there would have been no point in trying anyway, so I just whispered a quiet thank-you. Reza brought me a similar mattress to the ones the family were using and a big thick blanket. He closed the door and bade me goodnight. Moments later I was asleep.

In the morning, I was introduced to the rest of the family, who were all female and, apart from their mother, were much younger than Reza and Ashkan. Being the men of the household, the brothers didn't lift a finger at breakfast, which was served for us by their adorable little sisters on a plastic mat on the floor of the main room. We had boiled eggs, bread, real honeycomb, yogurt, and olives.

After breakfast, I was keen to go sightseeing, but I didn't want it to seem like I was setting the agenda, so I waited for the brothers to make a suggestion on where to go and what to do. Their suggestion was to go check out their PC in the room next door and for them to give me a full demonstration of how it worked.

What was it with young Iranians and their computers?

The computer was clearly their pride and joy and was fully rigged up to the Internet. They had downloaded loads of music videos and other crap, like fake WWE wrestling, all of which they were determined to show me. So my introduction to Yazd was not a tour of its splendid cultural and historical sights, but a couple of hours of watching stupid redneck wrestling nonsense and the likes of Britney sodding Spears shaking her butt about. This was all very kind of them to show me some prime examples of refined American culture, but it wasn't really what I'd come to Iran or to Yazd for. I'd come to Yazd because it was the country's quintessential desert city, sandwiched between the Dasht–e Lut desert in the south and the Dasht–e Kavir desert in the north. As deserts are one of my favorite environments, it appealed greatly. It is also home to the biggest Zoroastrian community in Iran, and has the country's finest old city, which is still inhabited. Yazd was described by Marco Polo as, "a very fine and splendid city and center of commerce." Yazd has always been renowned as a weaving town and was famed for its wonderful silks long before Marco Polo journeyed through on one of the multiple silk roads. After the Arab conquest, the city became a major stopping point along the caravan routes to India and Central Asia, and as a result its goods and crafts traveled far beyond the borders of Iran.

I eventually managed to convince the brothers to show me some of this fascinating city, and after I showed them the photos of Yazd in my guidebook, they agreed to take me to a Zoroastrian fire temple. We all piled into the Land Rover and headed off. It was another roasting day with a big blue cloudless sky that seemed to stretch for eternity. What I saw of Yazd on the way to the temple I really liked. It had leafy tree-lined streets, beautiful and strange-looking buildings, and was neither an overcrowded chaotic city nor a quiet deserted backwater.

We arrived at the Ateshkadeh Fire Temple just as Mr. Private Jet and the rest of the British pensioners from the Persepolis tour group were leaving and boarding a private coach outside. I waved a quick hello but didn't want to enter into a conversation with them so walked on past.

The temple was a modest-looking building set in a small garden with a little circular pond out the front and a Zoroastrian winged symbol above the main entrance. The attraction of the place was its "eternal" flame, which has reportedly been burning since AD 470 and is situated behind a big glass case. In 1174, the flame was moved to the nearby desert settlement of Ardakan and then onto Yazd in 1474. It is kept going by attentive priests who regularly feed the fire with almond and apricot wood.

Although I found the temple mildly interesting, I can't say I was taken aback with amazement at the place. We were confined to a small hallway overlooking the fire and, apart from a few paintings of Zoroaster on the wall and the flame itself, there really wasn't much else to look at.

We got back in the Land Rover and drove to a far better Zoroastrian site just outside of the town called the Towers of Silence. Here in the dusty barren desert were two huge circular towers on top of adjacent rocky hills. In days gone by, these had been used by Zoroastrians to place their dead so the vultures could feed upon them. It looked an ancient and delicate site, but that didn't stop the brothers burning around doing doughnuts in the Land Rover, whilst I got out to look at the towers.

There was a fantastic view from the top, with mountains and desert in one direction and the city in the other. Also of interest at the site were the remains of several other ancient buildings, including a big well with a domed roof, which was scrawled with Persian graffiti. Next to this were two towers called *badgirs*. *Badgirs*, or wind towers, can be seen all over Yazd and are an ancient means of air conditioning designed to redirect the slightest of breezes down into rooms below. The towers consist of a main chimneylike trunk which houses a number of ingenious shafts, special air shelves, and flaps that direct hot air out of the building and air cooled over a pool of water into the building. Although not as effective as modern air conditioning, the *badgirs* do have a discernable effect and are far healthier than the modern equivalent as they keep fresh air circulating and don't use electricity.

I had a good look around the main site and clicked off a load of snaps before going to look at the domed well where the *badgirs* were situated. Leading into the side of the well's dome was a little pitch-black tunnel. I moved along inside this almost completely blind as my eyes had yet to acclimatize to the darkness after the brilliant sun outside. I stopped just in time before the tunnel ended abruptly and dropped straight down into the well itself. It gave me a bit of a shock. I flicked some pebbles down to see how deep in went. It wasn't huge, but it was more than big enough to break a leg or two. I thanked my lucky stars I'd stopped in time. I went back and found the brothers, who were now launching the Land Rover off a natural ramp-like mound of earth. It's a wonder it didn't kill the suspension such was the force they were landing with—a fine testament to good old British engineering.

We drove back to their house, where Ashkan dropped Reza and me off and explained that he had to leave us for a few hours so he could go do some studying. Inside, Reza treated me to more fun and games on the computer, this time in the form of a DVD of female American wrestling. It was terrible and so clearly faked, but Reza loved it and asked me sincerely, "You think real?"

I think not.

When his sister came into the room he immediately turned it off and sent her out.

"For woman, it is not allowed," he said to me with a smile.

After a painfully long dose of "wrestling," we settled down to a late lunch prepared by Reza's wonderful mother. I was very grateful for her kindly preparing a meal, but my heart sank when I saw what it was–vast industrial quantities of kidney and liver chopped up and mixed with rice. Now I'm not a fussy eater, but I absolutely detest both liver and kidney. And I don't just mean that I'm not particularly enamored by them, but that I bloody loathe the stuff, nearly to the extent of gagging at the very thought of eating it, let alone actually eating it. But as much as I detest liver and kidney, I wouldn't dream of turning down a meal so kindly prepared, so I took a deep breath, tried to compose myself, and had my first tentative mouthful. I tried to swallow immediately in an attempt to stop contact with my taste buds, but it was simply impossible to get the stuff down without a good few chews to break it up. Even then, it seemed to wedge in my twitching gullet and travel down at an agonizingly slow speed.

It was simply disgusting and I felt seriously ill. I did my best to give little fake smiles to Reza's mother as if to say, "Yum yum, this is good." It wasn't easy. In an attempt to help the stuff on its way, I took huge swigs of cola with the kidney and liver and masticated it all into a squishy pulp before swallowing. This made things a little easier going but not much, as believe me, a liver and kidney "cola float" is a far from a refreshing beverage. Coca-Cola may have occasionally flirted with the idea of cherry and vanilla flavors, and even that weird Tab Clear stuff, but I don't think the powers–that–be at Coke PLC will ever detect a niche gap in the market and consider bringing out "Liver and Kidney Cola," perhaps with the slogan, "It's offally good!"

It took a long while, but I eventually cleared the plate and finished the last mouthful with a sigh of utter relief. I smiled at Reza's mother as if to say, "Thank you, that was delicious"–big mistake! She grabbed my plate and then, to my abject horror, started piling on an even larger second portion. I have no words to describe how my spirit dropped on seeing this, but I guess winning the lotto and then losing the ticket must be a close feeling.

It was far harder to get through than the first portion, but eventually, after what seemed like an eternity, I made it to the end. This time, I purposefully left a little on my plate to indicate I was full. After the meal, I felt so bad I had to brush my teeth and lie down for a good hour to recover. Luckily, Reza was having a siesta anyway so no suspicions were aroused.

In the late afternoon, after Ashkan had returned with the Land Rover, Reza and I ventured out again, this time accompanied by his little seven-year-old next-door neighbor, who wanted to tag along with the big boys. He sat in the back of the Land Rover with a big smile from ear to ear. We stopped at one of the architectural highlights of Yazd, and one of the most distinctive buildings in Iran, the Amir Chakhmaq Complex.

The Amir Chakhmaq Complex is a three-story structure with two towering minarets, many beautiful sunken alcoves, and sparkling white and blue tiles. It is used as a sort of grandstand to watch theater performances in the square below of the Ta'zieh, or passion play, commemorating the martyrdom of Imam Hossein. It is situated in the heart of Yazd across from a little park containing a pond and a fountain. Reza dropped me outside the complex and told me to meet him in the park opposite in half an hour, after he'd found a place to park.

I bought a ticket and went inside the towering structure. It didn't really have any internal rooms, as it was an open-fronted building from which to observe the world below. Not only could you climb up to the structure's open roof on the third floor, but also to the top of its massive minarets. To scale these, I had to negotiate, in near total darkness, a painfully narrow spiral stone staircase twisting all the way to the top. I stepped out onto a rather rickety-feeling platform at the summit and was bowled over by the breathtaking and unforgettable view. I could see for miles all the way across the ancient city's mud-brick houses with their distinctive *badgir* wind towers to a vast sea of rolling sand, which looked as if it was straight out of the film *Lawrence of Arabia*. The dunes led to the base of a sprawling and rugged sand-colored mountain range many thousands of feet high. This was all bathed in the orange glow of the descending sun, which was just disappearing over the horizon. The evocative sound of the call to prayer rang out from the many mosques of the city, creating a vibrant and tingling atmosphere. Down below in the park, children were playing, people were chatting, and a group of soldiers reclined on the grass using their backpacks as pillows. Everybody looked so very happy, and there was a subtle yet perceptible feeling of contentment in the dry desert air. This seeped into and saturated me to the extent that I felt I could stay perched up here forever. The whole scene was so magical, but it was also so typical of the Iran I had come to love. I stood up here and wondered if, when I got back to England, anyone would believe me that this was the real Iran.

I spotted Reza and his little friend sitting in the park eating ice cream, so I headed down to see them. I bought myself an ice cream and joined them just as the colored lights of the square were turned on. Here we sat enjoying the atmosphere and just watching the world go by.

One thing I really wanted to do in Yazd was to go out into the desert and, if possible, to spend a few nights there under the stars. Yazd was going to be my final destination in southern Iran before I started the long journey north again, so I was keen to make it a good one, and was more than willing to splash out on an expensive desert tour. This was something it was wise to pay a little extra for, as the last thing I wanted to do was end up on a budget desert excursion that wasn't properly prepared. Before leaving the U.K., I had read that the Dasht-e Kavir desert was one of the hottest in the world, and that it had nearly finished off Alexander the Great and his army, so it was not a place to take lightly by cutting corners on cost. Reza said it was possible to book desert tours through the Yazd Internet café and agreed to take me there.

After sending Ricardo a quick e-mail to find out where he was, I inquired about the tours. The Internet café only did local day excursions, but I wanted to get right out there and into the thick of it, so they directed me to a nearby hotel where there was a guide who organized longer trips. The guide was a friendly young chap who spoke perfect English and explained that he only did overnight tours for groups of four or more, so I would have to find three others who also wanted to go.

He offered a three-night, four-day excursion deep into the Dasht-e Kavir, which would visit huge white salt flats, rugged mountain ranges, and the obligatory rolling sand dunes. It was just what I was after. I took his card and told him I'd give him a call if I managed to find the necessary volunteers. We didn't stick around in town any longer, as by now the little lad was beginning to feel tired. On the drive back home, he fell fast asleep in the back of the car. We dropped him off, then popped into Reza's house to catch up with his brother. Here Reza handed over tourist duty to Ashkan, who immediately whisked me outside again in the Land Rover.

Ashkan was all dressed up and looking as smooth as hell in a fresh white shirt, polished pointed shoes, and smart black strides. He told me we were going to a park where we could meet beautiful girls. I liked the sound of this. We drove to a place called the "Parsian" Hotel, which was situated in a peaceful and attractive garden on the other side of town. In the garden was an octagonal pond surrounded by many raised carpeted platforms occupied by smartly dressed attractive people in their early twenties. The platforms were either all occupied by girls or all occupied by guys, but none of them were mixed. Despite this gender separation on the platforms, there were a few couples discreetly standing nearby who were chatting together and holding hands. I got the distinct impression this was a popular meeting place for young people to go on "the pull"–Persian style.

Ashkan stopped at one of the platforms to say a gentle-manly hello to a group of girls he knew and introduced me in the process. The girls were all dressed in colorful hijabs and, with the exception of one of them, were all very attractive, fit, and slim. The exception was a big scowling chunky lass who looked the spitting image of the grumpy matron who Hattie Jacques played in the Carry On films.

Ashkan and I got a platform about ten feet from theirs. After a couple of minutes, "Hattie" came over and perched herself on the edge of the platform, nearly toppling it in the process. She was forthright and to the point. "Give me gift! You give me gift!" she barked at me.

"Charming," I thought.

Although a bit taken aback by this, I emptied my pockets for something to give her. All I had was my wallet, my "World's Best Dad" pocket watch, and my passport. She wasn't getting any of these. I apologized and showed her what I had. She grabbed my passport and said, "Gift!"

Like hell it was. I grabbed it back from her sausage–like fingers.

"You are scrooge!" she barked.

"Cheeky cow," I thought, but in the interests of diplomacy I asked her politely, "What can I give you?"

"Give me chocolate. I want chocolate!"

"I bet you do," I thought, but this was the last thing she needed!

When I told her I had none, she repeated again, "You are scrooge!" this time grimacing up her face and five chins in the process. I told her I simply didn't have any chocolate and then said, with the intention of stumping her, "Okay, you give me gift. Give me chocolate; you give me chocolate!"

She reached into her handbag and, with a triumphant look, produced two little candies for me and Ashkan. Hattie changed the subject and now asked me which of the girls on the platform I liked–ooh, Matron!

"Well they're all very nice, as are you," I said lying through my teeth about the last bit.

"But which one do you like?!" she growled.

"As I say, they're all nice."

"Do you not think they are beautiful?"

"Oh my goodness, no, I wasn't saying that for a second; they are all very beautiful," I ventured.

"Then which one do you like?!" she near shouted at me.

I gave in and said, "The one with the yellow hijab." That was it. Off waddled Hattie to do the Iranian equivalent of, "My mate fancies you."

The girls all giggled shyly as Hattie discussed the situation with them. She returned and asked, "Would you like to marry her?"

"Well, obviously, talk of marriage is slightly premature," I stated. She stared at me with a look of confusion on her face and then just repeated the question.

"Would you like to marry her?"

"Don't get me wrong–she's very nice, but I couldn't possibly contemplate . . ."

"But you say you like her. You no like her now?" she interrupted.

"No, no, she's lovely," I said.

"You want to marry her?"

I was going to try to explain again, but then I thought, "Oh, what the hell?" and just said, "Yes, I would like to marry her."

Off she went and returned with my fiancée, who Hattie introduced as Susan. Susan barely spoke a word of English, so Hattie did the talking for her–and by the looks of it, all the eating for her as well. Susan was twenty-two, a physics student, and as Hattie kindly pointed out for me, was also "very beautiful." The conversation kind of ground to a halt past these basic facts, but my future wife had an idea of how to get the marriage back on track. She left for a little stall serving food nearby and returned a minute later with a romantic little present for me–a juicy, foil-wrapped double cheeseburger.

I was genuinely touched by Susan's kindness. It was all so very pure and innocent. I thanked her and told her in Farsi that she was beautiful. She liked this a lot and in English said, "Thank you," before Hattie ushered her back to the girl's platform. I finished the burger and bought her one in return. Hattie was green with envy at the sight of this and licked her lips whilst salivating wildly–get your own burger, Jacquesy!

I returned to my platform, and a minute later two of Ashkan's male friends came to join us. One of them spoke good English and explained to me that only a few years ago, young people wouldn't have been able to meet in places like this. He said that back then it was "more forbidden" and that the rules were generally more relaxed now.

Ashkan's friends stuck around for about an hour talking to us, and after they left Hattie and Susan returned for a chat. Susan asked me through Hattie what my name meant. I said I had no idea of its meaning, which seemed to confuse them and was probably the equivalent of someone in England saying they don't know how to spell their name, as everybody seemed to know the meaning of theirs in Iran. Susan said that in Persian her name meant "hot" or "fire" and that in Hebrew it meant "beautiful woman." She asked me what Susan meant in English.

I just combined the two and said, "Hot beautiful woman." They all laughed.

The girls left before Ashkan and I did, and on the way back, we drove past them in the Land Rover and gave them a polite wave. At Ashkan's house, I was treated to a lovely meal of succulent lamb with soft buttered rice for the main course and some of the best fruit I've ever tasted for the second course. We had grapes the size of golf balls, honey–sweet figs, dates, and cucumber. After dinner, the phone rang and amazingly Ashkan passed it to me saying, "It's for you." On the other end of the phone was a girl who said hello but nothing else. I tried to communicate but it was no good, so I handed the phone back to Ashkan. He spoke to the person, then hung up.

Ashkan explained that it had been my fiancée Susan on the other end and that she and Hattie wanted to meet up with us tomorrow. This was getting out of hand.

The brothers insisted I slept in the same room as last night and I had it all to myself again. Since the computer was also in there, I was given another fascinating demonstration of it before bed. This time, it was a pirated DVD of Celine Dion, followed by some downloaded Eminem videos. Just like the Tehran lads, both the brothers sang harmoniously with Celine and then did the exaggerated rapper–style hand moves to Eminem. It was a good laugh all round, and just like Pedram and the boys, they saw no contradiction in being equally enthused with both styles of music.

CHAPTER SEVENTEEN

Who's A-knocking on That Door?

Although Susan and Hattie wanted to meet up with Ashkan and me today, I was determined not to go through with it, as I simply didn't want to get her into any trouble with the law. It was all very well for me to take risks, but I didn't like the idea of Susan being accused of anything untoward with a non–Muslim male, despite how innocent it all would have been. With this in mind, I told Ashkan that when I was in Shiraz, I had arranged to meet up with a friend of mine (Verity) who was arriving in Yazd today, and because of this I wouldn't be able to meet the girls.

He understood and said that he had to go to university for a couple of hours, so it would have been difficult to meet them anyway. This was good news; I had a few things to organize today, including finding three people to come on my desert tour. I hoped that if I could meet up with Verity, she'd also be keen to come along on the excursion. I also needed to find out about train times going north and had been told it was necessary to book these long in advance. Reza kindly took me to the train station to make the necessary inquiries.

It was an interesting situation at the station, as the girl behind the counter spoke far better English than Reza, but he was reluctant to let her speak with me and seemed determined to prove his linguistic skills were up to the task. He struggled valiantly to translate for me but couldn't do it, and I don't think he even grasped exactly what I wanted to find out. In the end, he admitted defeat and the girl explained all I needed to know. He apologized to me for not being able to help. His brother's English was far better than his, and I think it annoyed him that I had near-normal conversations with Ashkan, but with him it was much more basic. I told him a white lie and said he'd actually been a lot of help with the translation. I don't think he understood this either.

I booked my train journey heading north and opted for a first class ticket, which I was delighted to learn was an overnight sleeper train with cabins and beds. I'd never been on anything like this before and imagined it to be very sophisticated and Orient Express–like. To me, it sounded the sort of train Roger Moore would catch in a James Bond film with some gorgeous Soviet spy, and in my rather deluded head, I imagined a similar scene in a couple of nights time, with my own spacious cabin, a magnum of champagne, and a busty Bolshevik to entertain.

Whilst leaving the station, I nodded a little hello to two Western backpackers I saw getting off the train who nodded likewise in return.

Like his brother, Reza also had to go to university today, so he offered to take me into town before he went. As I fancied a bit of a walk, I asked him to drop me on the main road heading into town so I could do a bit of sightseeing on the way. When he pulled over, I thanked him for the ride and said I'd catch up with him some time in the evening.

Whilst walking down the road, a guy on a moped pulled over and said hello to me in English and asked where I was going. I hadn't really made up my mind as to my destination yet but was considering going to a famed prison of Alexander the Great, so said, "Alexander's prison."

"Jump on," he replied, so I did. I loved the fact that in Iran a complete stranger would happily stop and offer me a lift, even when I hadn't asked for one, then go out of his way to take me to my destination, and all simply because I was a foreigner and, as he saw it, a guest in his country. I say this sincerely: Iranians are the nicest people I've ever met. It was just so easy to get to know people there that I can never imagine being lonely in Iran.

We shot off on the bike at a suicidal speed, weaving in and out of the traffic as we went. I held on with one hand and with the other secured my hat on my head so it didn't go flying. He dropped me at the prison, wished me well, and was gone as quickly as he'd arrived.

Outside the prison was a group of five young guys all around twenty years old who were hanging out together. Just like my friend on the bike, they came up and started talking to me without any prompting whatsoever. Two of them spoke good English and, after going through the normal list of intro-ductory questions, asked if I would like to come for a drink with them. I politely declined and explained that I was going to have a look inside the prison first. They said that the prison wasn't up to much and recommended I didn't waste my money. They were right.

It didn't take more than fifteen minutes to browse around, and there was very little to see. It looked nothing like a prison; in fact, it didn't really look like anything in particular, being little more than an old building with a few empty rooms. It had once had an infamous reputation and was written about by Hafez, but it was very hard to picture it back then as there were no cells or any sign that it was once used to incarcerate people. I left and found the guys still messing about outside.

They asked me if I would like a lift anywhere in their car, which predictably was a Hillman Hunter. I took them up on the offer and got a lift to the main square. In the car, there was a lot of good-natured banter, and when we got to the square, I was surprised to find they apologized for this and said they hoped they hadn't made too many jokes at my expense. They were a nice bunch of guys. I thanked them, assured them it was fine, then strolled down to the Internet café that I'd briefly popped into the night before.

I had a reply to the e-mail I'd sent Ricardo, who was now in Pakistan after visiting the remains of the ancient city of Bam, which had been devastated by an earthquake in 2003 that killed up to 40,000 people. He wrote:

> Hi Jamie!
>
> That's great! You can see, again, how does Iranians really live. I'm in Quetta, Pakistan. This is the Third World! And I'm sure in India it will be even worse. From the border, I came in a fourteen hours bus trip on an unbelievable piece of junk with four wheels. From Yazd, I took a morning train to Kerman, then a bus to Bam. The city is completely destroyed. I didn't see one single house not damaged. Most of the people is living in tents and cabins. But I was happy for being there, seeing people trying to live again after losing everything. I was looking forward to see Mr. Akbar, from the former Akbar Guesthouse. He also lost everything but now he built a very small house for his family and has three tents for the guests. He's such a nice person with a very positive attitude. From Yazd, I traveled with Charlie, a nice young guy. I don't think he realized the real situation in Bam. He asked for an Internet café (obviously, there was any); in the only kind of restaurant (an Inn) he asked for a menu (there wasn't any menu, just two "meals") and the first thing he

asked to Mr. Akbar was the price for a night, which is somehow rude. Mr. Akbar answered very well: "Why are you asking for the price? You should be glad for having a place to stay after what happened here. I'm not asking for money, just accept what people give me." If you go there, please tell Mr. Akbar that I told you about his guesthouse. I promised him I would tell everyone I know.

Have a nice journey,

Ricardo

I'll tell everybody, too, Ricardo; I'll put it in a book.

Whilst at the Internet café, I got talking to the two Westerners I'd seen this morning at the train station. They were both New Zealanders of about my age called Tim and Justin. I mentioned the desert tour to them and both were immediately interested, and after a bit of a sales pitch from me agreed to come along. This was excellent news. I now needed only one more person to make up the numbers, but if I couldn't find anyone, then I was prepared to pay the difference myself.

Tim and Justin wanted to go and look at the historic old part of Yazd and asked if I wanted to join them. I did.

The United Nations Educational, Scientific and Cultural Organization (UNESCO) describes Yazd as one of the oldest towns in the world. The old part of the city was hugely atmospheric and extremely difficult to navigate through. It was a mishmash of interconnecting alleyways through an area of sand-colored mud-brick houses, nearly all of which had the characteristic *badgir* wind towers. It was fantastic and like stepping back in time.

An interesting feature on many of the doors in the old town was that they had two doorknockers instead of one. These were both different shapes, one round and wide and the other elongated and thin, designed this way to create different sounds. I wasn't sure which was which, but one was used by women and the other by men, so the person indoors could tell what gender the person knocking was. It could therefore be decided who was going to get up and answer the door, or indeed if it was worth answering at all.

We wandered around chatting away, taking photos, and getting hopelessly lost in the process. We walked past a person doing a novel bit of DIY to the outside of his house. He was applying a fresh covering of slushy mud and water to a damaged section of the property's wall. This acted like a huge application of Spackle paste, which would dry rock hard in the baking sun. Eventually, we found our way out onto a main street again and made it back to the New Zealanders' hotel. Here I bumped into good old Verity again, who was chatting away in the courtyard with a group of other travelers. It was great to see her once more and have a chat about her experiences in Persepolis, and for me to tell her about the family I was staying with here. Unfortunately, she wasn't keen on the three–day desert tour and wanted instead to do the standard day excursion. As dusk approached Verity, Tim, Justin, and I, along with a couple of others from the hotel courtyard, went to watch the sunset from the roof of a nearby carpet shop.

This had amazing views of the old town, a huge mosque close by, and the distant desert mountains. I left the rest of the group after the sun had slipped away and went to try to contact the desert tour guide. I had met him the night before at the hotel where Verity, Tim, and Justin were staying, but when I turned up now, he wasn't there. The hotel manager called him on his cell and asked him to come over. When he arrived, I introduced him to Tim and Justin and between us we all agreed on a price. The New Zealanders were happy to split this evenly three ways despite my offer to pay for half, since I hadn't managed to find a fourth person. We arranged to meet first thing in the morning outside the hotel. I was delighted and very excited at the prospect of going deep into the Dasht–e Kavir desert. As far as I was concerned, this would be the last big highlight of my trip in southern Iran before I headed north.

I spent the next couple of hours in the hotel's courtyard rambling on excitedly to Verity and a Swiss girl she had met. Just when I was about to leave and get a taxi back to Reza and Ashkan's house, the tour guide returned but this time with bad news. There had been an earthquake in northeastern Iran where his friend's family lived, and although they seemed to be okay, they needed some sort of assistance from him. The trip was thus canceled, and my opportunity of seeing this amazing desert on a four-day tour was over. I was gutted.

Justin, Tim, and I still wanted to see a bit of the desert so we agreed instead to do a day excursion together with one of the many guides who went to the Zoroastrian pilgrimage site of Chak Chak, which was on the outer periphery of the desert. Verity was up for this trip as well, so we all arranged to meet in the morning at a different hotel where these tours were offered. I bade them goodnight then caught a taxi back to Ashkan and Reza's house.

I invited the brothers to join us on the trip to Chak Chak, but unfortunately they declined, explaining that they had to study again and had previously been there. I guess because they lived so close by, it didn't hold the same attraction for them as it did for me. We got to share a nice evening together, though, and stayed up late into the night chatting away and drinking their treasured Nescafé.

I had sort of assumed that a robust four-wheel drive would be taking us into the desert, driven by a similarly robust khaki-clad explorer type. It was therefore something of a surprise when our guide turned up in attire more akin to a bank clerk's than an explorer's, and led us to our chariot for today—that trusty two-wheel drive Iranian favorite, the Hillman Hunter.

I wondered just how wild the terrain we were about to visit was going to be.

I needn't have worried, as although we drove on a road suitable for any standard car–in the form of a gravel track–we ended up in a hauntingly silent landscape of parched sandy mountains accentuated by a deep blue sky and penetrating sun. The journey there was magnificent and just what I needed after all the mosques and historical sites.

Eventually, our track led us into a hidden valley where the village of Chak Chak was located, situated in the most amazing location imaginable halfway up a towering mountain range in the absolute middle of nowhere. We parked at the foot of the range and got out. There was an overpowering silence and next to no breeze. The place looked completely deserted, like a ghost town. We made our way up the steep path and steps in the intense heat to the village itself. The only person around was an old janitor sitting in the shade next to the Zoroastrian fire temple. Outside the temple was a sign stating that women who were menstruating were not allowed inside. The old man unlocked the temple's big polished brass doors, which were decorated on both sides with a depiction of Zoroaster, and led us inside. I respectfully took off my sun hat as I entered, but strangely the janitor indicated that I should keep my hat on as a sign of respect. This seemed odd, but it must have been a Zoroastrian tradition, because there were a number of spare hats next to the door for people, like our tour guide, who weren't wearing one. At the janitor's request, the guide put one of these on.

The temple was very small and situated right up against a jagged rock face. Much of the interior was covered in thick black smoke stains from the "eternal flames," which weren't particularly eternal as they were all out. I asked the janitor about this, who pointed to some tiny candles burning in the corner of the temple. These apparently counted, and, smartly, the powers that be had hedged their bets and had four of them on the go–just in case.

The temple serves as a focal point for Zoroastrian pilgrims, who gather in the thousands here every year at the start of the third month after Noruz, or Iranian New Year, which occurs on the first day of spring. There wasn't much to see in the temple, but the location itself was the main attraction, and after a brief look around, I headed out to sit by myself and soak in the scenery. Down in the valley there were lots of parched little meandering tracks that looked like they were formed by water, presumably in the wetter winter months. They looked very out of place, and sitting surrounded by such a dry landscape, it was hard to imagine the place with streams or in cooler climes. As was typical for Iran, there was lots of trash chucked about the village, which ironically, had presumably been left by the earth-loving Zoroastrian pilgrims, as no one seemed to live out here at other times of the year. We all did pretty much our own thing at the village, with most of us, at one stage or another, finding a good vantage point to sit down by ourselves and take in the view. When it was time to leave, Tim and Justin managed to persuade our guide to take us back via a different route through the town of Ardakan. According to our identical guidebooks, it was possible to get a camel kebab here, which all of us were keen on, apart from Verity, who was worried about the camel's notoriously high toxin content.

The landscape on the way back was even more spectacular than on the way there, and stretching across much of it were hundreds of strange circular pockmarks. These had been created by the construction of *qanats*. The *qanat* is an ingenious ancient Persian system of underground tunnels that uses gravity to transport water from deep highland aquifers to dry areas on the surface many miles away. Some are over thirty miles in length. The earliest Iranian *qanats* date back some three thousand years; these formed the beginning of a network that was built on a scale so massive that it equaled and even surpassed those of the great Roman aqueducts. Unlike the Roman aqueducts, the Iranian *qanats* continue to be used extensively today. It is estimated that Iran has some 50,000 *qanats*, which make up a staggering 200,000 miles of underground waterways. It is a remarkable achievement and has had a dramatic effect on the agricultural potential of the Iranian plateau, which on average receives the same rainfall as Australia's dry and barren center. Most other similarly parched areas of the globe are devoid of agriculture, but Iran is a thriving farming country, which grows vast quantities of food, not just for domestic consumption but also for export. This great achievement is in large part thanks to the development of the *qanat*.

At one time, many archaeologists thought the Romans invented the *qanat*, due to discoveries at several ancient Roman sites of similar underground waterways. More recent archeological digs, as well as information contained in surviving records, have proved beyond doubt that the *qanat* originated in ancient Persia. The *qanat* was first reported outside of Iran in the seventh century BC by Assyrian King Sargon II, who stumbled upon one near Lake Orumiyeh in western Iran, during one of his warring campaigns. This Persian knowledge was later exported to various parts of the ancient world. Today, there are areas of the Sahara desert made habitable through the *qanat*'s oasis–creating irrigation, whose inhabitants continue to refer to them as "Persian works."

Although three thousand years old, the techniques used today to construct a *qanat* in Iran are very similar to the original ancient methods. The first task undertaken is a detailed survey of an elevated location that is thought to contain an aquifer. A trial well is then dug by a pair of diggers, known as *muqanni*, who set up a hand–operated winch to bring the excavated material to the surface. The spoil is piled around the mouth of the hole creating the distinctive pockmark. If the *muqanni* are having a good day then they may hit an aquifer around the fifty foot mark. However, some reach down more than four hundred feet. Once they strike a moist stratum, the *muqanni* dig down past this to reach the impermeable rock beneath. Buckets are then lowered into this hole to test the quantity of water produced and the hole's potential as a source for the *qanat*. The down-hill route of the underground conduit is then mapped out. The gradient for this must be very gentle so that the water flows at a slow rate. If the angle is too great, material can be eroded from the base of the conduit and cause substantial damage.

No fancy instruments are used by the surveyor for this, who relies on a level and a long piece of rope. A narrow underground tunnel is now dug from the proposed destination of the water up toward the aquifer well. At standard intervals, holes are dug down along its length and the spoil excavated by further hand-operated winches. This is deposited around the hole, creating mile upon mile of pockmarks across the desert.

The digging is a dangerous job, as not only do the *muqanni* have to contend with sections of the tunnel collapsing, which then have to be reinforced with ceramic supports, but with lack of oxygen and the prospect of flooding when they finally break through to the aquifer itself. To minimize the risk of the *muqanni* being washed away in a surge of water, the aquifer well must be bucketed out as much as possible before it is tapped. Due to the inherent risks involved in the construction of a *qanat*, the *muqanni* refer to it as "the murderer." Many will not work on a day they deem to be unlucky, and prayers are often offered by those about to enter a *qanat*. Although relatively simple in theory, *qanats* have transformed Iran's landscape and turned some areas that would be virtually uninhabitable into lush centers of agriculture, a prime example being the desert town of Ardakan, which we arrived at now.

The camel kebab shop was closed, so after a brief look around the place, we decided to head back to Yazd and grab some food there instead. Our guide was a nice guy and even threw in the

Towers of Silence that I had visited a couple of days beforehand with Ashkan and Reza. Verity, Tim, and Justin had yet to visit the towers. We parked up at the bottom of one of these where our guide stated, "This tower is the easier one to climb, suitable for women," pointing to the smaller of the two towers, "and this one is the harder one suitable for men."

Verity wasn't having any of this and announced forcefully that she would bloody well climb the hard tower, thank you very much! The guide tried to stop her. "No, it is too difficult for woman; you will not manage."

That was it. "Hold my water bottle, Jamie," she demanded, thrusting it into my hands. She marched off toward the men's tower at a right old speed. I shouted out after her sarcastically.

"Come back, Verity! You won't manage it; it's too difficult for a woman. Stick to the easy one!"

She turned around laughing and gave me the middle finger. Verity was first to the top and stepped into the circular tower with a triumphant look on her face.

The guide stayed at the bottom listening to music in his car, which blared out across the landscape, making sure that the Towers of Silence were anything but. At the tower's summit, we were treated to a fiery orange sunset, which seemed to set the sky ablaze. As the sun slipped past the horizon, we headed down, and a few minutes later we were in the center of Yazd and bidding each other goodbye.

Back at my Iranian friends' house, I was treated to a wonderful dinner of succulent lamb, mixed vegetables, mountains of buttered rice, and delicious fresh naan bread. When the meal was over, Reza gestured me into the computer room and locked the door. "Super film," he said with a cheeky grin, putting a DVD into the computer–it was Persian porn time again.

In all honesty, I wasn't particularly interested and wrote up my diary notes, whilst Reza watched intently. Whereas a young student in Britain watching porn would probably make crude comments along the lines of, "Go on, give it to her good and proper!" Reza made analytical observations like, "This is, how you say, effective. I try with girlfriend," and, "This be interesting. She is very wide open, yes?"

After about fifteen minutes, he got bored with it and swapped the disk for something even more offensive–Chris de effing Burgh live in concert! The Irish warbler was beginning to seriously get on my nerves.

CHAPTER EIGHTEEN

Den of Espionage

In Yazd's historic old city is the splendid Jameh Mosque, where a rather bizarre but delightful ritual can be witnessed on Friday mornings. The tradition is for an unmarried woman to climb up to the top of one of the mosque's towering minarets wearing a weird sort of padlocked hijab, and then to toss the key to this down into the courtyard below. The aim is then for a man, any man, to pick it up, at which point the woman will make her way down and let the lucky fellow unlock her. The next bit I really like–they then go off and have cakes and candy together and possibly get married. I visited the mosque but alas it wasn't Friday, so I missed out on getting any free cakes or candy.

Despite my wanting to spend some time with the brothers today, their studies got in the way again, so I met up with Verity instead and after visiting the Jameh Mosque together, we set off for the bazaar in search of a suitable present that I could buy Reza and Ashkan's mother as a thank–you for her hospitality.

I had some hard bargaining on my hands after setting my heart on a big decorative plate with an attractive peacock design. I must have been losing my touch, because I couldn't get the trader to drop his price one iota. Whilst attempting to cut the deal, I noticed an identical dish in the stall opposite, so headed there after negotiations broke down. The crafty salesman from the first stall yelled something to his buddy opposite, and as a result, he wouldn't drop his price either. About four stalls down, it happened again, this time with both of them yelling something to the third stall owner, and presumably it wasn't to give me a good deal. I'd made the mistake of really setting my heart on the thing, and in the end I coughed up the full amount.

We took it easy for the rest of the day, strolling around visiting teahouses and other bazaar stalls and enjoying each other's company. When Reza and Ashkan were due back from college, Verity and I swapped e-mail addresses and wished each other well. After a fond farewell, I headed to the brothers' house to present their mother with the plate. She was over the moon with it and laid on a special meal for my last evening with them of burgers, gherkins, soft bread, grapes, and watery, salted cucumber. It was absolutely delicious.

My train left around two in the morning, but as was typical of Iranian hospitality, Reza insisted that I would not be getting a taxi to the station, and he would be taking me instead. Like the night before, I stayed up with him and Ashkan drinking Nescafé and chatting away as best we could. I got to ask them both about their political views, which were almost identical to Pedram's and the lads' from Tehran. Bush, bin Laden, and prime minister Tony B–Liar came in for significant criticism and were lumped together and described as terrorists. I told them I agreed.

I left for the train station with Reza and arrived there at about one forty-five. Rather bizarrely, there was a group of four people enthusiastically playing badminton at this hour in a small court opposite. God knows where they got the energy. Reza and I took a seat in the station a few places down from a Western–looking female traveler. Reza turned to me, and in a voice definitely loud enough for the poor woman to hear asked, "Is she attractive? Is she good or is she bad?"

I cringed, but what could I say other than, "She is good." I hoped she didn't speak English.

The train was late and when it finally pulled up, I was looking forward to getting some much-needed sleep. Reza and I parted with hugs and promises to keep in touch. I climbed on board just before the train pulled off. Inside, it wasn't quite the first class Roger Moore affair I'd rather unrealistically been hoping for, but was instead a bit on the rickety side with cramped cabins sleeping six apiece. As I walked down the corridor, I was amazed to find people still awake. In one cabin, an inconsiderate individual was reading a newspaper with all the lights on, whilst the rest of the cabin tried to sleep. I checked the number on the door and was relieved to find it wasn't where I'd be spending the night. Even worse was a couple of cabins down, where some idiot was listening to music—not with headphones as you might imagine but on a stereo with speakers for all to hear. Lucky this wasn't where I'd be sleeping either; if it had been then the man's sound system would have become better acquainted with an open window. I located my cabin, which thankfully was at the end of the carriage and far away from this one-man disco.

On quietly opening the door, I discovered five people asleep, with the only available bed being a top bunk. It was just the spot I would have chosen had I been the first one in there, and I quickly scaled the small ladder. After storing my luggage in an already packed luggage bin, I lay back with a big smile on my face. I really liked the novelty of being in a bunk bed on a train rocking gently back and forth whilst traveling through a vast desert. It seemed very civilized and was far superior to an uncomfortable night bus where you sat upright.

The only downside was a small, lit orange lightbulb that had no switch to turn it off. It shone directly on my face. I decided to cover it up and saw the perfect thing for the job. Crammed in the luggage section was one of the train company's empty zip-up plastic cases used to hold the pillows, sheets, etc., which were supplied for the bunk beds. I managed to wedge half of this in the luggage compartment above the light, so that the other half flopped down and neatly enclosed the bulb. It worked perfectly. The cabin was now in near darkness, and moments later I was asleep.

I awoke to the dawn's soft pink light lazily filtering through the cabin's curtains. I didn't want to miss out on some potentially awesome scenery, so I roused myself and went to investigate in the corridor. Out the window lay mile upon mile of wavy sandy desert accentuated by the light of the low morning sun, which transformed great swathes of sand into carpets of sparkling tiny jewels. Despite its beauty, to fully appreciate the view, I first needed a warm caffeinated beverage to stir me to life again.

I found a guard at the end of the carriage who was sipping a cup of tea and sitting next to a big warming urn–this seemed promising. I made a polite request for *chay* but the guard shook his head. I didn't know if it was his private supply or if he just didn't want to sell me a cup. I asked again and gestured as if inquiring which way I needed to go to get one. He shook his head again then tried to zip up the same type of case I'd used to cover the lightbulb in my cabin the night before. He struggled with the zip, so I helped out and held the bag together while he did it up. He owed me one now, so again I said, "*chay*" and gestured to the urn. He nodded this time and poured me a cup. I thanked him and went back to my magical desert.

We arrived by midmorning in Tehran, where I would have most of the day to kill before my connecting train to Tabriz this evening. I considered calling Leyla or Pedram but decided against it in the interests of some much-needed time alone. One place I wanted to see in Tehran, which I'd not seen on my first trip here, was the former U.S. embassy, now renamed and known officially as the U.S. Den of Espionage.

Outside the train station was total and utter chaos. I took my life in my hands and negotiated a crossing to the other side of the main road where there was a nice little park. I sat down and looked at my guidebook's map of Tehran and the location of the Den of Espionage.

As I was many miles away yet, I flagged down a shared taxi, which already contained a passenger and was heading in roughly the right direction. I rode shotgun and consulted my map as we swerved through the traffic. I disembarked at what I thought was the correct spot but was unsure since the layout of the street was slightly different to how it was depicted on my guidebook's map. To confirm it was the right place, I stood purposefully with a perplexed expression on my face, in the hope that someone would come to my assistance. Now I could do this in London and probably not receive any help for a week or two, but in Iran it was a different story altogether. With impeccable timing, no more than twenty seconds later, a smartly dressed man in his sixties, who spoke perfect English, stopped and with a warm smile asked predictably, "Can I help you?" He confirmed for me that I was in the right place and wished me a pleasant stay in Iran.

It was a bit of a walk to the famed U.S. Den of Espionage, which was a huge sprawling complex currently occupied by the Iranian military. It was surrounded by high walls, some of which were decorated with the murals mentioned in my guidebook. One depicted the Statue of Liberty with a skull for a face, and another had written on it, WHEN THE U.S. PRAISES US, WE SHOULD MOURN. But apart from these, I wasn't particularly impressed and had seen far more colorful and artistic propaganda murals else–where in the city. My guidebook referred to a mural depicting the shooting down of Iranian civilian aircraft Flight 655 by the

American naval vessel USS *Vincennes* and the resulting death of its 290 civilian passengers, including sixty-six children. I had a good look for it but couldn't find the mural, which had presumably been painted over.

The attack on the Iranian jetliner occurred in 1988 toward the end of the Iran–Iraq War, and caused huge international outrage. The United States had claimed that the aircraft was outside the commercial jet flight corridor, flying at only 7,000 feet, and on a descent toward the navy vessel. A month later, however, U.S. authorities admitted that the airbus had been within a recognized commercial flight path and that the Iranian jet was flying at 12,000 feet and not descending. In a sensitive move which no doubt went far toward appeasing the Iranian victims' families, all the crew of the USS *Vincennes* were commended and awarded combat action ribbons. The air–warfare coordinator, Lieutenant Commander Lustig, was awarded the Commendation Medal for, incredibly, "heroic achievement," and the vessel's Captain was bestowed the prestigious Legion of Merit medal.

Vice President George H. W. Bush famously stated a month after the event, "I will never apologize for the United States of America, ever. I don't care what it has done. I don't care what the facts are."

But, of course, there is far more bad blood between Iran and America than this incident alone, and a lot of it can be traced back to the building I stood in front of now. It was from a bunker beneath the U.S. embassy that CIA agents orchestrated the 1953 coup that ousted popular democratic Prime Minister Mohammad Mossadegh and installed the Shah as dictator. It was also largely from the U.S. embassy that the next quarter of a century's support and influence over the Shah was orchestrated. In 1976, Amnesty International noted that Iran, under the U.S. backed and installed Shah, had the "highest rate of death penalties in the world, no valid system of civilian courts and

239

a history of torture which is beyond belief. No country in the world has a worse record in human rights than Iran."

When the Shah was eventually toppled, the U.S. embassy was stormed by students who feared a repeat of the 1953 coup by the Americans. The students held fifty-two of the embassy's diplomatic staff captive, setting off the Iranian hostage crisis, which lasted 444 days.

Roughly six months into the crisis, America's elite Special Forces launched a rescue operation to free the hostages, but things didn't go according to plan. Former U.S. Special Forces soldier Richard Marcinko, who was tasked with forming a diversionary mission (ultimately rejected) that was set to coincide with the actual rescue operation, states in his autobiography, *Rogue Warrior*, that the rescue, "fucked up beyond all repair. . . . [W]e'd just failed in an operation that had been almost half a year in the planning and billions in the funding. . . . [F]rom the top down, it had been one humongous goatfuck. One big waste."

The basic plan had been to first fly a fleet of helicopters to a secret landing strip and refueling point in the Iranian Dasht-e Kavir desert north of Yazd. Here the choppers would refuel and transport the American Special Forces to a mountain hideaway near Tehran. Operatives on the ground would then meet and infiltrate with them into Tehran by truck. Once there, they would storm the embassy, kill all the students, release all the hostages, and escape in the helicopters, which would land in a nearby soccer stadium.

It didn't quite work out like that. On the way there, two of the choppers got lost in sandstorms and a mechanical failure took out a third. The secret landing strip in the Dasht-e Kavir desert wasn't particularly secret; a bus full of forty-five Iranian civilians drove past the Americans. The civilians were detained and the suggestion to murder them in cold blood was forwarded by Marcinko who describes the incident in the aforementioned book.

"What should we do with the Iranians from the bus?" somebody at desert one asked General Vaught in Egypt. I answered for him. "Kill the sons of bitches." My colleagues looked at me incredulously. "Just kidding," I told them. I wasn't kidding at all.

Further insight into the mentality of this charming man is gained in the same book when he states, "War was great!" What a lowlife.

After the civilians arrived in the bus, an Iranian oil tanker rolled up and joined the party. This, perhaps a little unwisely, was blown up, sending flames hundreds of feet into the clear desert sky. The mission was aborted soon after, but things went from bad to worse when a collision between aircraft occurred during the withdrawal. The resulting fireball destroyed most of the helicopters and refueling craft parked on the ground. Eight aircraft were lost and the same number of American soldiers killed. Many more were horribly injured. Several of the dead were left behind.

The spectacular failure of the mission, along with the fact that the hostages had still not been released, eventually cost president Jimmy Carter the upcoming U.S. election against Ronald Reagan. Within minutes of Reagan being sworn into office the American hostages were released from the embassy.

The embassy was a sobering place.

After staring at the "Den" for a while, I headed across the road to a little café where I ordered a cool drink, which the friendly café owner offered to me for free. Considering I was in a massive city and there were loads of customers behind me, I assumed it wasn't a serious offer but a *ta'aruf* one. I refused three times but the guy was adamant, so I sat down and enjoyed my free drink. Iran is the only place I've visited where complete strangers will give you something for free simply for being a foreigner.

I thanked the owner and headed for the subway not far off down the street, which would then take me to the train station. The subway was clean, modern, spacious, and generally far nicer than London's grimy, decrepit Tube system. It was also far cheaper and a ticket cost me the equivalent of about ten cents. I now learnt that the strict separation of the genders observed on buses and the like is completely abandoned on the Tehran metro, where it is every man and woman for themselves. The metro was so delightfully air conditioned that I could have stayed there far longer than my journey's time—not something a sane person would willingly do in London's chokingly hot non-air-conned Tube in summer.

One group of people who actually make a habit of spending long periods of time on London's Tube are, amazingly, members of Mensa (according to my father). Although the Mensans are supposedly those with a super-high IQ, like my old man, what the jolly Mensans do is periodically take over a subway car on the Circle Line, where they then hold a proper party complete with music, food, booze, paper hats, and party games, as they travel endlessly around London. In circles. All night. How very intellectual.

When I stepped out of the Tehran metro, it was like walking into an oven. By the time I got to the station, I was hot, tired, and ready to crash out just as soon as my train came in. The lack of sleep from the night before and today's wanderings had caught up with me. I was pleasantly surprised when the train arrived, as it was much nicer and more spacious than the one I'd caught from Yazd, having cabins that slept four, not six. I said a quick polite "Salaam" to my fellow passengers, then without further ado pulled down one of the cabin's upper bunk beds and passed out.

CHAPTER NINETEEN

English Expert

I awoke before dawn the next morning when a guard popped his head inside the cabin and announced that we would soon be approaching Tabriz. I started to get myself organized, as did another one of the guys in the cabin. One of the guys popped out into the corridor and returned a minute later with a couple of teas. We drank these together in silence. I spoke more Farsi than he did English, and since all I could really say in Farsi past "hello," "thank you," "how much?" and "damn it" was "you are beautiful," I decided it was best to remain mute–after all, he was no looker.

I stepped off the train into a surprisingly chilly and damp morning. After booking into a hotel, I headed off to the tourist office to make some inquiries. On the way there, it struck me that the roads of Tabriz no longer seemed quite so chaotic and dangerous as when I'd first been here. Certainly they weren't as bad as Tehran, but I was also becoming much more adept at crossing the road Iranian-style and now felt confident enough to casually step out in front of the traffic and just let the cars work their way around me. I near-skipped across the heaving main road in front of the tourist office without a second thought.

Inside the office were two Polish guys and a big ginger-haired Canadian guy waiting to talk to fountain of tourist knowledge Mr. Nasser Khan. I got talking to my fellow travelers and told the Poles of my desire to visit Babak Castle. They had already been there and highly recommended it, describing the castle as one of the highlights of their eight-week stay in Iran. They sang its praises so much that the Canadian guy sitting next to them decided to cancel his planned trip to another location and come along with me to the castle instead. He introduced himself as Ian, and we both hit it off immediately. Ian was a big friendly confident guy who brought to mind a lumberjack, such was his towering powerful stature, beard, and head of flaming red hair.

The Poles gave Ian and me the details on how to get to the castle, which they explained could be reached by two separate hiking routes. One of these was easy and over rolling hills, the other hard and through dense forest. They highly recommended the hard route on the way up due to its wondrous views and the easy path on the way down. The trip, they said, would take all day, and it was necessary to catch an early morning bus that left at 6 AM for a village near the castle. From the village, we would have to catch a cab to the start of the forest hiking path. Mr. Nasser Khan invited me to join him and the Poles for a tour of one of the nicer areas of Tabriz this evening. I accepted and arranged a time and place to meet them. Like me, Ian was keen for lunch and fancied some traditional Iranian *abgusht*, so Nasser offered to take us both to a suitable café. On the way there, I asked him what a suitable present to buy Shahram and Kimya would be, both of whom I hoped to meet up with later. He recommended a huge box of nut-laden confectionery on sale in the bazaar.

Over a delicious *abgusht*, Ian and I discussed tomorrow's trip to the castle. His hotel was within walking distance of mine, so we arranged to meet outside my place at the unappealing time of 5:15 AM, then to get a taxi to the bus station and catch the 6 AM coach.

I bade Ian good day and set off for Shahram's workplace, stopping off briefly en route to buy the recommended confectionary. He was shocked to see me and exclaimed, as best he could in English, that he'd been very concerned for me and had planned to wait a week longer, then telephone the police to launch a search. This was all very sweet of him, although a tad melodramatic. He calmed down when I gave him his present, which he seemed delighted with. We sat down, and I told him of my travels and plans to visit the castle tomorrow. He said to phone him tomorrow evening when I got back from the castle so I could collect my camping gear and we could go out for a meal together. Shahram had a ton of work to do, so I left him to get on with it and spent the rest of the afternoon pottering around doing nothing in particular except browsing around the bazaar.

In the evening, I met up with Nasser and the two Polish guys who were waiting for me outside the tourist office. We caught a taxi down to a salubrious part of Tabriz where all the women looked far more Western than their counterparts in the center of town. Here, instead of wearing layers of black clothing, they wore layers of makeup and colorful "skimpy" hijabs. Our first stop was an ice cream parlor where I tucked into a "sunshine sundae," consisting of loads of Jell-O but precious little ice cream. Whilst eating, Nasser saw two women he knew and said to them in Farsi what I thought was, "You are beautiful." He said it quickly, but I was sure I recognized the phrase, so after the girls had left I asked him if this had been the case. Nasser confirmed it was and explained that it was quite a normal compliment to pay a girl in Iran, and that it was not as cheesy as it would be in Europe.

He was impressed with my pronunciation of the phrase and the other tidbits of Farsi the Tehran boys had taught me. Nasser explained that around the corner was an English school and that he had arranged for us to attend for a little while to say a few words to the classes. As I had to be up first thing in the morning, I considered declining. I didn't want to seem rude, though, so I reluctantly tagged along and hoped it would be quick.

It was a small school that ran evening classes on the first and second floor of an office block. Nasser led me and the two Polish guys into the reception, where we were greeted by five staff members. The Poles were introduced first and got a warm welcome from the staff, but when I was introduced as Mr. Maslin from England, it was as if all their birthdays and Shiite religious festivals had come at once. The Polish guys were whisked off to the staff room, but I was far too valuable an asset for this, and was taken instead upstairs to talk directly to the students.

"Come in," said the teacher in English as the staff member who'd taken me upstairs knocked on the door. As we entered the room, the whole class, who were all girls between about sixteen to eighteen, rose to their feet respectfully. This was extremely cool and a world away from when I was last at school.

"This is Mr. Maslin, English expert from England!" announced the staff member. I liked that very much indeed. The staff member left, and I was asked by the teacher to introduce myself to the class. I did so and was then asked to take a seat whilst the girls asked me questions. First up was a tricky one: "Which is better, Iran or England?"

I answered diplomatically. "That's a difficult question to answer. It's a bit like me asking you which is better, an apple or an orange. They are both good but different."

She looked at me confused. "But an orange is better."

"Ah, yes, well, er, to you an orange is better, but to many the apple is the superior fruit."

All the class, including the teacher, looked confused at this. "No, but orange is better!" she repeated again.

My analogy wasn't working, so I quit discussing fruit salad and said, "Iran and England are as good as each other."

"But which is better?" asked another one of the girls.

Good God, it was like being back with Hattie trying to find out if I wanted to marry Susan.

"Iran has better weather," I said, "but England has better, er . . . soccer." This they all agreed on, and for the next few minutes, I was asked if I knew David Beckham and the like. The questions got easier after this, and I decided from now on to answer them in as straightforward a manner as possible. They included, amongst many others, "What Iranian food have you tried?" "Did you have culture shock when you come to Iran?" "What do people think of Iran in England?" and "What do you think of the hijab?"

The last two were interesting and I answered honestly, saying that a lot of people in Britain thought Iran was dangerous. I told them that I had even been warned not to go to Iran because I might get shot. The class roared with laughter as if this was the most absurd thing they'd ever heard. After order was reestablished, the teacher confirmed for the class that this was in fact the case and that many people in America and Britain thought Iranians were all terrorists. They seemed genuinely upset at this.

The hijab question was revealing when instead of answering what I thought of it, I asked them what they thought of it. One girl pointed to a small television camera up in the corner of the room and said, "It is not safe." And it wasn't; big brother was watching.

The teacher answered for them, saying, "For girls it is better to wear hijab, I think more safe for them."

We ended on a much lighter note, with me talking about my experiences in the country and the places I'd visited outside of Iran. One of the girls asked jokingly, "Are you Marco Polo?" Everybody laughed at this. There was a knock on the door and the same staff member who'd brought me into the class now came to take me on to another one. The class all protested and asked if I could stay. My ego swelled. They were overruled and I was taken next door, this time to a class of slightly older girls. They all stood for me again and once more I was introduced as, "Mr. Maslin, English Expert from England."

It was the same routine as before, and I was asked to introduce myself but by now I was really getting the hang of this teaching lark and said confidently, although a little tongue in cheek, "Please be seated class. My name is Mr. Maslin, I'm from England and will be answering your questions for the next fifteen minutes, so please fire ahead. Who's first?"

They reeled off pretty much the same queries as before, which I answered as best I could. I was in the zone now and managed to get the class laughing on a number of occasions. It was great fun, and I felt like I was a comedian on stage. There was another knock on the door and in came Mr. Nasser Khan. All the class, including me, stood up. Nasser took a seat nearby and listened to the rest of the questions, one of which was, "Have you learnt any Farsi?" After going through "hello," "goodbye," etc., Nasser leant over and whispered, "Tell her she is beautiful," so I did.

"*Shoma khoshgelly,*" I said, mustering up a look of sincerity. Everybody was in fits of laughter and began applauding. I was encouraged to do it several more times, which I did and received the same response. I was really getting into the swing of it all when there was another knock on the door. It was the same staff member who now wanted to take me away again. This wasn't popular, and there was a near-rebellion in the class with all of them begging to let Mr. Maslin stay.

When it was all over, I was taken downstairs to meet the school's head honcho who shot from the hip with his first question. "Which teacher was the best, and which teacher was the worst?"

I loved the irony, as teachers from my old school would be mortified at the thought of Jamie Maslin, of all people, being asked to critique their profession. Although the thought of playing school inspector for them would have greatly appealed, this was Iran, where classes were filmed—probably to keep an eye on the teachers as much as the pupils—so I didn't want to put anyone in it, and answered that both were exceptional teachers with very good English. The principal seemed satisfied.

Mr. Khan, the Poles, and I caught a cab back to the center of town, where we wished each other well and parted company. Minutes later, I was in my hotel. I requested a morning call for 5 AM and went to bed. I got bugger all sleep though, as for some reason, just like in Maku, I was paranoid that the call wouldn't come. When the phone finally rang, right at 5 AM, I was exhausted.

Fifteen minutes later, I was in a cab with Ian on the way to the bus station. We arrived there around five thirty, but for some reason the early bus was cancelled and we had to wait until 7:10 AM. It had been one big waste of a lie-in.

The scenery on the way there was awesome, with dramatic hills in layers of rusty red and murky cream, made all the more beautiful by the pink tinge of the early morning sun. I was pleased now that we'd traveled later; if we'd traveled in the dark, we'd have missed much of this wonderful landscape.

Ian and I chatted away on the journey there like old buddies and told each other about our trips and experiences in Iran. Ian worked for an airline and thus got cheap flights, so he had done a lot of traveling, and although Canadian, had been educated for a time in England. He was only in Iran for two more days and, if I remember correctly, had spent about a week here visiting the north of the country. On the way to our destination, the town of Kaleybar, we passed through a town where every vehicle, without exception, was an old style Land Rover. There were rows upon rows of the things all over the place. I'd never seen so many in all my life. We started counting them but gave up when we got into the hundreds.

Kaleybar was a sleepy little isolated town in the heart of Iran's rugged Azerbaijan region. It was surrounded by steep green mountains, the peaks of which remained unseen, shrouded in a slowly drifting alpine mist. It was a great location and once again so very different from most people's perception of Iran– not dry and parched like its central deserts, but as lush and green as merry old Mother England.

Ian and I were both hungry, and since we had many hours of hiking ahead of us, we went to a café to fill up on carbs. After our breakfast, we went looking for a taxi. On the way, we were invited into a complete stranger's house but as we were already well behind schedule, we reluctantly had to decline. We caught a cab up to the start of the trail.

The trek started along a twisting forest trail past a number of abandoned campsites, which, sadly, were strewn with trash. It was a real shame as it was a stunning piece of scenery, which clearly the people who'd camped out here had come especially to see, but for whatever reason had seemed determined not to leave that way. Past the campsites, the trail meandered uphill through the trees and along a boulder–riddled riverbed, toward the looming cloud–capped mountains in the distance.

All was going well on the hike until we arrived at a waterfall next to a steep craggy rock face, to which the path appeared to lead up. We were both unsure whether this was the correct route, as the rock face was steep and dangerous as hell. Ian didn't like the look of this one bit or the prospect of climbing it. Since he was built more for chopping trees down and I was built more for climbing them, I volunteered to scramble up the rock face and check it out, whilst Ian backtracked to see if there was another route.

To me, the climb seemed a little hairy, although perfectly doable if taken slowly and carefully. I didn't find it too hard and got to the top without drama. At the summit, the path skirted around the waterfall and connected to a much more gradual and safer track leading through the forest. As I descended to pass on the good news, the clip attaching my water bottle to my belt gave way, sending the bottle careering toward the ground, bouncing off and smashing into jagged rocks as it went. This did nothing to encourage Ian, who the water bottle just missed, that the climb was a safe one. Surprisingly, the bottle was in one piece.

Ian hadn't found another track, so the choice seemed simple: either he did the climb or we went back to the start again and located the easier route.

There was no point in him trying something he wasn't comfortable with, and what's more, we were in a very isolated location along a deserted mountain path and should something have gone wrong, than it could have gone wrong badly.

We started the depressing walk back, but a minute later, Ian fortuitously spotted another trail going all the way around the rock face and waterfall. We took this and in no time were both looking down on the waterfall. The path then led along another boulder–strewn riverbed toward a rocky peak jutting majesti- cally out of the forest hundreds and hundreds of feet above. It looked like the location where the castle was perched, although it was difficult to tell because a thick curtain of mist obscured the peak. The mist would part tantalizingly for a fraction of a second, leaving Ian and me straining for a glimpse of the castle before it closed again and enveloped the mountain. What we saw was mesmerizing. It was stunningly beautiful, like some mythical enchanted fortress out of a fairy tale or *The Lord of the Rings*. I couldn't wait to get to the top.

We arrived at a fork in the road, with both paths leading up the rocky peak in different directions. Ian favored the one to the right; I favored the one to the left. We decided to go check out our favored tracks and report back to each other a few minutes later before making a decision. A couple hundred feet up my trail, I became convinced it was the right one. I was just about to yell out to Ian and tell him this when he beat me to the punch and shouted to come back. I found him with a group of six or so Iranian hikers. They spoke little English but indicated that Ian's path led to the castle, and since they'd all just come from there, they were obviously right.

Another half an hour on and we came to the very steep rocky mountainous section. It was one hell of a place to build a fortress and would have been bloody difficult to attack as the hike up there was no stroll in the park. Sadly, we still couldn't see the castle clearly, such was the mist blanketing the summit. The Polish guys who'd recommended this route had described similar weather conditions and had said that, suddenly, out of the blue, the clouds had completely parted for them, revealing the castle in all its glory above. Ian and I waited for a while hoping to get the same awesome view from below but the clouds remained steadfast.

The Poles had also told us that it was possible to get a drink at the top, which seemed a bit unlikely given the castle's inac–cessible location up an isolated mountain in the middle of a forest. Jokingly, in stupid overexaggerated upper–class English accents, we shouted up toward the cloud–tipped peak, "I say, would someone be kind enough to put the kettle on up there!" and other inane although quite amusing nonsense. It echoed around the valley for miles.

"I hope there's no one who understands English at the top," said Ian.

A little farther up, we came across another path that joined onto ours, coming from the direction of the one I'd first favored. It was almost certainly the same trail and had led up to the castle after all. Being a bit of an outdoor enthusiast, I felt relieved to know I hadn't got my navigation completely wrong.

From out of nowhere, the strange sound of a large group of males singing harmoniously emanated from the castle's still unseen, cloud-covered peak. Suddenly, a boulder came crashing down the side of the mountain, accompanied by several shouts. We yelled up to let the choir above know we were down here. A couple of minutes later, a group of about twenty Iranian kids of around fourteen years old came down the mountainside, along with an adult who looked like their school teacher. They were having a great time and looked like they were on a school outing.

They went crazy when they saw us and all came over and shook our hands enthusiastically. They were a great bunch and hyper-energized. Ian told one of them he was from Canada and they went berserk.

"Canada! Canada! Canada!" they chanted together at the top of their voices, which echoed repeatedly all around the valley.

"Iran! Iran! Iran!" Ian yelled back.

"Canada, Iran! Canada, Iran! Canada, Iran!" everybody, including me, started to yell for no other reason than it was bloody good fun and we were all enjoying it. By this stage, they'd all assumed I was Canadian too and were giving me little pats on the back whilst enthusiastically shouting, "Canada! Canada! Canada!" again and again. I responded with "Iran! Iran! Iran!" It was insane and pointless but a great laugh.

After the chanting, a number of them produced cameras and we all lined up for some group photos. Every time we were about to part and go our separate ways, a couple of the group would run back to shake our hands again or to have one more snap taken with us. This happened about ten times before they finally headed down and disappeared into the mist below. Although out of sight, they were far from out of earshot, and for the next few minutes, the surreal sound of "Canada, Iran!" echoed all around the mist-shrouded mountains of Iran's East Azerbaijan Province.

Eventually, we got close enough to the castle to see it through the clouds. It had taken a good couple of hours but was well worth the effort. The castle was perched right at the top of a near-vertical rock face accessible only via a steep twisting path that led to the summit. We climbed this and were delighted to find the place completely deserted.

Although what remained of the castle was a ruin, many of the walls and structures were intact, several parts of which were roofed. Others were in the process of being rebuilt, but I kind of liked using my imagination to try to picture it back in its heyday.

We had a good look around the site, then sat with our feet dangling over the edge of a section of walling with a massive drop below. We waited here, hoping upon hope that the curtain of cloud would draw, even if just for a second, so we could glimpse the glorious vista we both knew was all around us but could not see.

Although Ian and I had the place to ourselves, it would have been a different story had we been here in late June. At that time, the castle and the surrounding area would have been packed with several tens of thousands of people coming to commemorate the birthday of Babak Khorramdin. Babak Khorramdin was a ninth-century Zoroastrian Iranian nationalist who fought fiercely against the imposition of Islam and the Arab invasion of his country. He was based at the castle, and it was later named after him.

The celebration of Babak Khorramdin's birthday is a rather disorganized event and follows no particular official program, with Iranians turning up and congregating in small groups for discussions, poetry readings, lectures, musical performances, dancing, and to campout overnight at the castle. The Iranian authorities have been none too happy about the gatherings in previous years, in large part because of what Babak Khor-ramdin symbolized as a popular nationalist who promoted an Iranian religion and fought against Islam. Some mullahs have criticized the participants in the birthday celebrations, saying that it is unethical to commemorate someone who killed Muslims. According to some reports, there have been multiple arrests at past ceremonies by the security forces.

Ian and I stayed at the top of the castle exploring around for a good long time, still hoping that the clouds would clear, before making the decision to head back. Whilst looking for the easy path down, we came across the "café" mentioned by the Polish guys where you could get a drink. It consisted of a couple of big urns, a gas burner, a box of tea bags, and a couple of kettles. It was all kept under a tarp and was deserted today. We considered getting the gas burner on the go and leaving some money for a *chay*, but decided against it when we couldn't locate any cups.

We found a path on the opposite side of the castle to the one we'd come up and assumed it was the easier route that led down toward the town. It could have led anywhere though, such was our disorientation from the terrible visibility, which was now down to about thirty feet. We started along the trail, but after a while it petered out, leading us to question if it had been the right path after all. In hindsight, we should have turned back to establish this for sure, but since this part of the walk was downhill and wasn't through the forest, we decided to continue. It was the wrong decision to make, especially since we could see next to nothing in the fog, and we paid for this dearly by walking for hours on end. It ended up taking us far longer to get down on the "easy path" than the "hard path" had taken us to get up to the castle. The heavens opened and it started to rain, soaking both of us. To add insult to injury, my water bottle that I'd thought had survived its fall intact, was actually leaking and had left a big round wet patch in a rather embarrassing place on my trousers next to where I'd reattached it to my belt.

In the mist, much of the visible landscape looked like an English moor, so much so that I could easily imagine a local country pub emerging from the fog, where I could get roast beef, Yorkshire pudding, and a real ale served in front of a cozy fireplace. Being familiar with the delights of English pubs, Ian found the idea extremely appealing, especially since we were now tired, wet, cold, and hungry.

Eventually, we found our way back to the place where the taxi had dropped us this morning. Wouldn't you know it, but as soon as we arrived, the clouds started to clear. Located nearby was a little café, so we dropped in for a well-earned hot drink. A few minutes later, we were joined by the "Canada, Iran" boys, who were staying at a campsite around the corner and were as enthusiastic as ever. Whilst Ian and I nursed a couple of hot coffees, the boys learnt to smoke cigarettes–none of them inhaled. After a while, Ian popped outside and called a taxi from a phone box down the road, which turned up a few minutes later. When we tried to pay for our drinks, the café owner refused payment. We thanked him and headed back to town.

After being dropped off in Kaleybar, we bumped into our first cab driver who'd given us a lift up to the trail this morning. He and Ian started to chat together again and, despite the language difficulties, got on like a house on fire. A few minutes later, we were all sitting in another nearby café together. We asked the driver, whose name was Farhad, how much it would cost for him to take us to Tabriz, as by now we'd missed the last bus back and it was beginning to get dark. Farhad recommended we didn't go with him as he worked for an agency of some sort that charged a lot more for longer journeys than normal taxis. He said his price would be fifteen Khomeinis, whereas a normal one would cost between four and five Khomeinis (a Khomeini being the green IR10,000 notes with a picture of said fellow on them). Before we went in search of a cab, Ian tried to give Farhad a gift consisting of a bundle of bank notes which he strenuously declined.

It was now completely dark and both of us were still wet, cold, and looking forward to getting back to our hotels. We found a taxi going our way that had one other passenger, who was about eighteen years old and sat in the front seat. He turned out to be a really nice guy, as demonstrated en route when we stopped briefly so he could pop into a little village store. He returned a minute later and presented Ian and me with a big bag of cheesy–puff–like chips, a couple of cool drinks, and a chocolate bar each. I certainly didn't take these kind gestures for granted, but they no longer surprised me, for I'd been encoun-tering this sort of thing every day since arriving in Iran.

Ian and I swapped e-mail addresses back in Tabriz and parted company with promises to send each other copies of our photos from our day out together.

I got back to my hotel feeling tired but very satisfied. I tried calling Shahram several times but alas there was no answer. I resigned myself to meeting up with him tomorrow.

CHAPTER TWENTY

Strange Encounter

Sadly, today would be my last full day in Iran. My visa ran out in a couple of days' time, and my train for Istanbul in Turkey left Tabriz early tomorrow morning. As such, I planned to do nothing more than meet up with Shahram and Kimya, pick up my camping gear, send a few e-mails, and find a present for my friend Chris, who had said to me before I left England, "Maza, send me something fucked up from Iran!" I intended to oblige.

While I was eating breakfast at the hotel restaurant, something strange happened. Sitting a few tables down were two Iranian-looking guys and a hauntingly attractive woman of indistinguishable origin with blue eyes. The men were talking in English and one had definitely lived in the U.K., such was his accent. The other spoke with an Iranian twang, and the girl remained silent. Apart from the professor I met at the library in Tehran, this was the only time I'd heard someone in Iran speak with an English accent. I eavesdropped for a while, but it was just general chitchat about nothing in particular. Suddenly, the two guys got up from their table and came and approached me.

"I recognize your face," said the one with the Iranian accent. "You got your visa through IranianVisa.com, didn't you?" He then added, "I work for them and see all the passport scans."

Considering Iran was a country of 71 million people, and IranianVisa.com was based in Tehran not Tabriz, this was a massive coincidence. Also, my passport photo was taken when I was nineteen and had much shorter hair and looks nothing like I do now—or at least I hope it doesn't since I look a complete dork in it. I cautiously confirmed I had got my visa through them, but was on my guard and immediately wondered if they were secret police.

"What is your name?" asked the Iranian.

I told him.

"Yes, Jamie, I remember."

"Are you enjoying your stay in Iran?"

"Yes, thank you."

"Where have you visited?" I answered his questions as succinctly as possible and couldn't quite work out if I was being mega paranoid or was justifiably concerned. He rambled off a list of queries, including how long I had left in the country. I lied and said another week.

I'd been warned by Leyla to be very careful when sending e-mails in Iran, but I hadn't really heeded this warning completely. I made sure to omit Iranian names in my correspondence with friends at home, but had made no secret of the fact I'd be writing a book about my Iranian adventures when I returned. Could the powers-that-be have intercepted these? Were they worried about what I'd write? Or was I just creating another Roger Moore James Bond fantasy in my head? I didn't know, but tried to think what Bond would do in a similar situation: probably end up shagging the chick, I figured—I could live with that.

I decided to say as little as possible, and after a couple of minutes, they went back to their table. They all spoke together in Farsi now. Half of me was convinced it was all just silly paranoia but the other half of me wasn't so sure. I knew foreign journalists had been arrested and even killed in Iran. Canadian photojournalist Zahra Kazemi had died in custody from "a stroke" after being arrested taking photos outside Iran's Evin Prison, although her body showed signs of brutal torture–so these things happened, but whether I was being singled out because of my e-mails, or I was completely losing my mind, I didn't know. Before I could ponder this anymore, the men returned again.

"Have a nice stay in Iran," the English one said, offering me his hand to shake. I shook his and then the other guy's hand.

They began to walk off, but then the Iranian guy turned and faced me. "How long did you say you were staying in Tabriz?"

"A week," I replied.

"Have a good time," he said, and with that they were gone. It was all a bit weird, and the chances of me meeting the one person I'd sent a scan of my passport to out of 71 million other Iranians seemed very unlikely indeed, but then again I'd had other strange coincidences occur while traveling before.

I got up to leave and walked past their empty table, then returned to examine it after wondering if they'd been waiting there a long time for me. I looked at the cigarette butts in the ashtray–there were seven. I'd only seen the woman smoking. What did this mean? I didn't have a fucking clue but it seemed the sort of thing Columbo would look at. I gave up and went outside in search of something "fucked up from Iran."

Not a minute down the road and I was at the shop which sold the horrendous thalidomide disco-dancing DVD I'd seen on my first visit to Tabriz. It was the perfect gift for Chris and certainly qualified as something "fucked up from Iran." I felt guilty at the thought of buying one, but then figured it was considered funny in Iran, and therefore said something, although I'm not sure quite what, about the place. I made the purchase and went down to the post office to stick it in the mail.

Sending a DVD through the mail is no straightforward transaction in Iran. I had to hand it over to a guy behind a counter who skimmed through the disk's scenes on his computer to check if there was anything illicit or banned on it. Even though it was just a minor infringement of my civil liberties, it really got on my nerves. They were nice about it though and in true contradictory Iranian style gave me a nice cup of tea, whilst they searched for subversive material and ascertained whether I was a dangerous enemy of the state. They concluded that it was no "super film" and gave it the all clear. I put it in the mail.

I had a pleasant surprise at my next port of call, which was a money changer in the bazaar. I handed over my wedge of Iranian notes that I'd been unable to spend and discovered to my amazement that my whole trip, all the way from France, had cost in total an amazing $450! I was astonished. I knew I'd had quite a bit of currency left in the bottom of my backpack, but I didn't expect it to be this much. I wondered if I could have made it all the way to China on $1,400 after all.

In return for my huge wedge of Iranian notes, I received a minuscule sliver of U.S. dollars, which immediately made me feel poor and strangely hard done by. It's interesting to note that despite the Iranian government's aversion to all things American, until recently their preferred foreign currency for international trade and exchange was the U.S. dollar. This has now changed, with the Iranian government insisting on non-dollar currencies for its oil and planning to open its own oil exchange where, crucially, oil will be traded in euros instead of U.S. dollars.

Some people believe that in breaking the monopoly previously enjoyed by the dollar for all OPEC oil trades, Iran will significantly devalue the U.S. currency, which is already suffering from a national debt in excess of $11 trillion.

The theory goes that if the dollar is to remain the world's favored reserve currency then it is crucial that oil is solely traded in it. That way, the euro would be unlikely to become a major reserve currency, as there's not much point in central banks stockpiling euros if they have to change them into dollars every time they purchase oil. By offering the euro as an alternative, as did Saddam Hussein just before he was ousted, Iran could potentially lead the world's central banks to drop the dollar as their reserve currency and switch instead to the stronger euro. The resulting sale of dollars would send the U.S. currency into freefall and cause complete havoc.

Whether or not Iran's proposed non-dollar oil exchange can lead to the above scenario is disputed. However, what is far less disputed is that the U.S. economy would go through a period of vast upheaval were the dollar to ever lose its de facto reserve status. Some analysts claim it would be catastrophic and eventually force the U.S. to dramatically change its tax, debt, trade, energy, and ultimately, military policies–no longer, they say, would the U.S. be able to spend 42 cents in every tax dollar on the military.

After my visit to the money changers, I walked over to pick up my camping gear from Shahram. I arrived and found to my dismay that the company he worked for was closed and all locked up. Whoops.

The only telephone number I had for him was his work phone, so this was serious. My train left tomorrow morning, and my visa ran out the day after that. If I couldn't get hold of him today then it looked like I'd be saying bye-bye to all my precious camping equipment. Not only was it all of enormous sentimental value but was worth well over a thousand dollars.

The office on the floor above was open, so I stuck my head in and inquired after Shahram by saying his name and pointing downstairs. One of the staff pointed out to me what I already knew, namely that the door was locked and that he wasn't in. I gestured that I needed to call him. Luckily, he looked like he knew what I was after and went back to discuss this with a colleague. His colleague picked up the phone and called Shahram's cell for me. Ten minutes later, Shahram and Kimya were outside with all my camping gear.

We went for a wonderful *abgusht* lunch together in a smart little restaurant around the corner run by a very animated man wearing big chunky sunglasses. Over lunch, Shahram tried to discuss some sort of investment in Iran's stock market with me. I think he wanted me to invest some money in the market as a whole, as opposed to stock of an individual company. He said it was extremely safe and that the Iranian stock market was "the number one stock market in the whole world." His proof? "It has officially been declared the best by the Iranian government."

I told him I'd think about it.

Outside the restaurant, we bade each other farewell and promised to stay in touch. Before I left, Kimya said to me, "I hope you can come back and visit again someday with either your wife or sister." I told her I'd like to.

The rest of the day I spent packing, getting some of my diary notes written up, and generally taking it easy.

I had an early start on my final morning in Iran as my train left just before dawn. I'd asked the hotel's reception staff the night before to order a cab for me. I waited and waited in the lobby, watching the clock. The car was very late. After twenty minutes of nervously biting my fingernails, I gave up and went out into the chilly near-deserted predawn streets in search of another one. It was still dark and there was next to no life about. After ten minutes of panicked searching, I spotted one and flagged it down, waving my arms about like a madman. I didn't know the Farsi for "train station," so I did silly little choo-choo train impressions with the appropriate hand moves and noises. The driver turned around and looked at me like I was a fool.

"Do you want to go to the train station?" he asked in perfect English. I told him yes and that I was seriously late. He put his foot down and burned off at racecar speed. And thank goodness he did, because I arrived only a couple of minutes before my train left. If I'd missed it, I would have been in serious trouble; my visa lapsed the following day, and I definitely didn't want to be in Iran illegally.

I shared a spacious cabin with just one other guy who spoke no English whatsoever but was a warm and friendly chap who shared his bag of candy with me. I spent the next few hours gazing out of the window at wonderful mountain gorges and the huge sprawling surface of Lake Orumiyeh, which the train skirted past. Northwest Iran has some mind-blowing scenery.

Before long, we crossed the Iranian border and were into Turkey. It was party time. The girls suddenly took their hijabs off and changed into revealing Western outfits. The guy from my cabin who'd shared his candy with me rolled up and smoked a spliff. He puffed away while I checked for guards in the corridor. Afterward, he crashed out listening to his Walkman. Even through the headphones, I could tell it was none other than our Irish friend. Could I ever get away from the guy?

I was both sad and excited to be at the end of my Iran adventure and the end of my journey. Everywhere I traveled, I encountered the friendliest people I'd ever come across and constantly had to remind myself that I was in Iran—part of the so-called Axis of Evil. Although I obviously make no apology for the abysmal Iranian government and its terrible human rights abuses, the Iranian people were just incredible.

On the long journey back to Istanbul, I met a group of Iranian girls in their late twenties in the train's restaurant car who belonged to the minority Baha'i religion. Being part of this religion would have meant death or imprisonment in Iran until recently, and its followers are still prevented from employment opportunities or attending university. The girls had managed to obtain visas through the UN and were leaving Iran for Istanbul, then heading to Canada for a better life. This would be their last time in Iran for many years, and possibly their last time ever. I said how happy they must be to be off to Canada, but the eldest one shook her head.

"No. There is no place like home."

I could well understand. It wasn't my home, but I was certainly made to feel welcome. It was, however, time for me to take my leave as well. After all, you can only take so much Chris de Burgh.